THE FOREST BROTHERHOOD

DAN KASZETA

The Forest Brotherhood

Baltic Resistance against the Nazis and Soviets

HURST & COMPANY, LONDON

First published in the United Kingdom in 2023 by
C. Hurst & Co. (Publishers) Ltd.,
New Wing, Somerset House, Strand, London, WC2R 1LA
© Dan Kaszeta, 2023
All rights reserved.

Distributed in the United States, Canada and Latin America by
Oxford University Press, 198 Madison Avenue, New York, NY 10016,
United States of America.

A Cataloguing-in-Publication data record for this book
is available from the British Library.

ISBN: 9781787389397

www.hurstpublishers.com

Printed and bound in Great Britain by Bell and Bain Ltd, Glasgow

CONTENTS

PART 4

AFTER THE FOREST BROTHERHOOD

DEBATES, REVISIONISM, LEGACY

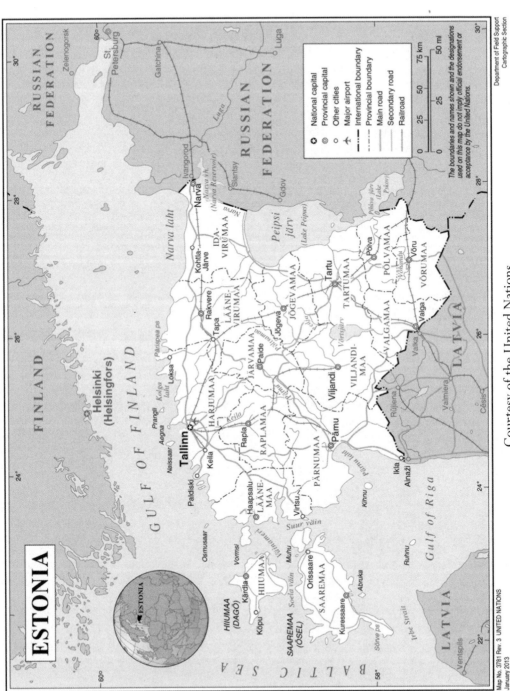

Courtesy of the United Nations.

Contemporary Latvia

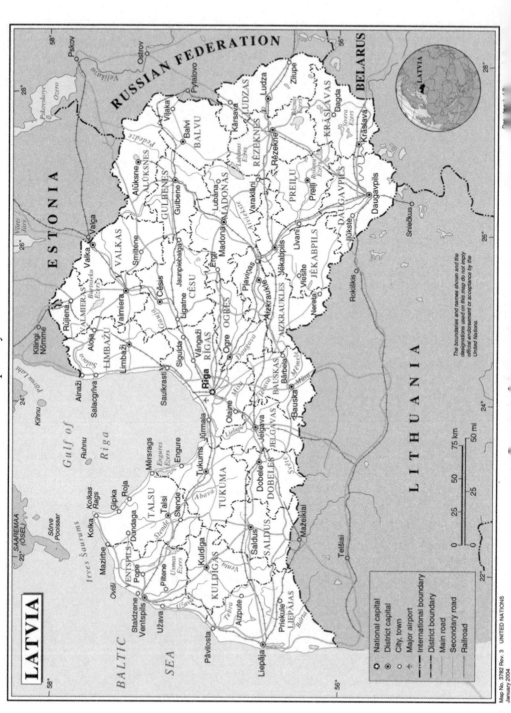

Courtesy of the United Nations.

LIST OF ILLUSTRATIONS

1. Lithuanian Forest Brother leader Juozas Lukša 'Daumantas'. Unknown photographer. Photo from the Genocide and Resistance Research Centre of Lithuania.

2. Forest Brothers in southern Lithuania in the late 1940s. Unknown photographer. Photo from the Genocide and Resistance Research Centre of Lithuania.

3. Latvian Forest Brothers in the Kabile forest, early September 1946. Unknown photographer. Photo from the Centre for Documenting the Effects of Totalitarianism, Constitution Protection Office of Latvia.

4. A Forest Brother grave in Perloja, Lithuania. Photo by author.

5. The Forest Brother memorial in Merkinė, Lithuania, the site of a heated battle in 1945. Photo by author.

6. A memorial to August Sabbe, the last Estonian Forest Brother. He drowned while escaping capture by the KGB in 1978. Photo by Laanõ Valdis via Wikimedia Commons. (CC BY-SA 3.0).

7. Estonians taking up arms in 1941. Unknown photographer. Photo from VALDEF.

8. Archival CIA documents, now declassified, have revealed much about Western attempts to liaise with Baltic Forest Brothers. Image from CIA Freedom of Information Act Electronic Reading Room.

9. Many Forest Brothers were imprisoned in Gulag camps. This is one of the last remaining examples, in Perm, Russia. Photo by Gerald Praschl via Wikimedia Commons. (CC BY-SA 3.0).

LIST OF ABBREVIATIONS

BBFPS   British Baltic Fishery Protection Service. A British-led group that ostensibly enforced fishing regulations in the Baltic Sea but was a cover for British intelligence operations.

BDPS   Bendras demokratinio pasipriešinimo sąjūdis. Joint Democratic Resistance Movement. A Lithuanian partisan organisation active principally in the 1944–9 period.

CIA   Central Intelligence Agency. The United States' principal civilian foreign intelligence agency. Established in 1947.

EVRK   Eesti Vabariigi Rahvuskomitee. National Committee of the Republic of Estonia. Established in 1944 as a provisional government. Fled into exile and wound up in the 1950s.

GULAG   Glavnoe Upravlenie Lagerei. Main Directorate of Camps. An early name of the Soviet government agency responsible for prison camps. The abbreviation became common slang for the vast punitive labour camp system. The actual name of the organisation changed several times.

KGB   Komitet gosudarstvennoy bezopasnosti. Committee for State Security. Principal security and intelligence arm of the Soviet Union, 1954–91. Successor to MGB and NKVD.

LAF   Lietuvių Aktyvistų Frontas. Lithuanian Activist Front. Lithuanian resistance group with a wide membership base, active 1940–1.

LIST OF ABBREVIATIONS

LCP	Latvijas Centrālā Padome. Latvian Central Council. Umbrella resistance group in Latvia, active 1943 to 1951, latterly in exile.
LLA	Lietuvos Laisvės Armija. Lithuanian Forest Brotherhood organisation, active 1944–6.
LLKS	Lietuvos Laisvės Kovos sąjūdis. Union of Lithuanian Freedom Fighters. Final national Forest Brotherhood organisation, active 1949–53. Built from remnants of LLA and BDPS.
MGB	Ministerstvo Gosudarstvennoy Bezopasnosti. Ministry of State Security. Soviet internal security ministry, 1946–53. Replaced by KGB.
MI6	The United Kingdom's primary foreign intelligence service. Also occasionally referred to as SIS—Secret Intelligence Service.
MVD	Ministerstvo Vnutrennikh Del. Ministry of Internal Affairs. The ministry in the Soviet Union responsible for policing and the Gulag system, 1946–91.
NKVD	Naródnyy Komissariát Vnútrennikh Del. People's Commissariat of Internal Affairs. Main security organisation of the Soviet state, 1934–46
OSS	Office of Strategic Services. US wartime intelligence and special operations organisation. In existence 1942–5. Considered a predecessor to the CIA.
RVL	Relvastatud Võitluse Liit—'Union of Armed Struggle'—the most organised of Estonian Forest Brotherhood groups.
SOE	Special Operations Executive. British government special operations and sabotage organisation in the Second World War. In existence 1940–6.
SS	Schutzstaffel. Major paramilitary organisation in Nazi Germany, 1925–45. Principal perpetrator of the Holocaust.
USSR	Union of Soviet Socialist Republics. Formal name of the Soviet Union.

Vaps   Strictly speaking, not an abbreviation. Nickname in Estonian of the Vabadussõjalased, a nationalist movement in Estonia active in the late 1920s and early 1930s.

VLIK   Vyriausiasis Lietuvos Išlaisvinimo Komitetas. Supreme Committee for the Liberation of Lithuania. Umbrella political group established in Lithuanian in 1943. Continued in exile from 1943 until wrapped up in the early 1990s.

AUTHOR'S NOTE

This book was born in the days after Russia's invasion of Ukraine in February 2022. However, it has been floating around, partially gestated, in my head for a very long time. Half of my family tree originates in Lithuania. My own surname ties me to a fairly small rural region in the far south of Lithuania, and I have ancestors from other parts of Lithuania as well. I grew up with an understanding of where Lithuania was, and a bit of an idea that there were two other 'captive Baltic nations' under the yoke of Soviet tyranny. But I have also learned that these countries are not necessarily well understood, even by their neighbours, let alone America or Britain. I actually knew very little about Estonia or Latvia until I made an active effort to learn. More than once in my youth, I heard the insult 'they're just not real countries', the simplification 'they're all basically the same', the region getting muddled with the Balkans, or, the worst trope of all, 'they're all just Russians, aren't they?' This is a book about armed struggle, and it is important to understand who these people are and what they were fighting for. We see the exact same questions being asked in Ukraine of Ukrainians, so it seems clear to me that the issues are still relevant.

When I was young, I could not find Lithuania on a map. The atlases at my home and school showed a place called the 'Lithuanian Soviet Socialist Republic' as part of this thing called the USSR. The country that gave birth to my forebears and gave them a language and culture had been stolen. A whole country. How does a whole country disappear? How could I be of Lithuanian descent, when there was no Lithuania to be found? Did it vanish without a fight? If you were to read the history books that were commonplace in school libraries in the United States in the 1970s and 1980s, Lithuania faded out. At best, you might find some mention that bad things happened there in the Holocaust. I became fascinated with what happened. Part of the story of what happened is resistance to foreign occupation, as part of a broader five-decade-long story of captivity and national reassertion of independence. As I grew older and met Estonian-American and Latvian-Americans, I realised they had faced the same struggle as Lithuanians. There was a story to tell, and not many people were telling it.

This book attempts to tell that story. There are inherent problems in putting together a historical account like *The Forest Brotherhood*. Much of the narrative is permanently lost to us. Most of this struggle happened in obscurity. Many people died without fanfare in lonely forest outposts or remote prison camps, without their stories being told. Some abandoned the struggle and took many secrets with them to the grave. It is very difficult, then, to treat this war as if it were a conventional military campaign. I have started at the beginning of the war and ended at the end, but the middle is very much divided up into hundreds or thousands of small actions by small groups of people. An encyclopaedic account is probably impossible. If I had more time, this book could have been much longer, but the overall tale would not be any different. I must, therefore, apologise for the many interesting events I have left out, for lack of time, language skill, or source material. I apologise if I have not included a story about your grandfather or uncle that you were keen to read about.

Resistance in Ukraine and elsewhere

The Baltic Forest Brothers were not the only partisan resistance movement in the region, although the other groups are beyond the scope of this book. Armed resistance movements, which were, at points, anti-German, anti-Soviet, or both, popped up across Eastern Europe.

The history and legacy of the partisan movement in Ukraine is both a rich and controversial subject. A large partisan resistance evolved in Ukraine, particularly in the west of the country. The Organisation of Ukrainian Nationalists (OUN, which had factions) and the Ukrainian Insurgent Army (Ukrayins'ka Povstans'ka Armiia—UPA) as well as other groups fought a struggle as full of interesting stories as that of the Baltic Forest Brotherhood.

Numerically, it was a larger movement. Much, but not all, of the Ukrainian nationalist resistance was led by or affiliated with its leader Stepan Bandera. Bandera is, by any account, a controversial figure worth exploring. Depending on who says it and in what context, 'Banderist' or 'Banderite' is praise or insult.

There are many prominent differences between the Baltic resistance and the Ukrainian resistance. One factor is that Ukraine did not have much of a political existence as a state between the two World Wars, unlike Estonia, Latvia, and Lithuania. Various governments that purported to Ukrainian statehood in the Russian Civil War were short-lived. The Ukrainian nation, as opposed to a state, was mostly divided up between Poland and the Soviet Union, with some Ukrainians in other states as well. This divided Ukrainian nation had divisions along other fault lines as well, particularly religious divides between various strands of Catholicism and various denominations of Eastern Orthodoxy.

In the mid-1920s, patriots and nationalists were running political parties and getting elected to power in ethnic-majority states in Estonia, Latvia, and Lithuania. Ukrainians of a similar mind were deprived of this privilege. Ukrainians were oppressed to a great extent in the Soviet Union and to a lesser extent in Poland. The Ukrainian nationalist movement developed both openly and clandestinely, and the roots of Ukrainian partisan resistance date back to underground movements that had their birth well before the Second World War. Plotting, organising, developing armed underground movements, and preparing for partisan resistance in Ukrainian-speaking regions was all seriously underway years before partisan resistance started in the Baltic states.

At the risk of serious understatement, the legacy of the Ukrainian nationalist resistance is fraught with minefields. Ukrainian nationalism was in a place, historically, where the various Baltic nationalists were decades earlier. Ukraine's nationalists were seeking to create a state by carving it out from other states. Much of the movement was revolutionary in nature and espoused some radical philosophies. There were extremists. Anti-Semitism and anti-Polish beliefs could be found. Add into this mix that the Germans ruthlessly exploited Ukrainian nationalists for their own ends. While Ukrainian nationalists did at points resist Nazi

Germany, at other points they supported the Germans in the faint hope of establishing an independent state. The relationship between Ukrainian nationalist partisans and collaboration with Nazi occupiers is more muddled and has more overlap than it ever did in the Baltic states. Germans openly aided the UPA, trading arms for intelligence information. The situation is further darkened by atrocities directed against Jews, Poles or both.

There is a tendency to compare, contrast, or aggregate the quite potent Ukrainian resistance effort with the Baltic efforts. At times, this has even gone to the point of political invective, referring to Baltic Forest Brothers as 'Banderites'. However, while there are many points of comparison between the movements, there were many differences as well. It is a category error to refer to Balts as 'Banderites'.

It is also worth noting that partisan resistance existed to a lesser extent in other parts of Eastern Europe and the Soviet Union. A much smaller anti-Soviet partisan resistance movement existed in Belarus but is less well documented in English. At the time, Belarusian nationalism was a weaker and less organised phenomenon than that of any of the surrounding countries. Belarus was the site of quite active Soviet partisan and Jewish partisan resistance to German occupation. In addition, the Germans infiltrated some 'Black Cat' stay-behind teams that were briefly active in 1945. Lithuania borders Belarus, and it is known that some Lithuanian Forest Brotherhood units operated on both sides of the border. Also, much of post-1945 Belarus had been part of Poland before 1939. Some Polish Home Army units were active in the area.

Poland had a post-war Soviet resistance based largely on Second World War movements continuing to struggle for Polish statehood. Again, it is beyond the scope of this book but an interesting episode in its own right. Resistance movements in places like Albania, Romania, and Bulgaria eked out their fights before ending in relative obscurity.

A note on sources

There are few works in modern English for the general reader on this period of Baltic history. Some books have been published in recent decades, but they tend to be single-country studies like Mart Laar's excellent *War in the Woods* (1992) or works locally published in the Baltic states without much circulation outside their respective homelands. Broader works on history mention the subject in passing or even devote a few pages to the topic. Entire works on the history of some of these countries sometimes give very little detail on the subject. Since the early 1990s, there has been a veritable deluge of archival material, particularly from American and Soviet sources. I have barely been able to scratch the surface of this material, but some recent scholarship, particularly in Lithuanian, is now available, including a number of partisan memoirs that can be accessed online, and Lithuanian, Latvian, and Estonian archives have also made Soviet records and partisan documents available. During the more open era of the 1990s, significant Soviet documentation was available for examination, and some scholars have studied the subject from the Soviet angle. Of equal importance, online translation tools have made many of the period's documents more accessible to English speakers.

A note on language and spelling conventions

Estonian, Latvian, and Lithuanian are interesting languages. Comparatively few people outside the region have any facility in them. To one extent or another, they have characters or diacritical marks unknown in English. Characters like ā, ū, č, and š are found in these languages. I endeavour to use the correct words with correct spelling when appropriate. This becomes particularly relevant with names of people and places, as not including a diacritical mark literally misspells a proper noun.

As far as place names are concerned, it can get very complicated very quickly. A lot of places have multiple names, reflecting the numerous former overlords of the region or inhabitants of a particular place, who may have changed over time. Tallinn was known for a long time as Reval, its German name. At various points, Kaunas, the one-time capital of Lithuania, has been Kovno, Kowno, Каунас, Kauns, Коўна, Kovna, Kovne, and עֲנוּאָק. At least these words sound broadly similar, unlike Tartu (Estonian) and Dorpat (German), which are the same city. A particular choice of spelling of a place name can, deliberately or inadvertently, be a political statement. To avoid confusion, I use the current Estonian, Latvian, and Lithuanian place names and spelling within those countries unless I am directly quoting something that uses a different spelling.

Another area of terminology trouble is what to call the armed resistance fighters. Some of the books written in the West during the Cold War call them 'guerrillas'. Perhaps 'partisan' was tainted by its Second World War association with Communists. In Soviet historiography, many books and articles ensured that 'partisan' only meant officially directed Soviet irregular units. 'Freedom fighter' has a good feel to it as well. 'Resistance' and 'underground' are not bad but need additional qualifiers to differentiate between a largely but not completely rural armed resistance and a largely but not completely urban unarmed resistance that outlived the armed struggle. The restoration of independence in the Baltic states has witnessed an earnest effort to reclaim the term 'partisan' as a valid way to refer to armed resistance fighters. My own opinion is that there is no particularly good reason why Communism should claim a monopoly on the term 'partisan'. As such, I am going to agree with recent Baltic usage of the term. I use the term 'partisan' freely in this book to describe people engaged in armed resistance against foreign occupation. Many of these groups referred to themselves as partisans. Where necessary, the phrase 'Soviet Partisan(s)' is used to designate the Soviet-armed and -led irregular forces during the Second World War.

The main state security agency of the Soviet Union has had several names over the course of its existence, and I have tried to use the commonly used Russian-language abbreviation of the agency (NKVD, KGB, etc.) at the actual time of a reported event. For most of this book, it is the NKVD.

Acknowledgements

Many people have helped me with this book.

Some people helped me over thirty years ago when I first developed an interest in the subject of Lithuanian partisans. The late Stasys Bačkis and his successor Stasys Lozoraitis Junior, as elder statesmen in the most literal sense as the remnants of the Lithuanian diplomatic corps in exile, and the late Antanas Dundzila, editor of the journal *Lituanus*, deserve credit for sparking my interest in this subject in 1987. They were incredibly generous with their time and information resources. Any one of them could have said, 'get lost, kid', but they didn't.

Not long afterwards, I became a bit of an Estonia-phile as well. Tunne Kelam, Mari-Ann Kelam, Mart Laar, and a whole host of other friendly Estonians embraced me in the early days of my pan-Baltic enthusiasm. The late Olaf Tammark gets credit for being the only Forest Brother I ever met in the flesh. He spent an afternoon in the early 1990s explaining German weaponry to me and describing how to build a bunker in a forest. I wish I'd kept the sketch he drew for me on the back of a bit of junk mail.

Arthur Snell, Edward Lucas, Martin Toomas Ilves, Aidas Palubinskas, Martin Brown, Roger Moorhouse, Alina Nowobilska, Mart Kuldkepp, Ben Wheatley, Mari-Ann Kelam, Tunne Kelam, Nick Zambellas, Cheryl Rofer, my wife Sophie Tyler, and many others have all helped with various aspects of the work.

I have never met him, but my distant relative Algis Kašėta did a lot of time-consuming research in this subject, and without the groundwork laid by himself and other enthusiasts and scholars in the three Baltic states, this work would have been much harder to do.

I would also like to thank Michael Dwyer and the entire team at Hurst publishers, who are lovely people to work with. Special thanks go to the incomparable British Library and the long-suffering staff in both the Oriental Club and Cask Pub in London, where I seem to have become, over the years, their writer in residence.

PROLOGUE

DECEMBER 1950

Jurgis was known by the codename 'Lapė' (Fox). He was the leader of a small group of five men. There had been more. As many as ten at times. The first winter wasn't so bad.

Then, they lived in the lofts of nearby farms and survived off food from the farms. At first, they had spent more time farming, paying their way in labour. But as more Soviet secret police (NKVD) troops were stationed in the district, and there were more searches of farms for partisans, they retreated into the woods.

The dugout was called a bunker, but it wasn't much of one. It was a place to hide and keep dry and to try to keep warm in the winter. Spring, summer, and autumn were times to gather food and other supplies. Winter was for surviving. The forest yielded honey and mushrooms, which could be gathered and traded with farmers. The farmers still provided what support they could, but times were hard. A bucket of milk here, a basket of apples there, and the occasional loaf of stout sour rye bread that would last ten days before it went stale, left out on a windowsill. When the weather was good, life in the forest wasn't bad. Once, they even shot a deer. But they would not dare risk a gunshot now. Jurgis had grown up in a similar forest, only 20 kilometres away. His right-hand man, Algis, but known as 'Kikilis' (Finch), had been a scout in these woods as a youth and taught much woodcraft to the others.

Fox was the leader, having been a young lieutenant in the Lithuanian Army. He still had the greatcoat and shoulder insignia of the republic's army that he had deserted with after the 1940 Soviet occupation. They were a valued memento of better days and kept him warm. Fox had led the group from the beginning. This was initially because of his military experience, though he had not actually had all that much. He stayed in charge because he was a natural leader with good sense and, most important for a brother of the forest, good luck.

Their armaments were an odd mix. Three Mauser rifles of various vintages, two Soviet PPSh submachine guns. Six different pistols, but only one of them, a Tokarev they took off the NKVD, had much ammo. One German 'Schmeisser' submachine gun, but only one damaged magazine for it. Finally, they had an actual German Army machine gun, an MG-42, left over from the 1941 Nazi occupation, but only one belt of ammo left for it. It was for a last stand should the bunker be compromised. Seven hand grenades. Keeping rust at bay was a constant struggle. Since their radio had died in 1947, their most valued item was the tin of oil. And shoes. Footwear was at a premium. Word had long gone around the Forest Brothers that some groups had received radios and radio operators parachuted in from the West. But Jurgis joked that the best thing the CIA could do for them was five pairs of boots, a bottle of gun oil, and a sack of potatoes.

Cold, boredom, and hunger were bigger enemies than the NKVD or the Red Army. When the Brothers acted, which was not frequently any longer, they made sure to go at least 5 kilometres from the bunker. This was like a war in slow motion, in deep freeze. Once a month, Fox went out to meet with the district leadership and came back with a bundle of papers—someone had a mimeograph machine and could make copies of their underground newspaper. Last year, they'd shot up some NKVD guys. Six months ago, they'd thrown a grenade. These days, their struggle was largely to survive. If they could covertly hand out some newspapers, hold up a commissar and take his money (and boots), and raise the flag in a village on 16 February, Lithuanian independence day, they felt like they were still doing something. They were still fighting a war just by staying alive and occasionally reminding the Soviets that they were still there.

They'd been ten. One, Vytautas (known as 'Owl'), died from pneumonia in 1946. One of the Brothers, and their one 'Forest Sister', managed to slip back into civilian life before it got harder to regularise the paperwork. 'Bear' had been shot in early 1947, but it was a minor wound and he got better. More than once, though, someone went out and never came back. Nobody knew what happened to 'Eagle'. He never came back. Maybe he was caught? Maybe he was killed? Maybe he had had enough. Maybe he joined a group with better prospects and more farms nearby. He probably hadn't given the rest of the group up, because nobody came looking for the dugout. Eventually, the food was going to give out. The Communists were 'collectivising' agriculture and turning all the small farms into 'kolkhozes'—collective farms that really served as rural jails for the farmers. Every time this happened, it became harder for groups of Brothers to feed themselves. Unless another world war broke out, this destruction of farms was going to be the end of the Brothers.

So, there they were. Keeping the dream of Lithuania alive. Eating old potatoes and stitching up the holes in old clothing. How did it come to this? Well, there's a story to tell …

INTRODUCTION

THE BACKGROUND

The prologue described a person named Jurgis and a few others in a forest. They are fictional, but only barely. There really were thousands of people exactly like them in real life, hiding in forests. They were the so-called 'Forest Brothers', and they have often been forgotten by history. Where are the Baltic states? Who are these peoples? Why were they fighting in the forests? What happened? Why is it still important?

Where?

To fight for one's homeland and country is a natural impulse. So let us, at the outset, locate the countries. Estonia, Latvia, and Lithuania are the so-called 'Baltic states': three separate countries on the eastern shore of the Baltic Sea. In their own languages, they are called Eesti, Latvija, and Lietuva, respectively. There is no correct order in which to mention them, so for lack of a better scheme I will refer to them in alphabetical order unless there is a reason to do otherwise. They are not the same as each other, but they do share many common experiences.

'Baltic states' is not a perfect phrase, but it is less flawed than the other ones I have heard. It is used collectively like 'Scandinavia', 'the Low Countries', 'the Nordic countries', or that troublesome term 'the Balkans' to refer to a collection of smaller states. 'Baltic republics' is technically correct. They all call themselves 'republics' and have such a form of government. But that term might be just a bit too redolent of the Soviet era when the three were 'republics' in name only as part of a union of such fake republics, the Soviet Union.

'Baltic nations' is similarly problematic. Ethnographers and linguists will tell you that Latvians and Lithuanians are 'Baltic peoples', ethnically and linguistically, whereas the Estonians are Finnic people, speaking a Uralic language. To use the word 'Balt' or 'Baltic peoples' in a strict sense might mean, in some contexts, excluding Estonians. The words 'nation' and 'nationality' can imply ethnicity, and all three have significant ethnic, linguistic, and religious minorities. And if we are going to talk about nations and ethnicities in the region, there are others than just Lithuanian, Latvia, and Estonian. Some, like the Curonians and Prussians (the Baltic people of the original name, not the Germans who took their lands) are extinct. Others, such as the Livonians in Latvia and Setos in Estonia, are small and dwindling but have national identities of their own. In addition, it's largely a matter of convention that we do not refer to Finland as a 'Baltic nation'.

I suppose 'Baltic countries' might work, and I've even used that conversationally. 'The Baltic' or 'Baltics' is too vague. The Russian word for the region 'Pribaltika' is a bit like 'the Ukraine' or 'the Balkans'—a geographic term, not a political or national one. So we are left with 'the Baltic states' as the best general term to use.

The 'where' question also invites questions about borders. The borders of all three Baltic states have been relatively stable between each other but have had a number of shifts at their outer edges. This is a fascinating tale, but one beyond this book. Border shifts will be mentioned as relevant. Consider the current-day borders as a general guideline but not an absolute statement as to where each of these states begins and ends.

Who?

The three main nationalities in this narrative are the Estonians, the Latvians, and the Lithuanians. To a greater or lesser extent, all three of them are modern nationalities that grew out of smaller regional and tribal groups over the last two millennia.

Estonians are closely related to Finns, and more distantly related to Hungarians and a number of less widely known ethnic groups across the former Soviet Union. They speak Estonian, a complex language in the Finno-Ugric language family, a subset of the Uralic languages, and not related to most of the other languages of Europe. Early Estonia formed its own culture and identity, but from the medieval period onward its history is heavily influenced by Vikings, Denmark, and Sweden. Because of strong German and Swedish influences, since the Protestant reformation, the prevailing religion in Estonia has been Lutheranism.

Latvia is directly to the south of Estonia. Latvians are 'Baltic' peoples and speak one of the only surviving languages in the Baltic-language group of the Indo-European languages. The Latvians, referred to in older documents as 'Letts', lived in what is now Latvia alongside the Livs (or Livonians), a now mostly extinct group. The region now known as Latvia was composed of areas historically referred to as Courland and Livonia. As with the Estonians, Latvians came under foreign domination, in the form of Germans and Swedes. The prevailing religion among Latvians has thus also been Lutheranism, for as long as Lutheranism has been a thing, although a significant proportion are also Roman Catholic.

Physical geography affects the cultural geography of Estonia and Latvia. Both have extensive coasts, which made them vulnerable to marauding Vikings of Danish and Swedish origin. Both were on the way, more or less, to the interior of Eastern Europe and were thus part of the complex system of rivers and portages that provided trade routes to the Black Sea and thus Constantinople and the East. Germanic and Nordic traders used these routes, settled along them, and developed ports. This arrangement led to the formation of the Hanseatic League and to significant settlement and religious conversion in the areas now known as Latvia and Estonia. Riga and Tallinn, the respective capitals, as well as a number of other towns, were members of the league. To make a broad simplification, Estonian and Latvian history and culture looks west to Germany and Sweden.

Lithuanians are also Balts but have some interesting added complexities to their history. The Lithuanian language is, perhaps, one of the oldest in Europe. Many Lithuanians and even some Indians will tell you that it is the closest living language to Sanskrit, but such a belief may be more of a romantic notion than linguistic fact. Nevertheless, scholars of early Indo-European language flock to Lithuania to study this language seemingly frozen in amber. The reason the language is as old as it is has much to do with geography. While Estonia and Latvia were highways for commerce, Lithuania with its scant coast—and at points in history, a coastline measured in feet not miles—and dense forests, was a barrier. The dense primeval forest of Lithuania, which figures a lot in the narrative of this book, offered refuge but relatively little prospect for commerce. There was, simply, little reason not to bypass the Lithuanians. So, they remained relatively unmolested while the rest of Europe changed around them. They solidified as a Grand Duchy, and one that became quite powerful.

Religion is an important thread in the Lithuanian fabric of identity. The dense woods allowed defence against the outside, which meant that it was easier to resist conversion by crusading Teutonic knights who more easily conquered and converted their northern neighbours. Lithuanians remained solidly pagan until the late fourteenth and early fifteenth centuries, the last major group in Europe to convert to Christianity. But when they did convert, it was to Roman Catholicism. The Protestant reformation did sweep through Lithuania as well, but it receded in the face of a counterreformation, leaving a small Lutheran minority and an even smaller Calvinist reformed minority in its wake. Lithuania's history looks more south-west to Catholic Poland than across the Baltic. Catholicism remains strong to this day, and the Catholic Church played a role in the resistance movement.

A series of adventurous grand dukes gave Lithuania its own empire that once spanned as far as the Black Sea. Lithuanians proudly point out that, at one point, Lithuania was one of the largest countries in Europe. Political and dynastic affairs ended up intertwining Poland and Lithuania, first loosely, and then tightly. The Polish–Lithuanian Commonwealth lasted until 1795, although the Lithuanian part of this polity became something of a backwater over time. A grand history full of military victories over Russians and Germans gives a bit of skeleton to the Lithuanian national self-image.

It is important also to understand that people of other ethnicities and nationalities have long resided in the same space. Larger multi-ethnic polities, such as the Polish–Lithuanian Commonwealth, the tsarist Russian Empire, and the Soviet Union had some degree of internal movement of peoples for a variety of economic and political reasons. Armenians seem to have got all over these empires, for example. Tatars ended up settling in some places in Lithuania. Swedes ended up in Estonia as an artefact of the Swedish Empire. Roma live here as well, as in other places in Europe. Poles ended up in south-eastern Latvia, where they live to this day in some considerable number. Even smaller ethnic groups occur in pockets of these countries.

Four groups of particular relevance to this book are Jews, Baltic Germans, Poles, and Russians. The Polish–Lithuanian Commonwealth had a significant degree of religious tolerance. Many Jews settled in lands of the Grand Duchy of Lithuania. The footprint of the old Grand Duchy became, roughly, the borders of the Pale of Settlement, that bit of the Russian Empire where Jews were allowed to live. Significant Jewish populations developed in Lithuania, with Vilnius becoming a major centre of Jewish culture in Eastern Europe. Smaller populations of Jews settled in Estonia and Latvia later on.

Baltic Germans (there are very few left in the Baltic states) were the descendants of crusaders and traders who settled in Estonia, Latvia, and a narrow coastal bit of Lithuania. They formed a landowning nobility class for hundreds of years and were the basis of middle- and upper-class city dwellers in Estonian and Latvian cities well into the twentieth century. They were a relatively well-off minority in all three countries.

Poles have been an ethnic minority in parts of Lithuania for many centuries. It is not as if there is a sharp traditional border where one side is always Polish and the other Lithuanian. There's a gradient at the edges. This gradient has grown steeper at points, but for example there has been a significant ethnic Polish population in the Vilnius region for a long time, as well as the Daugavpils area in south-east Latvia.

Settlement of ethnic Russians is not just a post-war Soviet phenomenon. To some extent or another, there have been some Russians in the Baltic states for many centuries. In the 1600s, Russian 'Old Believers', an Orthodox sect that rejected various changes in the Russian Orthodox Church in the seventeenth century, migrated to all three countries, forming rural communities. After the 1700s, when all three countries were under the tsar, Russian officials, businessmen, and their families moved in. According to the 1897 census, Estonia had about 37,599 ethnic Russians and a few hundred Ukrainians and Belarusians. Riga was a major seaport for export trade with the rest of the world and had developed some industry. Latvia was 8 per cent Russian in 1897, much of this population peasants along the border. By contrast, Lithuania was only 2.5 per cent Russian according to its somewhat later 1923 census. All of these minorities become important later in this story.

The Baltic states up to 1940

In the late 1700s, imperial Russia's westward expansion brought almost all of the Baltic states, barring a small sliver of the west of Lithuania, into the Russian Empire. The bit of Lithuania around Memel, now Klaipėda, became part of the Kingdom of Prussia and is often known as 'Lithuania Minor'. All three Baltic states, with the exception of that small fragment under Prussian and then German rule, endured tsarist rule from the 1700s until the First World War. Religion and language suffered repressions of varying extent during this period as various Russification policies were pursued. Hardship made people leave. The end of serfdom in the Russian Empire in 1861 meant that peasants were not legally tied to the land, and a significant number of Lithuanians managed to emigrate to places like the United States, Canada, and South America between the 1860s and the First World War. Lithuanians had a relatively porous border with Germany and could literally walk off to the West. Emigration was less numerically significant in Latvia and Estonia, but it still occurred.

The latter part of the nineteenth century saw the rise of national identity in all three countries. The Lietuvių tautinis atgimimas ('Lithuanian national awakening'), Pirmā Atmoda (Latvia's 'First Awakening'), and the Estonian Ärkamisaeg (roughly, 'the time of waking up') were contemporaneous and even occasionally cross-pollinated movements. These occurred at a time when similar movements and revivals were emerging across Europe and even other parts of the world, such as the rise of Arab nationalism. In the same context, this is the period in which Germany and Italy unified as nation-states with ideas of ethnic and linguistic identity.

INTRODUCTION

The not uncommon trope used against the Baltic states is that they are somehow 'fake countries' with no identity, but their identity was formed at the same time as German, Italian, and even Irish identity. Nobody calls those countries fake.

The First World War began in 1914 and ripped through the region. Much of the territory of the Baltic states was under German occupation at one point or another. A high percentage of the military-age males served in the Russian Army. While those of us in the West have a clear demarcation of that war ending on 11 November 1918, the point at which we declare the end of the war in the East is up for discussion. At the risk of oversimplifying a very complex period of history, Germany largely bested Russia on the Eastern Front, and tsarist Russia gradually folded and imploded. Two revolutions happened in 1917. The second of these two saw the Bolshevik party take control of Russia. The resulting Russian Civil War dragged on for some years. This chaotic situation created an environment wherein a lot of nationalities within the now former Russian Empire could try to achieve independence. Some of these escape attempts—Finland, the three Baltic states, and Poland—were successful; others, like Ukraine, Belarus, Georgia, and Armenia, ultimately failed.

Estonia, Latvia, and Lithuania had complicated wars of independence, each of which is worthy of a detailed account. There were numerous sides in these conflicts, and they were, in various ways, wars of liberation, the last gasp of the First World War, a failed attempt to extend the 1917 Bolshevik revolution, a secondary front in the ongoing Russian Civil War in the East, a border conflict with Poland (in the case of Lithuania), and conflicts within and between factions. Even an enthusiast like myself has occasionally lost the plot when trying to understand all of the events of the 1917–20 period.

At the risk of handwaving over a complex period better covered by other books, all three Baltic states achieved their independence in 1918 and had a fraught time maintaining it for a few years. But by the dawn of the 1920s, world maps had two new countries on them for the first time, Estonia and Latvia. A third one was back from the grave, Lithuania.[1]

By the early 1920s, Estonia, Latvia, and Lithuania were functional multi-party democratic republics whose citizens enjoyed a reasonable degree of economic and political freedom. But in all three instances, by the start of the main events of this book (1939–40), all three had degraded into some form of undemocratic rule, albeit nowhere near as harsh or totalitarian as the Nazi, fascist, or Communist regimes. To understand later resistance efforts and interpretations of motivations, it is worth taking a quick tour through the interwar period in the three countries.

Estonia

Estonia started out as a multi-party democracy after its independence. After defeating the Bolsheviks and the Germans, it secured peace and independence with the Treaty of Tartu in 1920. A constituent assembly was elected in 1919 that drew up a democratic constitution. Elections in 1920 to the new Riigikogu empanelled 100 parliamentarians from a wide range of political parties. The history of this period is greatly influenced by two political figures, Konstantin Päts (1874–1956) and Jaan Tõnisson (1868–1941?).[2] Another prominent figure was General Johan Laidoner (1884–1953), a highly talented military leader and a hero of the war for independence.

The economy was still largely agrarian, and agricultural exports formed the basis of the economy. Land reform broke up the old Baltic German rural estates, creating thousands of smallholder farms that would provide the subsistence basis for a rural partisan movement, as recounted later in this book. One criticism that could be levelled at Estonia during this period was that it had a surfeit of democracy. It originally had a strong legislative branch and a weak executive. There was a multiplicity of parties, many short-lasting, with none close to getting a majority. Governance shifted between coalitions, with few governments lasting very long. The average government lasted less than a year during this period.

Despite Estonia getting its independence from Bolshevik Russia in 1918, Communism was still viewed as a serious threat to statehood throughout the 1920s, and efforts both by Estonian Communists and by the Soviet Union reinforced these fears. In 1924, the Estonian government arrested and tried 149 members of the Estonian Communist Party. In December of that year, Estonian Communists supported by Soviet agents attempted a coup in Tallinn.

The coup attempt, later billed as an 'uprising' in Soviet histories, failed. General Laidoner helped restore order.

The period after the 1924 Communist coup saw the development of the Estonian Defence League, the Kaitseliit, which was trained and equipped as a reserve force for national defence. Boy and girl Scout movements were associated with it as well. Thousands of Estonians received some degree of military training through the Kaitseliit, a factor that later gave some basis for armed resistance. By 1940, the strength of the organisation was 42,000, an impressive figure for a small country.

Another development was less positive. A mass group called the Vaps movement was founded in 1929.[3] Nominally a group for veterans of the independence struggle, it was led by former tsarist military officers and quickly veered into right-wing politics. Some of its affectations, such as black berets and a Roman-style salute, carried the whiff of fascism about them. Some members supported the rise of Hitler, although the group openly denounced racial ideology and the oppression of Jews. The Vaps movement, which wanted a more strongly presidential form of government, forced a referendum on constitutional reforms that took much power away from the legislature.

By the 1930s, the Great Depression had started seriously affecting Estonia as well. The toxic brew of far-right politics and economic despair caused problems. The Päts government started to feel threatened by the Vaps movement. In early 1934, the Vaps movement won a lot of seats in local municipal elections. In effect, Vaps got what they wanted—a strong presidential government when Päts and Laidoner effectively threw a 'self-coup' and established a dictatorship. They threw over 400 members of Vaps into prison. Ironically, the state of emergency declared by Päts was legal under the new 1934 constitution that Vaps had advocated.

The 1934–8 period is often called the Era of Silence. Political parties were suppressed, and right-wing corporatist policies were pursued to try to shore up the economy. While authoritarian, Päts' rule was not considered harsh. Yet another constitution came into effect in 1937, and opposition candidates were allowed to run in the following year's elections, albeit as independents, polling nearly 43 per cent of the vote. In 1938, Päts released all jailed political prisoners.

Latvia

Latvia emerged into independence in 1918 heavily in debt and somewhat depopulated. The population had sunk to 1.6 million in 1920 from a healthy 2.5 million in 1914.[4] With over half the land still belonging to the German nobility, but with lots of landless people, land reform was a key agenda in the early years. The Ritterschaft— the association of German gentry and landowning nobility— resisted the reforms, but the organisation was ultimately abolished and the nobility's estates, many of which dated back centuries, were broken up. Smallholdings proliferated and agriculture flourished.

By 1922, a new Latvian constitution had been adopted. A legislature, the Saeima, was established. Political parties and democracy proliferated, albeit to a somewhat ridiculous extent, as any association of five persons could register as a political party. Representatives of twenty-two political parties were elected to the first Saeima. The political spectrum was broad ranging, from socialist and social democrats through to liberals and then on to Christian nationalists. Consensus and compromise, in the form of coalition governments, became the norm for a few years.

The 1920s was a period of relative prosperity for Latvia. The economy grew, debt was reduced, and significant development of infrastructure occurred. Riga became the most cosmopolitan city in the region. Many countries had their principal diplomatic and commercial outposts in Riga, with mere satellite offices and consulates in Tallinn and Kaunas. Arts and culture flourished.

As with Estonia, an auxiliary paramilitary organisation developed as part of the national defence strategy. The Aizsargi (roughly, 'the Guards') developed as a national movement. By the end of Latvian independence, it had over 30,000 members and significant youth and women's auxiliary wings, thus laying some of the groundwork for later resistance.

The leading figure in Latvian politics was Kārlis Ulmanis (1877–1942). Ulmanis served as prime minister four different times, although two of those terms were quite brief. Originally an agricultural expert, Ulmanis had studied in Switzerland, Germany, and the United States before the First World War. He founded the Latvian Farmers' Union, which became a prominent conservative party after independence. The party polled in second place in the five Saeima elections in the 1920s and 1930s, behind the Social Democrats.

Both politics and economics took a downward turn in the 1930s, largely because of the worldwide Great Depression. The prosperity of the 1920s was over. The compromise and consensus model led to many changes in government and declining confidence in the generation of leaders that had brought about independence. As elsewhere, far-right organisations started to crop up. The Pērkonkrusts (the 'Thundercross', after their symbol) were, possibly, the most fascist of the right-wing movements in the entire region.

In 1934, Ulmanis conspired with the war minister Jānis Balodis (1881–1965) and the Aizsargi to stage a coup. He installed himself as both president and prime minister. The constitution, political parties, and the parliament were all suspended. The new Ulmanis regime cracked down on political opposition of every stripe. Leading Social Democrats were locked up, but so were pro-Nazi Baltic Germans and ninety-five members of the Pērkonkrusts. Corporatist policies based on those of Päts in Estonia and António de Oliveira Salazar in Portugal were implemented. Ulmanis made no attempt to rewrite the constitution and ran the regime unilaterally on the basis of his personality. However, while authoritarian, his rule was by no means fascist as Ulmanis largely avoided ideology

Lithuania

Lithuania's early years of independence were plagued by a war with neighbouring Poland. Newly independent Poland disputed the borders of Lithuania and wished to expand at the expense of the new Lithuanian republic. Poland's leader, Marshal Piłsudski, had a broad vision of re-establishing the old Polish–Lithuanian Commonwealth. But geography, demographics, and the Polish exceptionalism afoot at the time would mean that Lithuanians would always take second place in such an arrangement. Enthusiasm for this concept among Lithuanians was scant to say the least. A brief war was fought between Lithuania and Poland, which was so contentious that even to this day Lithuanian and Polish scholars cannot even agree on the end date of the conflict.

For most of the interwar period, relations between Poland and Lithuania were awful. Diplomatic relations were suspended, and the region around Vilnius, the official capital, was occupied by Poland and annexed into their country as Wilno. This meant that Lithuania was stuck with a provisional capital in Kaunas. Also, due to the occupation, interwar Lithuania did not actually border upon the USSR.

One aspect of the early days of the republic was, like in Estonia and Latvia, the development of an auxiliary paramilitary force, the Riflemen's Union. It taught marksmanship to thousands and served as a reserve component of the military. It grew to over 30,000 members. Importantly, it actually owned a variety of firearms.

Early independent Lithuania also claimed the formerly German city of Memel and surrounding region, referring to them by their historic Lithuanian names of Klaipėda and Lithuania Minor, respectively. Independent Lithuania desperately needed a seaport and had historic claims to the city. In the immediate aftermath of the First World War, the Klaipėda/Memel region was occupied by French troops and administered by the French as a League of Nations Mandate. In early 1923, Lithuania staged a revolt in the territory, which met little resistance from either local police or French occupation troops. The Riflemen's Union participated in this action. In 1924, the Klaipėda Convention regularised the status of the region as Lithuanian territory, and the Lithuanian state finally had its seaport.

Lithuania's interwar history is similar to that of Latvia and Estonia in that it can be broadly divided into a democratic period and an authoritarian period. As with the other two countries, a centre-right authoritarian government grew out of a diverse political environment. In the republic's early days, the foremost political party was the Christian Democrats, a centre-right party that espoused patriotic and Catholic values. Roman Catholic clergy had been involved in the founding of the party in tsarist times. Other prominent parties included the centre-left Peasant Popular Union, the left-leaning Social Democrats, and the right-wing Lithuanian National Union.

One key figure in interwar Lithuania was Antanas Smetona (1874–1944), a leader of the Lithuanian National Union. This party had its roots in a merger of two smaller parties, the Party of National Progress and the Lithuanian Farmers Association. The party had little electoral success, despite Smetona and another figure, Augustinas Voldemaras (1883–1942), being prominent and popular personalities.

Smetona had been a Lithuanian nationalist since his student days, when he was forced to utter prayers in Russian, not Lithuanian. Although he nominally worked in a bank in tsarist-era Vilnius, he spent an active career in Lithuanian nationalist politics and was the first editor of the *Lietuvos Aidas* ('Echo of Lithuania') newspaper while Lithuania was under German occupation in the First World War. He was chairman of the Council of Lithuania that signed Lithuania's declaration of independence and briefly served as interim president from 1919 to 1920.

The other figure in the nationalists, Voldemaras, was a rival to Smetona. Voldemaras had started his career as an academic, studying history and philosophy and earning a PhD. Like Smetona, he had been active in nationalist causes before and during the First World War and was part of the Council of Lithuania. He briefly served as prime minister after independence. However, he was very critical of the government in the 1920s and even served a brief sentence of hard labour for his political writings.

The 1920–6 era showed a lot of promise. Democracy started to flourish. Party politics meant that there were shifting coalitions. Nine different governments ruled during this period, albeit with significant overlap between them. The economy started to grow. With new construction, Kaunas ceased to be a provincial backwater. Much of the modernist architecture of the era gives Kaunas a great deal of its current charm and appeal. Land reform helped keep the country from being a backward, peasant-based society run by wealthy landowners. President Aleksandras Stulginskis (a Christian Democrat) was in office from 1920 to 1926. He was unassuming but got on with the job. One of his ministers, Father Mykolas Krupavičius, served as agriculture minister and was quite a reformer.

The brief democratic era basically came to an end in 1926. The nationalists did poorly in that year's elections, and the Christian Democrats won thirty out of eighty-five seats. The Peasants Popular Union and Social Democrats formed a coalition with a variety of small parties representing ethnic minorities. Kazys Grinius was elected the third president of Lithuania and Mykolas Sleževičius was prime minister. Both were from the Peasants Popular Union.

The nationalists took umbrage at this state of affairs, and elements of the military started planning a coup. In December 1926, army troops under one Colonel Povilas Plechavičius (who will enter the narrative again in a later chapter) launched the coup during President Grinius' birthday celebration. They used the generally implausible excuse of an imminent Communist coup. After a session of the Seimas held without the Peasants Popular Union and the Social Democrats, Smetona was installed as president and Voldemaras as prime minister.

From 1926 to 1940, Smetona ran Lithuania as an authoritarian state along single party lines. The Christian Democrats left the coalition, and Smetona gradually came to consider himself a 'Father of the Nation' figure. Voldemaras crept further to the right politically. He formed a far-right, quasi-fascist group, the Geležinis Vilkas ('Iron Wolves'), which by 1929 had over 4,000 members and was intended to oppress dissent. This was evidently too much for Smetona, who sacked Voldemaras as prime minister in 1929 while he was out of the country. Voldemaras was rusticated to rural exile under police surveillance. In 1930, the Iron Wolves were suppressed, though some of them continued to operate underground.

The Smetona regime spent much of the remaining decade facing threats from the far right. Voldemaras and his supporters attempted a coup in 1934, but the coup failed, and Voldemaras was jailed and then exiled to France. A number of military officers were imprisoned. It should also be noted that the Smetona government also faced sedition from Nazis in Klaipėda, which had a significant German population. Lithuania prosecuted and jailed Nazis, a rarity in pre-war Europe. As the decade ended, Smetona, now in his sixties, remained the sole ruler of the country.

Laying the groundwork for resistance

Conditions in the Baltic states in the 1920s and 1930s laid significant groundwork for armed resistance movements. First, one can look at geography and topography. All three countries are heavily forested, with forests and swamps accounting for a relatively high percentage of land in Estonia, Latvia, and Lithuania. Many of these forests were and are coniferous, providing cover and concealment in winter as well as summer. There is a long history, both in documented instances and in popular folk history, of fleeing invaders by seeking refuge in dense forests. My own experience in and around one of the villages of my ancestors in the Dzūkija region of Lithuania is that it can be dark as night on a bright day a mere five minutes' walk into the densest bit of primeval forest. This is terrain that suits a partisan. A secondary factor in Estonia was access by sea to Finland, which had some secondary roles in the development of resistance there.

Economics also affected the rise of resistance movements in the 1920s and 1930s. The foremost factor was land reform. In all three states, older estates owned by landed gentry and nobility, often in absentia, were broken up into smallholdings. Peasants, the eldest of whom might have been born into serfdom, which ended in the Russian Empire only in the 1860s, found themselves landowners, running small and medium-sized farms. The breakup of the large estates meant that the proliferation of small farms, with a relatively dispersed agrarian population, could clandestinely feed a population of resistance fighters. The eventual collectivisation of agriculture was one of the factors that saw the decline of armed resistance.

From political, cultural, and social perspectives, one can look at the 1920s and 1930s in the three Baltic states and see that many developments had an impact on resistance movements in the following decades. The development of the three as independent states, with their own languages, institutions, religious entities, and educational curricula, cemented the national identities that had started to emerge in the nineteenth century. The national identities gave people something to fight for. Few partisans were fighting principally for the restoration of the substandard pre-war regimes. They were fighting for the idea of nationhood. Nationalism and national identity manifested itself in many different ways across the political spectrum, not just in terms of right and far-right parties. National identity was embraced from left to right across the political spectrum.

Some institutions arose or grew stronger during this period in ways that eventually benefitted the resistance. All three developed armies during this period. The armies did not end up resisting foreign invasion by much stronger opponents, but they did serve the purpose of training thousands of people who went on to fight in the resistance movements. The 1920s and 1930s saw a lot of men in all three countries rotate through military service.

In addition to formal active military service, auxiliary and paramilitary organisations were prominent. The Lithuanian Riflemen's Union had tens of thousands of members in the 1930s and taught marksmanship to many eventual partisans. The Aizsargi were a home-guard-type paramilitary organisation in Latvia, and the Kaitseliit in Estonia were similar. These organisations helped provide a basis for resistance. Scouting movements taught outdoor living skills that made life in the forest easier for many a partisan. In some instances, Scouting movements were formally affiliated with the paramilitary units. Institutional development worked both ways, though. Such groups usually had membership lists, which made good fodder for the secret policemen of the Soviet and German invaders.

As the 1930s drew to a close, things started to unravel across Europe. The Baltic states, hopeful that they could stay out of the upcoming war, were soon to be disappointed.

PART 1

THE BALTICS BETWEEN GERMANY AND RUSSIA

1

NIGHTFALL

A continent in crisis

By the late 1930s, Estonia, Latvia, and Lithuania had ceased to be functioning multi-party democracies. None of their governments were particularly fascist, although some members of their respective governments certainly had far-right tendencies. As a general rule, the three governments feared far-right extremist groups in their own countries to a greater degree than any domestic Communist threat. By the late 1930s, the Communist parties in all three were small. Indeed, in 1938 President Päts had pardoned imprisoned Communists and no longer considered them a serious threat.

In a broad sense, the situation in the three Baltic states was little different from a lot of what was going on in Eastern Europe at the time. This was a region where the optimistic attempts at democracy and constitutional rule after the First World War had come off the rails. The states sandwiched between Germany in the West and the Soviet Union in the East were on a decline into authoritarianism if not totalitarianism or fascism.

This is a fascinating period of European history that is worth exploring in its own right.[1] Starting from the north and working down, it is worth having a bit of a refresher on the political geography of 1939. Finland was arguably the best example of viable democracy in the region, although even Finland had a far-right uprising in 1932 led by the far-right Lapua movement.

The Second Polish Republic was no beacon of democracy at the time either. After 1935, it was ruled by a group called Piłsudski's colonels, a fragment of the earlier Sanacja movement. It suffered under the shadow of authoritarian tendencies left in the wake of the death of Józef Piłsudski in 1935. Democracy was not dead but was certainly limited by 1939. After the 1938 parliamentary elections, the Sejm—Poland's parliament—was almost completely dominated by the nationalist Camp of National Unity party.

Austria had been incorporated into Nazi Germany in 1938, but it had been an authoritarian far-right regime for years prior to the Anschluss. Czechoslovakia had been dismembered, with the Czech half of that democracy being subsumed into the Third Reich. The Slovak half was carved off into the Slovak Republic, which was a one-party fascist state ruled by a Roman Catholic extremist dictator, the priest Jozef Tiso. He later collaborated heavily with Nazi Germany, and Slovakia became a de facto German puppet state.

Hungary was, technically, a monarchy. But it was ruled as a regency without a monarch by Admiral Miklós Horthy, ironically in a country with no navy or seacoast. He was a regent who served as a dictator. The 1939 elections, which were the closest Hungary had seen to a free election, resulted in a parliament in which a majority of seats were held by the far-right Party of Hungarian Life.

Yugoslavia was a relatively modern creation, having been formed out of various (mostly) Slavic ethnic groups in the Balkans after the First World War. It was a kingdom, but in 1939 King Peter II was only sixteen years old, and the country was run by a three-person regency council on his behalf. It was not a robust democracy by any stretch. The 1938 elections had put the Yugoslav Radical Union—an alliance of right to far-right parties—into power in parliament.

In the interwar era, Romania was the continuation of the Kingdom of Romania that had been in existence since the 1880s. It was a monarchy under King Carol II, a German noble from the House of Hohenzollern and a second cousin to Britain's George VI. Romania had managed to function broadly as a constitutional monarchy with a functional multi-party political system. However, by 1939, under threat from far-right extremists (the 'Iron Guard'), Romania was under one-party rule by the National Renaissance Front created by the king.

Bulgaria was a kingdom as well, but no democracy. Tsar Boris ruled the country through his tame prime minister Georgi Kyoseivanov. Albania was taken over by Italy in 1939. Greece was nominally a monarchy but was run by the authoritarian dictator

NIGHTFALL

Ioannis Metaxas. Turkey was a republic. Mustafa İsmet İnönü had taken over after the death of Atatürk in 1938, but there was no attempt at multi-party democracy until 1945.

In the context of the time, Estonia, Latvia, and Lithuania all rate in the middle of the league table for the state of their politics in 1939. Aside from Finland, that entire half of the continent had either never been particularly democratic or had lapsed into some degree of despotism. Individual liberties, where they existed, were fragile.

The global and regional situation in 1939 would easily have made all three Baltic states a bit neurotic. All three governments saw existential threats around them. The rise of Germany and its aggrandising behaviour on its frontiers was apparent from the mid-1930s onward. The risk was acutely felt in Lithuania, which directly bordered Germany. But it was also felt in Latvia and Estonia, which had significant German minorities.

All three were near to the USSR and felt that risk as well, even though their own domestic Communist parties had largely been suppressed. The struggles against the Soviet Army and red terror in the early days of the three republics were still fresh in the minds of most residents. Lithuania continued to face a strained relationship with Poland, its neighbour to the south-west. It considered Vilnius to be its capital, but a swathe of south-east Lithuania had been under Polish occupation for two decades. Finally, all three faced internal threats from groups that were more far right than the existing regimes—the Vaps, the Pērkonkrusts, and the Iron Wolf faction.

Unravelling of independence

Over the course of 1939 and 1940, the independence of the Baltic states was eroded and then destroyed. This happened in the context of the beginning of the Second World War. Geographically, the Baltic states were sandwiched between two large aggressive powers, Germany and the Soviet Union. These two, despite some historic animosity, were starting to secretly plot an alliance, the terms of which would not be favourable to the countries sandwiched between them.

The Memel/Klaipėda crisis

The first point at which Baltic independence started to unravel was in the west of Lithuania. Lithuania's only significant access to the sea was the Baltic seaport city of Klaipėda, which also housed about a third of Lithuania's industrial output. Given the largely frozen land border with Poland, this seaport was the key route for external trade.

Klaipėda is a good example of the region's geopolitical issues. You can look at a place like Klaipėda through several different lenses. From the standpoint of the Republic of Lithuania, it was a major city. But from a German standpoint, it was the old trading city of Memel. It was an old seaport dating back to the time of the Hanseatic League. It was the easternmost bit of the Kaiser-era German Empire, and before that, it was the easternmost outpost of the Kingdom of Prussia. Scholars can point to this Prussian border having been fixed in the Treaty of Melno in 1422. But both the city and the surrounding countryside gained a reasonable population of ethnic Lithuanians over the years.

The loss of Memel to Lithuania in the early 1920s was one of many events taken as an indignity by German nationalists. When people study the pre-war expansion of Germany, the given examples are usually the remilitarisation of the Rhineland, the Anschluss of Austria, the seizure of the Sudetenland, and then the dismemberment of Czechoslovakia. Hitler's annexation of Memel in early 1939 should be viewed as yet another act of aggression on that list.

Ethnic Germans, as well as some local Lithuanians who resented being ruled from Kaunas, had been agitating for years. Nazi groups and groups that were pro-Nazi in sentiment had the region on the brink of a crisis. Knowing that Lithuania would be powerless to stop it, Joachim von Ribbentrop, Hitler's foreign minister, issued an ultimatum in March 1939: Lithuania was to cede the lands or face invasion. The Smetona government found no sympathy elsewhere as appeasement of Hitler was still the prevailing policy. On 23 March, the Lithuanians, feeling they had no choice, gave up the region in a one-sided treaty. Hitler sailed in on the naval cruiser *Deutschland*, and German troops annexed the region; 10,000 refugees, mostly

Jews, fled into Lithuania. The dismemberment of the Baltic states had begun.

The wicked pact

Hitler then set his sights on Poland. Germany contrived a dispute about the 'Polish Corridor', the part of Poland that connected it to the sea but also cut East Prussia off from the rest of Germany. This crisis eventually brewed up into the actual outbreak of the Second World War in Europe. It was, of course, obvious to Hitler that a successful annexation or invasion of Poland would put Germany on the border of the Soviet Union. This was one of many reasons for several months of quiet diplomacy between Hitler and Stalin, which culminated in a treaty on 23 August 1939.

The Hitler–Stalin Non-Aggression Pact had many consequences. The most immediate was that it paved the way for Hitler's invasion of Poland, the planning and execution of which was very much underway before the ink was even dry. Despite Soviet-era revisionism and denials—the Soviets long denied the pact's existence—a variety of military and commercial relationships opened up. For all the glory that rightly accrues to the Soviet Union for its heroic efforts to defeat Nazism in Europe, we must never forget that, for the first 661 days of the Second World War, the Soviet Union was on the side of the Axis.[2]

The Secret Protocol

The specific bit of paper that sealed the terrible fate of Estonia, Latvia, and Lithuania was the 'Secret Protocol' appended to the Non-Aggression Pact. It reads as follows:

> Article I. In the event of a territorial and political rearrangement in the areas belonging to the Baltic states (Finland, Estonia, Latvia, Lithuania), the northern boundary of Lithuania shall represent the boundary of the spheres of influence of Germany and U.S.S.R. In this connection the interest of Lithuania in the Vilna area is recognized by each party.
>
> Article II. In the event of a territorial and political rearrangement of the areas belonging to the Polish state, the spheres of influence of Germany and the U.S.S.R. shall be bounded approximately by the line of the rivers Narev, Vistula and San. The question of whether

the interests of both parties make desirable the maintenance of an independent Polish State and how such a state should be bounded can only be definitely determined in the course of further political developments. In any event both Governments will resolve this question by means of a friendly agreement.

. . .

Article IV. This protocol shall be treated by both parties as strictly secret.

The two countries effectively divided Eastern Europe between themselves: Finland, Estonia, and Latvia were to be part of a Soviet 'sphere of influence'; Poland would be dismembered and divided; and while Lithuania was initially allocated to Germany, a second secret protocol a month after the signing of the Non-Aggression Pact reassigned it to the Soviet Union. It did not take long for the Soviet Union and Nazi Germany to put the pact and protocol into operation.

On 1 September 1939, Germany invaded Poland. On 3 September, Britain and France declared war on Germany. Two weeks later, the Soviet Union invaded Poland from the east, entering the war on the side of Germany. Poland was effectively eradicated. It was divided between the Soviet Union and Germany along the lines agreed in the Secret Protocol. The Vilnius region was temporarily ceded to Lithuania, although some bits of territory that Lithuania had claimed were occupied by the Soviets.

Annexing the Baltic states

The Soviet Union clearly intended to annex territories broadly equivalent to the territorial extent of the Russian Empire in 1914, and the invasion and occupation of eastern Poland in September 1939 was the beginning of that effort. Contemporaneous with the Soviet invasion of Poland in September 1939, Stalin put 160,000 troops on the Estonian border in a show of force. This was a force ten times larger than the Estonian Army.

Pacts of Defence and Mutual Assistance

The Soviet Union leaned heavily on the Baltic states, starting first with Estonia, which caved in on 28 September 1939. Latvia followed suit on 5 October, and Lithuania on 10 October. The Soviets extorted what they called, rather euphemistically, Pacts of Defence and Mutual Assistance. These pacts allowed sizeable Soviet military bases in the three countries. The number of troops allowed in these treaties were 25,000 in Estonia, 30,000 in Latvia, and 20,000 in Lithuania. Some troops arrived quickly, but there was no means to verify headcount of arriving forces. Vilnius and its surroundings were gifted to Lithuania, and it moved its capital. Germany's silence in all of this was taken as a signal of consent. Likely, the three Baltic governments felt that they had little choice, and that these deals would at least preserve their independence and neutrality while the rest of Europe was gradually going to war.

War progressed elsewhere in Europe. To the north, Stalin's attempt to intimidate Finland was rebuffed, resulting in a bitter 'Winter War' in late 1939 that lasted 105 days, with the Finns inflicting heavy damage and, against all odds, fighting the Red Army to a standstill. However, by the end of fighting, Finland had lost a lot of territory on its eastern frontier. The Baltic countries watched this happen. Finland had better resources and more strategic depth to defend itself. The world complained but did not come to Finland's rescue. The much smaller Baltic states rightly reckoned that they would not be able to replicate Finland's success, particularly with Soviet garrisons within their borders.

Annexation

The Soviet Union took advantage of the German war in Western Europe in 1940 to use both skulduggery and brutal intimidation to take over all three Baltic states.

While the rest of the world's attention was focused on the fall of France in late May 1940, the Soviet Union contrived a crisis with Lithuania. The Soviets accused the Lithuanians of kidnapping two soldiers from the new Soviet garrison in Lithuania. This degenerated into the Soviets accusing Lithuania of not abiding by the terms of the Mutual Assistance Pact and they named the interior minister and the head of its security service as having anti-Soviet attitudes. Vyacheslav Molotov, the Soviet foreign minister, demanded the arrest of the two officials, the formation of a new government, and the entry of more troops. The Lithuanian cabinet bickered.

President Smetona argued for at least token resistance but was outvoted. Prime Minister Antanas Merkys resigned, and Smetona fled the country. On 15 June 1940, the day after Hitler's troops entered Paris, the Red Army occupied Lithuania.

Estonia and Latvia were then confronted with emissaries who issued ultimatums similar to that issued to Lithuania. They were given less than a day to respond. Molotov accused the Baltic states of intriguing with Britain and France to sow mistrust between the German and Soviet allies. Estonia and Latvia had no choice but to yield. On 17 June, Soviet troops marched out of their garrisons, and additional troops swarmed over the border, occupying Latvia and Estonia.

'Popular Governments'

What happened next was a reorganisation of the governments in each of the three countries. Exact details and chronologies vary, but events followed the same broad plot in all three countries. The Baltic governments were confronted with lists of new cabinets and forced to accept them. As actual Communists were rare on the ground in all three countries, these new government cabinets were a mix of broadly left-wing figures with whatever actual Communists they could scrape up. No opposition to this was allowed. When Ulmanis and Päts were reluctant to adopt the new cabinet lists, the Soviets contrived demonstrations. Despite the Soviets' later claims that these were popular demonstrations, in reality the demonstrators were Soviet soldiers in mufti, civilian workers from the Soviet military bases, and a leavening of actual Communists. In Tallinn, there was a brief skirmish between Estonian soldiers and 'demonstrators' invading their barracks.[3]

Lithuania was in a strange legal position in that, with President Smetona having fled the country, there was nobody with legal authority to approve a new cabinet. In Latvia, Ulmanis refused to sign the decree forming the new cabinet. However, the Soviets did it anyway. The new governments were still theoretically sovereign but were heavily influenced by the Soviet occupiers.

New 'People's Governments' or 'Popular Governments' (translations vary) were installed by the Soviets. Although they had the veneer of sovereignty and independence, it is now clear in retrospect that these 'People's Governments' were merely a mechanism to achieve annexation by the Soviet Union. Over the next two months, non-Communist public activity was gradually curtailed. Many organisations were suppressed or disbanded, such as the Scouts or political groups. Police chiefs and mayors were replaced. The armies were kept in barracks, and senior officers were laid off or retired.

'People's Assemblies'

The next step in the Soviet annexation of the Baltics was the establishment of 'People's Assemblies' in July 1940. The elections to these assemblies were complete stitch-ups. A very short period—only three days in Estonia, for example—was allowed for nominations. The overall intent was to only have single candidates, nominated by approved, that is, Communist-influenced, organisations. Although some opposition candidates were nominated, various grounds were used to disqualify candidates who were not approved by the Soviets. Newspapers carried intimidating messages. Ballots ended up with single names on them, no electoral register was used in Lithuania, meaning that people could vote multiple times, and in places Red Army soldiers guarded ballot boxes. The results of the rigged charade were predictable. The 'Working People's League'— the euphemism for the official candidates—somehow achieved an improbable 99.2 per cent of the vote on a 95.5 per cent turnout of a very ill-defined electorate. Only slightly less improbable claims were made in Latvia and Estonia. The new puppet assemblies were elected.

In all three countries, these new assemblies met on 21 July 1940. Unsurprisingly, their agenda had been set by Moscow. These assemblies were only a mere formality. They voted to enact a Soviet form of government, nationalise property and private business, and apply to join the USSR. They elected delegations to go to Moscow to 'ask' to be admitted to the Soviet Union. In yet another undemocratic charade, the Supreme Soviet, the Soviet Union's decidedly non-democratic parliament, met and 'considered' the 'request' for incorporation. The three republics were illegally done away with and replaced with impostor 'Soviet Socialist Republics'. Baltic independence was over, and the Soviet Union was enlarged.

This chain of events left a variety of Baltic diplomats stranded abroad. Some countries, notably the United States, never recognised the illegal incorporation of the Baltic states into the Soviet Union. A number of other countries acknowledged the incorporation as a de facto reality but let existing diplomats and diplomatic missions keep the cause of Baltic nationhood alive in exile. The youngest of these diplomats soldiered on for decades in these roles and outlived the Soviet Union.

Sovietisation and oppression

It would take thousands of pages to catalogue the true horrors wrought upon Estonia, Latvia, and Lithuania after their involuntary incorporation into the Soviet Union. However, a book about people fighting against their occupiers should address the 'why are they fighting' question. What made everything so bad that, a year later, many people viewed occupation by the Nazis as, well, not ideal, but quite a relief? Just how bad can one year be? In the case of the Baltic states, the answer is clearly 'very bad indeed'.

Economy

The new Soviet overlord rapidly disassembled free-market economies. Chronic shortages, queues in shops, hoarding, and speculation of basic goods became routine as economic output declined dramatically. Housing was chaotic. People lost their ownership of larger residences, and many were forced to move out as their housing was reallocated to make room for new arrivals. Anyone who was abroad at the time had their property forfeited by default. Currencies were devalued, and the Soviet rouble replaced the previous currencies at disadvantageous rates of exchange. Between this and the state takeover of banking, many people were robbed of their savings. Many bank account balances were simply taken.

Large and medium-sized businesses were nationalised and their owners dispossessed. Small businesses and independent tradesmen could, in theory, remain in business but were heavily oppressed. Middle and upper management for industry was transferred in from elsewhere in the Soviet Union, but many of these new managers had little education and no experience. People were no longer allowed to quit their jobs, and people who did quit without managerial permission were often jailed. Unpaid overtime was ordered. Labour unions became a tool for the new bosses to discipline the labour force.

Agriculture

In the countryside, the Soviet authorities viewed collectivisation of agriculture as their ultimate objective. Ultimately, the Soviet view was that all agriculture should be done by either state-owned farms ('sovkhozes') or collective farms ('kolkhozes'), but they also realised that it would take some time to achieve this. Although a handful of *kolkhozes* were started during this first period of Soviet occupation, the Soviet authorities proceeded with 'reforms' that were punitive to larger farmers. Because of quite good land reform efforts in all three countries during the years of independence, there were very few large landed estates left over from the tsarist era, despite Soviet propaganda. However, the Soviet authorities started redistributing land. Holdings larger than about 30 hectares (75 acres) were confiscated, affecting many thousands of farms and farmers. Many landless peasants were given land, but the plot sizes were small (10–12 hectares) and often could not support a family. This policy was actually intended to fragment the rural population as a class and divide it among itself, rather than achieve its stated aims of helping the poor.[4]

Politics, society, and culture

Daily life changed rapidly under Soviet rule. The education systems were forced to shift their curricula. Schooling was shortened by one year in Latvia and two in Lithuania. Textbooks literally had pages torn out as there was not enough time to produce Soviet textbooks in local languages. All publishers and printing shops were taken over by the state. Many newspapers and magazines disappeared, and others were heavily altered in content. Thousands of books were banned. Many writers were proscribed, even some leftists. Some authors were arrested. Politics in the conventional sense was not particularly freely flowing before the annexation due to the authoritarian tendencies of the countries' leaders, but after annexation, any political activity outside of the Communist Party was illegal.

Officially, religion was left untouched, and church hierarchies continued to operate, but in reality, oppression of religion was eased into place. Seminaries and theological institutions were closed. Party activists whipped up groups of 'atheist brigades' that harassed churches and congregations. Religious holidays disappeared from the calendar. Clergy were deprived of pensions. Clergy and churches were subjected to extra taxes and rents.

Repression

The Soviet police state descended heavily upon Estonia, Latvia, and Lithuania. The NKVD had secretly turned up the previous year along with Soviet troops and had been clearly planning for actual annexation for some months. It took a lot of time for the NKVD to develop plans to fully oppress the population. It had to spend months developing new networks of informants and building lists of people to question, arrest, and imprison. There were not many NKVD cadres who could work in the local languages, and it took time to develop the infrastructure of oppression. The relative weakness of local intelligence networks did allow some leeway for early resistance efforts to develop.

The first big wave of disappearances started on the eve of the stilted elections for the People's Assemblies in July 1940. I use the term disappearance rather than merely arrest. In July, in theory, the countries were not yet part of the Soviet Union. People answered a knock on the door and then nobody saw them again. Some neighbours, at first, even assumed that the disappeared must have fled the country. But most went to an interrogation cell. The majority were not actually tried but given a sentence without trial and either imprisoned or deported. Menachem Begin, future prime minister of Israel, was among those sent to the Gulag, having been arrested in Vilnius in September 1940.

Because the Soviet Union was an ally of Nazi Germany until June 1941, people with German ancestry could leave and go to Germany. Although many Germans had already left in 1939 during previous Nazi-sponsored repatriation efforts, tens of thousands of people now left for Germany. The days of Baltic Germans living in the Baltic states were numbered. Because of the military and commercial alliance between Germany and the Soviet Union, these were relatively amicable departures, not anything like the forced deportation of people to Siberia and other distant parts of the Soviet Union. The departure of Baltic Germans also had the effect of removing a lot of middle-class professionals and businesspeople from the economy.

Within a few months, the NKVD was finally in a position to draw up lists of categories of people to be arrested, either for imprisonment in camps or deportation to exile settlements. Various such lists exist in the archives. Some categories are predictable like former tsarist or White Army officers, clergy, and members of various political parties. But the blacklists contained broad and vague categories like 'industrialists' and 'unstable elements' as well as hyper-specific niches such as stamp collectors and people who could speak Esperanto. An NKVD official, speaking and reading only Russian, might have some odd interpretations of just who exactly was an 'industrialist'. Clearly a factory owner was. But a shift foreman? A pensioner who owned a few shares? Rather a lot of people were included arbitrarily or through similarities in spelling of names.

Up until June 1941, the arrests had been selective. But starting on 13 June 1941 in Lithuania and the following day in Estonia and Latvia, a reign of terror was inflicted upon all three countries. Tens of thousands of people, including small children and the elderly, were locked up. Hundreds of freight cars were used to send people east. People were shoved on to freight cars with minimal arrangement for feeding and sanitation. Some people were allowed a brief period to gather up food and clothing. Others literally had the clothing on their back and nothing else. Many people on the lists could not actually be located, so other people were locked up to meet the quota. Men were generally sentenced to imprisonment, usually without trial, and sent to Gulag camps. Women and children were sent into exile in remote parts of the Soviet Union such as Siberia.

The true extent of the June deportations is hard to document, and estimates vary on the numbers of people imprisoned or deported during these dark days. Older books made a variety of guesses. In more recent years, efforts to document these disappearances and deportations have made some headway. There are now thousands of names on lists, based on extensive research. Alexander Statiev, the Canadian scholar whose book *The Soviet Counterinsurgency in the Western Borderlands* (2010) drawing on Soviet-era records, arrives at the figures of 10,187 Lithuanians, 9,546 Latvians, and 5,978 Estonians deported in a four-day period from 14 to 17 June 1941. These were people forcibly resettled. In addition, thousands were arrested and sentenced to Gulag imprisonment. Statiev reports precise figures of 3,178 Estonians, 5,625 Latvians, and 5,664 Lithuanians arrested during the same period.[5] These figures are almost certainly incomplete, as arrests and deportations continued after 17 June. A Lithuanian archival effort has compiled a list of 23,869 named individuals who were either imprisoned or deported in 1941.[6] The vast majority would have been part of the June wave of terror. The magnitude is similar in Estonia and Latvia. Survival rates were not particularly good for prisoners or forcibly relocated exiles. Thousands died in transit, particularly the elderly, and many thousands more died from cold, illness, or starvation.

The wave of deportations in June 1941 occurred the week before the Germans invaded the Soviet Union. The toll of death, deportation, and imprisonment would have undoubtedly been higher if the German invasion had not happened when it did. Certainly, the exact timing of the German invasion saved some Baltic peoples from imminent deportation, and it temporarily halted a reign of terror, even if new terrors were soon in store for the Baltic states. This had a direct and timely effect on public attitudes towards the German invasion.

Estonia, Latvia, and Lithuania are not large countries. If we transposed these deportations at scale to the contemporary United States, we would be talking about millions of people. This was a sizeable fraction of these countries. There is a word for this sort of depravity on a mass scale, but the word was not widely used at the time of the 1941 deportations. That word is genocide. This was genocide. People were going to resist.

2

1940 AND 1941

RESISTANCE FORMS, BUT THE GERMANS INVADE

Forcible incorporation into the Soviet Union was not a pleasant affair. Although broad conditions provided some environmental factors that would assist resistance, the overall shock and rapidity of the Soviet annexation caught the people of the three countries by surprise. That it took some time for organised resistance to evolve suggests that few people had done any serious preparation for armed or even unarmed resistance. But it is also clear that the incoming Soviet regime would provoke many people into finding ways of resisting.

Lack of formal military resistance

The people whose formal job it was to resist invasion, the armies, did not fight. There was no repeat of Finland's heroic Winter War. Military history attests to some resistance movements developing in their earlier phases from the gradual fragmentation of conventional armies and small units and individual soldiers disappearing into hiding with their weapons. In other cases, a period of armed resistance can create a window in time for a partisan resistance movement to grow. Neither of these happened in the Baltics.

In Estonia, President Päts issued no orders for resistance. General Laidoner was sacked from his job on 22 June, only days after the Soviet occupation. Rather hopelessly optimistic about the situation, perhaps, Päts remained in office for nearly a month, signing many of the Soviet decrees that were put in front of him.

But only a small signal detachment of the Estonian Army put up any armed resistance, near a school in Tallinn.[1] To this day, the Signal Battalion of the Estonian Army celebrates that day.

A similar tale unfolded in Latvia. Aside from some isolated border police incidents, it appears that the Latvian military put up no resistance. This was a matter of policy. The minister of war, Jānis Balodis, had been fired in April 1940. Ulmanis, the president, gave a national radio address ordering no resistance and stating that he would remain in office: 'You stay in your place. I'll stay in mine.'[2] Preparations for armed resistance by various military officers were called off when the Soviet Union threatened to bomb Latvian cities.[3] Staying in his place ended badly for Ulmanis. He ended up dying in a Soviet prison in 1942.

In Lithuania, President Smetona found himself in a minority in an emergency cabinet meeting. He wanted to have at least some token military resistance and asked to have the former commander in chief of the army, General Stasys Raštikis, take over the government. This was unacceptable to Moscow.[4] Smetona decided to flee the country and slipped over the border into Germany and thence to Switzerland. His decision to flee is viewed by some as cowardly and by others as wise.

Several factors influenced these decisions. First, all three countries already had Soviet military forces inside their borders on the bases that had been extorted over the previous months. Second, they faced overwhelming force and were greatly outnumbered. Third, there was no prospect of foreign assistance, except maybe a faint glimmer of Finnish help for Estonia. The rest of the world was at war, and the allies who might come to their aid were tied up. Fourth, the three countries' militaries did not do much to coordinate with each other in previous years, so any kind of united resistance would not happen. Fifth, they all relied on mobilisation of reserves and auxiliaries to augment the national defence. Such mobilisation needs time if it is to be effective.

Gutting the Baltic armies

The new Soviet occupiers were faced with the question of what to do with the Baltic militaries. Although the exact details vary, the same basic plan seems to have been executed by the arriving Red Army and NKVD troops. The militaries were kept administratively intact in the short term but were more or less under house arrest in their bases and barracks. Armaments were locked up and secured. Depots of arms for the reserve components, such as the Defence League in Estonia, were seized or at least placed under Soviet guard.

Gradually, these standing armies, which were treated more like prisoners than armies, were formed into elements of the Red Army. The remnants of the Estonian Army were repackaged as the 22nd Territorial Rifle Corps of the Red Army. Plagued by desertions since July 1941, it had been disbanded by September 1941. The remaining units of the Latvian Army were merged into the 24th Territorial Rifle Corps, which was largely disbanded after the German invasion out of fear that the Latvians would turn their rifles on their Soviet masters. Many soldiers were arrested and imprisoned in Gulag camps. The Lithuanian Army was briefly re-branded as the Lithuanian People's Army and then transformed into the 29th Territorial Rifle Corps. It too did not survive long, and was disbanded by September 1941.

It should be noted that, along the way, many small arms and uniforms from these Baltic armies went missing. Although I was unable to identify serious systemic efforts to cache weapons for later resistance, it certainly happened on an individual scale. To this day, weapons from the 1920s and 1930s do turn up in rural locations. The War Museum in Kaunas, Lithuania, has a rifle that was found inside a tree that grew up around it.

Governments in exile

One way in which resistance to invasion can be promoted is by maintaining continuity of government through a government in exile. The speed and ruthlessness with which the Baltic states were forcibly incorporated into the USSR, combined with the fact that there was a world war already underway, meant that it was not easy to set up such governments. What the governments did have, though, were diplomatic missions and embassies abroad.

Latvian President Ulmanis had taken the prescient step in May 1940 of authorising two senior Latvian diplomats abroad, Kārlis

Zariņš in London and Alfrēds Bīlmanis in Washington, to continue to represent the Latvian state in the event of catastrophe. No government in exile was formally constituted, but various Latvian diplomatic missions continued to operate for decades as the only remaining fragment of the Republic of Latvia. In 1990, I met Anatols Dinbergs, an elderly chargé d'affaires, in Washington, DC, who had entered diplomatic service in 1932, and had continued to serve in exile since 1940.

Lithuania had a similar story. After fleeing the country through Germany, President Smetona met with Lithuanian diplomats in Bern and discussed forming a government in exile, though no action resulted. He ended up moving to the United States by way of Portugal and Brazil, all neutral at the time. The terms of his US visa prohibited him from officially representing any government. The Lithuanian diplomatic corps, operating out of diplomatic missions in Washington, London, Paris, Bern, and elsewhere and headed by Stasys Lozoraitis senior, took up the mantle and became the last bit of the Republic of Lithuania.

Lozoraitis held a meeting of diplomats in Rome in September 1940. Unlike Germany, Italy was not actually allied to the Soviets. This meeting formed a Lithuanian National Committee, which may have had the basics of a government in exile, but its constituent members were too spread out, and wartime complications meant that it never met again.

Some Lithuanian diplomatic missions survived all the way through to the restoration of Lithuanian statehood in 1990. Lozoraitis' son, Stasys junior, was still alive and in post in 1990 in Washington when I met him as a young intern.

Estonia was the only one of the three to establish an actual government in exile. Like Latvia and Lithuania, Estonia had diplomatic missions abroad, which continued the job of representing the idea, if not the reality, of an independent Republic of Estonia. Somewhat later, in 1944, an actual government in exile was formed. It operated in Sweden and Norway. Its role during the Cold War was nominal. Consul Ernst Jaakson, who began his career as a twenty-seven-year-old junior diplomat in New York, continued in post in New York city as Estonia's diplomatic presence for so long that I actually spoke to him repeatedly on the phone, still in role, in 1991 and 1992. He died in 1998, having served the Estonian diplomatic corps for seventy-nine years.

These efforts in exile proved to be a valuable conduit later on. Many efforts were made by the resistance movements to keep in touch with the various diplomatic and political elements in exile. Some diplomatic missions became valuable conduits between the Forest Brotherhood and Western governments. Others were shut down immediately or gradually. Yet others faded into the woodwork as their diplomats retired and could not be replaced.

Development of resistance

The harsh reality of Soviet occupation motivated the development of resistance. Much of this resistance was informal, amateurish, and/or symbolic. Armed resistance was not an initial feature of the embryonic anti-Soviet resistance at this point in the struggle, although some individuals saw that armed struggle would eventually be taken up by some. Across the three countries, it would be a mistake to describe this phase of resistance as highly organised, as even the groups that emerged tended to be small, ad hoc organisations.

Estonia

In Estonia, the Kaitseliit proved to be the basis of early resistance. The organisation was formally disbanded in June 1940, but individual members, particularly in the countryside, hid their weapons. A group named the Estonian National Club briefly attempted to form a legal opposition movement to stand candidates in the rigged elections, but the organisation was quashed. A member of the group, Ülo Maramaa, started an organisation called the Rescue Committee. The committee spawned subsidiary groups in some of the regions of Estonia and began planning for an uprising. They viewed war with Germany as a strong possibility and felt that such an event would be their opportunity to rise up. The group began accumulating arms, made contact with Finnish intelligence, and even made tentative contacts with the Germans. This shows that many Baltic people cynically but correctly saw the Hitler–Stalin Pact as a short-term arrangement. Once the Soviets got wind of this group, however, the crackdown was severe, and the group's members were largely in prison cells by the end of 1940.[5]

The honour of being the first member of the Forest Brotherhood in Estonia belongs to a young man named Enn Murulaid. He was a soldier in the Estonian Army, and he deserted in September 1940 at the point at which the army was being forcibly integrated into the Red Army. He hid in the forests near his home in the Viru district in north-eastern Estonia.[6]

Other efforts at organisation had to be small and compartmented for their own security. In the spring of 1941, a group using the Estonian Museum of Health Care as cover organised among students and others in Tartu, Estonia's second city. This group of about twenty members remained secure. A number of its members were military reserve officers with some training, and discipline was apparently tight. They covertly prepared for an eventual revolt when conditions were ripe. They met literally across the street from the NKVD.[7]

The most significant early development in resistance occurred in the Võru district, in the south-eastern corner of Estonia. In this rural district, former rank-and-file members and junior leaders of the Kaitseliit started reorganising. Their objective was to defend their homes and property. The group mushroomed in size in June 1941 when the Soviets started locking up Kaitseliit members. Many former Kaitseliit members in the area took to the woods. Allegedly, this group had 430 members, about half of them armed.[8]

Latvia

As in Estonia, early resistance efforts in Latvia were small and fragmented. Most people were caught out by the speed with which the republic crumbled. A number of small groups formed early on but had little or no experience in clandestine life and were basically discussion groups. Some of the better organised groups came out of youth movements like the Scouts. Early acts of opposition were symbolic or peaceful in nature, like hoisting the national flag or distributing leaflets. Many student groups got involved but were easily suppressed by the NKVD.

A larger, more serious resistance movement came in the form of the Tēvijas Sargi ('Defenders of the Homeland') group. It was founded by Vladimirs Kļaviņš, a Riga law student.[9] The group quickly grew in size, becoming a serious underground movement with a propaganda department, a foreign relations department, and a war department. The propaganda department developed one of the first underground newspapers, *Zinotājs* ('The Messenger'), which had a run of six issues, although it was never printed in more than eighty copies at a time. The group's war department started collecting weapons and gathering information on the Red Army. Key to this effort was one of its leaders—a man on the inside. Lieutenant Laimonis Sala was a Latvian Army officer who had been incorporated into the Red Army and provided vital information on Soviet military capabilities. German military intelligence, the Abwehr, became very interested in this group. The foreign relations department made contact with German intelligence, and the Abwehr provided a radio set for liaison.

Other groups started to spring up across Latvia. Given the number and moderate size of these groups, the Soviet authorities were not yet in a position of having enough intelligence collection capability to detect them and their specific plots. Former officers, who would likely be eventual targets for the Gulag, were active in many of these groups. The 'New Latvians' allegedly had 600 members and may have been involved in the sabotage of the Vulkāns match factory in Liepaja. The Latvian writer Juris Ciganovs claims this group was the most powerful of the 1940–1 era groups.[10] Yet another group was the 'Latvian National Legion', which wanted to unite other groups and made approaches to the Germans. Another group, "Kaujas organizācija Latvijas atbrīvošanai"—The Combat Organisation for the Liberation of Latvia—reached out to contacts in Lithuania and also made contact with the evidently by now quite busy German Abwehr agent in Riga. The KOLA leader, Teodors Gulbis, a student only aged twenty-three, and not to be confused with a Latvian Communist of the same name, even tried to organise a summit meeting with Lithuanian and Estonian leaders. KOLA also recruited women medical and nursing students.

If this wasn't enough, other groups started to spring up with a variety of poetic names like 'The Hawks' and 'The Iron Guard'. Competition was not fierce, and the groups started to coordinate with each other through covert couriers and messengers. But, as elsewhere, the NKVD finally started to get its act together. From December 1940 onward, arrests and interrogations started to roll up these groups. By March 1941, they were all no longer functioning, and many of their members had been arrested. Some eventually faced execution. The ones not caught were forced to lie low.

Latvians abroad were not idle. In particular, Latvia's former military attaché in Berlin, Colonel Aleksandrs Plensners, had been recruited by the German Abwehr. He started acting as yet another liaison between Germany and Latvia. Perhaps, given his position in Berlin, he could see tell-tale signs of the upcoming German invasion. By now, we can see that there were a number of contacts between Latvian groups and German intelligence. Was this a sign of fascism in the movement? Possibly in some individual cases, but not as a general rule. Although few knew it at the time, the Abwehr was an outpost of anti-Hitler sentiment and even conspiracy. As in Estonia and Latvia, an air of cynicism prevailed, and people viewed Germany, Nazi or otherwise, as a counterweight to Soviet Russia. By 1940–1, it was, to be both realistic and cynical, the only state to which such movements were able to turn.

Lithuania

Early resistance largely consisted of disseminating anti-regime leaflets, most of which were crudely produced. Examples of over fifty leaflets from the late 1940 and 1941 era are in archival collections. A number of small groups sprang up, many of them with aspirational names that might have given both their members and the security services wrong ideas about their size. Many were student groups. Invariably, the NKVD took a deep interest in these groups when they emerged. One of the largest appears to have been the Independence Party, twenty-six members of which were arrested by the Soviets, but even that seems to have been an exaggeration, as some were actually released, indicating that the dragnet was bigger than the group.[11] Several other small groups were identified and arrested. Some remain apocryphal mysteries to this day and may have been one-person efforts.

By far the biggest development was the Lithuanian Activists Front (Lietuvių Aktivistų Frontas—LAF), which was a hybrid of both domestic and exile resistance activity. The LAF was, rather suspiciously, started in a Berlin flat owned by Colonel Kazys Škirpa in late 1940. Škirpa (1895–1979) had served in the Russian Army in the First World War and then in Lithuania's forces during the war of independence. He served in several roles in the Lithuanian Army. Most importantly, since 1928 he had served as Lithuania's military attaché in Berlin, giving him extensive contacts in both Weimar and Nazi Germany. Also of interest, in 1926 he had drafted a national mobilisation plan for use during national emergencies.[12] Škirpa was also a member of the ill-fated Lithuanian National Committee and had been at its only meeting in Rome a few months previously.

The question comes up of whether or not Škirpa was a German agent, a Nazi-sympathiser, or both. It is almost beyond any degree of credibility to claim that the Lithuanian military attaché of twelve years standing did not have contacts with the Abwehr. It had been his job to have such contacts. It is likely that his intelligence contacts pre-dated the Nazi rise to power. It is also inconceivable that he would be hosting meetings to form a revolutionary movement in his front room without German intelligence knowing of it. If Škirpa was a German agent, he would almost certainly have been reporting to the Abwehr, not the SS. The Abwehr, as Germany's long-standing foreign intelligence agency, was running far more foreign agents, particularly at this stage in the war. Throughout the war, the Abwehr and the SS were strong rivals. Indeed, the Abwehr proved to have been a hotbed of anti-Nazi and anti-Hitler sentiment.[13] The SS, being in charge of internal repression in Germany and occupied lands, had far less experience in foreign intelligence operations and running espionage agents. This may be too fine a difference for some, but it is a big difference in other contexts.

Complicating the story of the LAF is General Raštikis, the Lithuanian military's senior officer. He turned up to help Škirpa. Smetona had wanted Raštikis to lead the country upon Smetona's retreat, but he had declined and had been put to work by the Soviets in integrating the Lithuanian Army into the Soviet armed forces. However, he fled to Germany a few months later, fearing arrest. Raštikis seems to have been in the company of an SS intelligence officer named Heinz Gräfe, further muddying the tale of the LAF. This gives rise to the possibility that the two rival agencies were both trying to get their hooks into the LAF.

Twenty-eight people signed the initial creation document of the LAF, ranging from centre-left to far right. The only real unifying idea was re-establishing independence. The thing that made LAF a bit different was that it had both a political office in exile and an operational arm in Lithuania that started to recruit and build cells. The LAF started to develop a large cell in Kaunas and a smaller cell in Vilnius, with activity elsewhere. However, contacts between the headquarters were difficult.

Operation Barbarossa: German invasion

In June 1941, Hitler reneged on his pact with Stalin and invaded the Soviet Union. Almost instantly, the three Baltic states became the front line in this new phase of the Second World War. Despite months of intelligence indicating an imminent German invasion, the German surprise was almost total, and Soviet defenders were caught out entirely. In the three Baltic states, which had been suffering under harsh Soviet occupation for a year, the first few months of this new phase of the war were a mix of nervous mobilisation, vindictive retreat by an occupier, some faint hopes for national restoration, some brave but futile uprisings, and an occupation by a despotic enemy as bad as the one that was just evicted.

Brutality on the way out the door

The Soviet Union's rapid defeat and retreat from the Baltic states during the early stages of the German invasion was characterised by absolute brutality on the way out. Viewing the German invasion in isolation is a mistake. The Nazi invasion occurred in the midst of a major wave of Soviet oppression and deportations across the Baltic states. The scale of the deportations would certainly have been larger had they not been interrupted by the Nazi invasion.

But one thing is clear. The Soviet occupiers of the Baltic states had clear orders to oppress the local population, yet, for days, they lacked orders to oppose the German invaders. The NKVD carried on arresting, deporting, and executing people in the days after the invasion. As the reality of the invasion dawned on the Soviet security forces, there was a sense of urgency to finish their business before retreating. Ammunition that could have been spent fighting Nazis was spent on Baltic civilians.

While much of the brutality of the final days of the Soviet occupation was likely never documented, several incidents stand out. One such event was the Rainiai massacre of 24–5 June 1941. In the north-west Lithuanian town of Telšiai, Soviet secret police were unable to retreat with their inventory of political prisoners. They had between seventy and eighty Lithuanians locked up and did not want to release them. The prisoners were a mix of minor political figures, Lithuanian Army officers, and young people. Some were students from a local crafts school, and some were teenaged Scouts. It was considered too burdensome to try to evacuate these prisoners to the Soviet Union in a general retreat, so the order came to liquidate them. The prisoners were taken to the forest near the village of Rainiai and tortured and killed. Their bodies were mutilated so badly that only twenty-seven of the seventy to eighty victims could be positively identified. The arriving Germans used this massacre for anti-Soviet propaganda purposes. Similar but less well-documented massacres of prisoners happened across the Baltic states.

Uprisings

Germany's surprise attack coupled with the defeat and retreat of the Red Army gave an opportunity for Baltic people to attempt to regain some control of their countries. Across the region, there was a brief period of time where neither the Soviets nor the German invaders were in charge in the three countries. Both optimists and opportunists could see this as a chance to do something. Geography dictated that the first of the Baltic states to see arriving German troops was Lithuania.

Uprisings in Lithuania

The largest and most well-organised attempt to exploit the brief interregnum took place in Lithuania. The LAF had been waiting for the right moment to launch an uprising, and within hours of the German invasion on 22 June 1941, Lithuanians were taking up arms against their Soviet captors. Kaunas was the centre of the revolt. A team of armed partisans, clearly working to a plan drawn up by the LAF, seized the radio station. A local LAF activist, Leonas Prapuolenis, gave a radio announcement declaring that the republic had been re-established and announcing the formation of a provisional government. By the end of the day, partisans had seized the telephone exchange, allowing a great deal of communication to happen around the city and disrupting Soviet communications.

Given the hatred of their occupiers, made ever stronger by the waves of arrests and deportations that started the previous week, it is not surprising that a lot of people rose up. However, although many people clearly joined the uprising spontaneously, it had been carefully planned in advance, even if communications between the LAF's office in Berlin and their cells in Lithuania were difficult. On paper, the LAF had established a broad provisional government. With his decades of useful contacts in the German military, Colonel Škirpa, the LAF's man in Berlin, was likely aware of the impending Nazi invasion—whether through active cooperation with the German Army, tip-offs, or simply his political intuition. Some sources allege collaboration between the Abwehr and the LAF. Other sources portray the LAF as a disorganised umbrella organisation with lots of groups not coordinating with each other particularly well, which is to be expected when operating under the nose of two totalitarian states. Both statements are, in fact, true. There was some German involvement, through Škirpa and likely a few others. But the mix and large number of people involved in the uprising also mean that it was a broad and somewhat disorganised movement.

For several days, street fighting occurred in Kaunas. Groups of factory workers formed battalions. There were raids to seize weapons and free prisoners of the NKVD. Various platoons of partisans were posted to protect shops against looting and generally harass the Soviets around Kaunas. The revolt quickly spread elsewhere in Lithuania in response to hearing the national anthem on the radio. Many Lithuanian conscripts in the Red Army deserted from their unit, the 29th Territorial Riflemen's Corps.

In Vilnius, ethnic Lithuanians were very much a minority at the time, and the city had just been transferred from Polish to Lithuanian rule. Not only that, but the local LAF cells had been seriously disrupted by Soviet security services. However, on the evening of 23 June, the post office and radio station were seized. Uprising activity was sporadic in the rest of the country. For example, stiff fighting occurred in the Panevėžys and Ukmergė regions, but it was quiet in some other places. It should be noted that not all of the fighting was against the Soviets. In Alytus, a town in southern Lithuania, someone shot several Germans, leading the German Army to conduct vicious reprisals.

In some places, the Lithuanian uprising took a sinister turn. The LAF and the provisional government that was trying to take power were umbrella organisations representing the broad spectrum of political views in the pre-war republic. As such, some of the individuals and groups were pre-war far-right extremists who had been bundled into the provisional government along with more reasonable people.

The most infamous event was the so-called Kaunas pogrom. Between 25 and 29 June, several thousand Jews were massacred in and around the Kaunas area. A vicious German SS commander, Franz Walter Stahlecker, a pastor's son and clearly one of the more damaged people to ever serve any country in uniform, turned up in Kaunas. He was the commander of the infamous Einsatzgruppe A. The Einsatzgruppen were infamous SS death squads whose job was to follow behind the front lines and massacre Jews.

Stahlecker started giving vitriolic anti-Semitic sermons to the new provisional police in Kaunas. Eventually, he found a shadowy Lithuanian named Algirdas Klimaitis, a minor right-wing journalist and follower of the extremist former prime minister Augustinas Voldemaras. (His followers were well represented in the ranks of Nazi collaborators and Holocaust enablers.) Klimaitis seems to have assembled a gang, ranging in size from fifty to 600 (estimates vary; the likely total was in the middle), which proceeded to commit a variety of atrocities against Jews in the Kaunas area. According to Stahlecker's own report, several synagogues were set on fire, around 3,800 Lithuanian Jews were massacred, and many houses burned.[14] One of the most infamous parts of this pogrom was the so-called 'Lietūkis Garage Massacre' in which sixty-eight Jews were murdered in a garage that had been used by the NKVD.

Histories often point to this pogrom as the beginning of the Holocaust in Lithuania. While Stahlecker and the SS seem to have played a leading role in instigating these events, there is still much debate about the extent to which violent anti-Semitism was a more serious trend in the Lithuanian resistance. It appears to me and many others that this particular Kaunas pogrom was very much instigated by Stahlecker and the SS.

The aftermath of the uprising meant that the arriving Germans would have to contend with a broad-based provisional government and armed partisans. Škirpa, the prospective head of the provisional government, was never allowed to leave Berlin to assume his new role. Hitler had no vision for either a Lithuanian government, even a Vichy-style one, or Lithuanian military forces. Both were disbanded. Many of the provisional government's members ended up being arrested. A few, from the far right of Lithuanian politics, ended up as collaborators.

Uprisings in Latvia

The Lithuanian uprising had clearly been planned. Further north, the uprisings were more ad hoc. Because they were further from the German frontier, it took longer for the approaching German Army to reach Latvia, and then Estonia. This allowed more time in the immediate aftermath of the beginning of the German invasion for ad hoc preparations, but it also allowed more time for the Soviets to conduct vicious acts of repression on the local population.

Latvians took up arms in the days following the invasion, but it was a more fragmented affair. Initial partisan activity consisted of sabotaging communication lines and railways. The most significant factor was the wholesale desertion of Latvian soldiers from the Red Army. Only a minority of the former Latvian Army, now re-badged as the 24th Territorial Riflemen's Corps, fought the Germans and retreated with the Red Army. Some entire units deserted, and many individuals. This led to trained and armed personnel hiding in the forests, which became the basis for the formation of partisan units. Various Latvian officers started to organise units and seize control of some towns, leading to clashes with Soviet units. Lt Colonel Kārlis Aperāts, formerly commander of the Signals Battalion, started to organise an actual regular Latvian Army unit and formed a staff on his own initiative.

While Škirpa had likely helped the Abwehr coordinate anti-Soviet activities in Lithuania, it seems that the Nazi intelligence agency played little role in the uprisings in Latvia. Although Plensners, the Latvian attaché in Berlin, had been cooperating with the Abwehr, there was little coordination between that organisation and either the invading Nazi forces or the occupation authorities who came after the front lines had passed through. Afraid that events in Latvia could get out of hand, Plensners was rapidly brought in to assert control over the newly formed partisan units, taking up where Lt Colonel Aperāts had left off, and organising as many as 8,000 Latvian soldiers under his command.[15]

It would not be long before Latvians realised that they had just changed overseers rather than regaining their independence. In July, the SS took over security of 'rear areas'—by which time, the front had passed on, and Latvia was a rear area as far as the Germans were concerned. The German vision for Latvia did not have a role for Latvians in Latvian uniforms under Latvian commanders. The new forces were dismissed and sent home. Latvians were disarmed where found. Lt Colonel Viktors Deglavs, Plensner's chief of staff who had served as attaché in Lithuania, was mysteriously found shot dead in the stairwell of Plensner's apartment block, reported as a suicide but possibly killed by the SS.[16]

Uprisings in Estonia

Estonians also reacted to the German invasion. It took longer for the Germans to get to Estonia, as they would have to progress through both Lithuania and Latvia. This small period allowed for several things that had an effect on the development of partisan resistance. First, the Soviets moved the remnants of the former Estonian Army, the 22nd Riflemen's Corps, out of Estonia to Russia, as part of their retreat. But many hundreds of Estonians, including junior officers and NCOs who had not yet been purged, deserted from the Soviet Army to become a useful cadre to form armed resistance.

Second, the Soviets instituted conscription of Estonians. Many young people ignored summons, and when authorities came to round up young men for military service, many fled to the forests. The Soviets also started punishing family members of conscription avoiders.

Third, the Soviets set up special irregular battalions to stop the irregular retreat and enforce discipline. These were the first *istrebiteli*—'destruction'—units of post-war infamy. The Soviets authorised these new hastily formed units to shoot Estonians on the spot without trial or investigation. This, naturally, enraged the populace and served as yet another impetus for rebellion.

One interesting aspect of the 1941 uprising in Estonia is the role of the Estonian border guards on the Estonian–Latvian border. These border guards, all Estonian, had not yet been fully incorporated into the Soviet infrastructure, as the Soviets saw that border as almost a non-border, internal to the USSR. The commissars had not actually gotten around to dealing with the eighty to 100 border guards who had long minded that largely peaceful and quiet border. These border guards had an intimate familiarity with the rural area along the border and were armed. They became useful in the Forest Brotherhood movement by becoming the nucleus of resistance cells in the areas where they knew the countryside very well.

In Tartu, the group that had been secretly using the Museum of Health Care as cover led an uprising. A battle broke out in Tartu and the city was, effectively, liberated by partisans.[17] A council led by former (and arguably still legally) Prime Minister Jüri Uluots met in liberated Tartu and entreated with the arriving Germans to restore the Estonian state.[18] This request was refused. As in Latvia and Lithuania, once German rule bedded down and German officials took up their roles governing Estonia, armed Estonians and organised groups were not part of the overall vision. But we will hear more from Uluots later in the book.

The retreating Soviets also laid the groundwork for partisan resistance of their own sort, particularly in Latvia and Estonia where they had more time to organise such efforts. A number of agents, weapons, and supplies were left in Estonia to help establish a Communist partisan network to harry the German rear areas. Indigenous support for such a movement was very limited, as nearly every Estonian sympathetic to the Soviet cause was either dead or had fled ahead of or with the retreating Red Army.

Verdict on the uprisings

The 1941 uprisings are complex stories that would require a deeper examination than the limits of this book permit. There are several ways in which they can be viewed. A Soviet-slanted (or even Nazi-slanted) perspective might view them as basically Nazi fifth columnists at work, with maybe some Finns as well in Estonia. A rose-tinted nationalist view, particularly of the Lithuanian uprising, might want to overlook some of the unsavoury characters, actions, and German connections.

It is right to point at atrocities and describe them for what they are. These were popular uprisings against an unpopular occupier, even if some of the planning, timing, and impetus were driven by German activity. A slightly less unpopular occupier arrived and hijacked some of the hard work. Opportunists of various bents did what opportunists do. A window of opportunity to exact revenge on oppressors opened up.

The idea that these were wholly German plots is unrealistic. The scope of German intrigue extended to liaison with, perhaps, dozens, of Balts. Yet tens of thousands of people with legitimate grievances took up arms and took to the streets. The size, scope, and diversified nature of the 1941 uprisings gives way too much credit to the German invaders, who, in the end, really did not want large Baltic military and paramilitary organisations with nationalist aspirations lurking about in their rear areas.

The tendency from some quarters to paint every one of the uprising fighters as 'Nazi collaborators' is an exaggeration. It seems utterly reasonable for the Germans, who did have a relatively sharp intelligence service, to assess that the population of the region was being done over pretty badly by their Soviet occupiers and thus were ripe for rising up. These uprisings, however, all hoped to re-establish states and governments that the arriving Germans did not want to exist.

In some writing about the period, it has become fashionable to say that the Baltic peoples openly embraced the new German occupiers as liberators. Although there is some truth to such a view, it is also a simplification that overlooks a few basic facts. First, the Soviet repressions of 1940–1 were so brutal that stopping the mass repressions, deportations, and wreckage to the economy, even for a few months, seemed a blessed relief to many people. Second, the Germans turned up at exactly the right point to maximise sympathy for a different occupier because of the severity of the June 1941 oppressions that were underway. Third, the German occupation during the First World War was within living memory. The Kaiser's occupation of the Baltic states was nowhere near as bad as what these countries experienced in 1940 and the first half of 1941. Indeed, there were even some positive aspects to that earlier German occupation when compared to the worst excesses of tsarist rule. Many people could honestly say to themselves: 'We remember the last time the Germans came. How bad could these Germans be compared to these Soviets?' For people to think this at that time in history is not an unreasonable position, particularly as the full horrors of the Holocaust were not yet known to many people in the Baltic countries. Fourth, the Germans were master propagandists: they were fully capable of exploiting this situation, and they did so.

It is possible that the 1941 uprisings, while sincere in intent, were premature. They flushed a lot of people out into the open, where they ended up on lists. The Germans wrote down a lot of names. Furthermore, as we will see, the Germans co-opted a lot of talented and motivated people into serving their own ends, usually through coercion, false pretences, or exaggeration. But the groundwork was being laid for partisan resistance.

3

THE SECOND WORLD WAR

The three Baltic states were in an awful position geographically. They were stuck in between two much larger countries governed by despots who did not view Estonia, Latvia, or Lithuania as having a right to exist. All three countries spent the next few years under a German occupation that was harsh but in many ways not as harsh as the Soviet occupation. There is a large exception to that statement, of course, which is the massacre of the Jewish population, a crime against humanity that casts a pall over this period.

The German occupation and local collaboration

By the autumn of 1941, the front lines had passed through the Baltic states. Active fighting was much further east. Many people initially greeted the arriving German troops as liberators rather than occupiers. It took some time before this naïve optimism wore off, and people realised that the 1941 German occupiers were not the ones from 1915. The enthusiasm to re-establish independence gave rise to the various revolts in 1941 that accompanied the German invasion. The Germans quickly quashed these false hopes.

Administration

Organisationally, Nazi Germany administered the Baltic states— along with Belarus—as Reichskommissariat Ostland, which came under the purview of the Reich Ministry for the Occupied Eastern Territories. The exception was the Lithuania Minor region around Klaipėda. It was renamed Memelland and incorporated into the Reich. The minister for the occupied eastern territories was

Alfred Rosenberg, a Nazi ideologue and himself a Baltic German. Hitler appointed Hinrich Lohse as Rosenberg's *Reichskommissar* for Ostland. Rosenberg and his staff had defined ideas about what to do with the conquered territories east of Germany.

The Germans could have exploited local anti-Communist and anti-Russian sentiment, and to a limited extent, propaganda made inroads along these lines. But no amount of wartime propaganda was going to make up for the Nazis having a vision for the Baltic states that was not good for the native populace. Nazi racial pseudoscience went through various gyrations as to how to classify the Baltic peoples. Rosenberg's pseudoscientists viewed Estonians as having a lot of German blood and thus being higher in their perverse hierarchy than Latvians or Lithuanians.

The eventual German plan was to remove much of the population of the Baltic states and resettle millions of Germans into the area. Ostland would be a new province of Germany. Germans would settle on Baltic farms and in Baltic cities. The population already there would be greatly reduced, likely by deportation further east. This, of course, entailed winning the lands further east. The forced Germanification of the Baltic states would stay largely on the planning documents awaiting a military victory that never arrived. Limited resettlement of some Dutch occurred as a pilot project by the end of 1943, occupying Lithuanian property that had belonged to Poles or Jews.[1]

In the interim, the three countries were considered as sources of resources that could be exploited to support the German war effort. Aside from Estonian oil shale, the principal resources were agriculture and labour. Pre-war Baltic agriculture had been prosperous, so the produce of Baltic farms was procured to feed Germany and its armies. Soviet dispossession of small farms and small businesses was reversed, and these properties were returned to their owners. Farms and small industry were expected to yield up much of their output to the occupiers, but they were left in private ownership. Larger industry was subsumed by German companies. For example, the German firm AEG took over the VEF radio and camera factory in Riga, known for manufacturing the Minox subminiature camera.

Local government

The conquering Germans did not bring enough German personnel to administer civil government as if this were a new region of Germany. Although local uprisings had given the Germans the option of having a ready-made local government, these were swept aside as being far too independent of German rule. Unlike Denmark or Vichy France, there was no pretence at a separate government, even a puppet one. Local administrations were to deal with local affairs and to assist the Germans. Some degree of local autonomy was a practical necessity from the German standpoint. The local levels of government tried to carry on as much as possible, reverting to pre-occupation local rules and laws unless they were specifically over-ruled or superseded by German edict. On the one hand, these local administrations carried on essential functions like health, welfare, and education as best they could under trying circumstances. On the other hand, when it came to public order or the war effort, they were at the mercy of their German overlords. The German-directed local administrations ran police departments, but these were also reinforced, supplanted, and often over-ridden by the German SS. They assisted the oppression and death of Jews and facilitated conscription efforts.

The Germans formed a 'directorate' and a council of locals in each of the three countries. In Estonia, the local directorate was run by a member of the Vaps movement named Hjalmar-Johannes Mäe, a minor politician from the pre-war era. His early criticism of President Päts, who despite being a despot was rather popular, made Mäe no friends. He was a puppet of the Germans. His director of home affairs was Oskar Angelus. Angelus closely collaborated with the Nazis and established a secret police force, nicknamed the Sipo, that was closely integrated with the Germans and had both German and Estonians on its staff.

In Latvia, the Germans appointed a retired general, Oskars Dankers, to run the directorate. He was well known as a military figure and had moved to Germany before the Soviet occupation in 1940 and became a German citizen. One of his key staff was Alfreds Valdmanis. They actually did a fair bit to preserve Latvian institutions, like Riga University. The Germans never fully trusted Dankers and his directorate as he was not the pliable figure that they really wanted.

Riga, the capital and home to a third of the population, was kept under more direct German control under a German mayor.

In Lithuania, the Germans could have turned to the provisional government formed during the 1941 uprising and made it into the local directorate. But they did not do so and appointed former army general Petras Kubiliūnas to run the local directorate. He had done much to improve and modernise the Lithuanian Army in the interwar era but had been one of the leaders of the unsuccessful far-right coup of 1934. The 1941 revolt had liberated him from prison, likely saving him from NKVD executioners. He tried to walk a line between being a Nazi 'yes man' and trying to maintain some Lithuanian identity, but he did a lot to help Nazi oppression and conscription.

Recruiting and conscription

The German occupier saw the native population as a source of labour, and significant efforts were made to recruit and conscript workers for the military, the paramilitary, the police, industry, and agriculture. By expanding the war to include the Soviet Union and the United States, Germany was facing enemies that were numerically superior, not just in terms of military power but also civilian labour to keep farms and factories running.

Industrial and agricultural labour

Conscript labour was, in effect, a form of slavery. Indeed, some Germans were tried in post-war tribunals for offences relating to the use of slave labour. Some of this was, in practical terms, a form of serfdom, tying Baltic peoples to their farmland indirectly by requiring a certain amount of agricultural output. Other labourers were technically volunteers, but much of this volunteering was coerced in some way or another. Still others may have joined the German labour force out of desperation or poverty. But most of the labourers were conscripted or literally nabbed off the street.

Germany had a variety of categories of foreign labour, ranging from a relatively small number of decently treated *gastarbeitnehmer* ('guest workers' from friendly or neutral countries, a category that may have included some Baltic Germans) to various forms of prisoner and de facto slave labour. Further, there were people who were imprisoned in concentration camps, and they were usually put to hard labour as well.[2]

Like other aspects of Nazi horror, the true scale of this enslavement is not fully accounted for, and there have been various estimates of the number of foreign labourers used in German industry and agriculture. Post-war reckoning is made more difficult because some sources aggregate the Baltic states into the Soviet Union. However, one authoritative study by the International Labor Office in the immediate aftermath of the war puts the number of forcibly detained labourers from the Baltic states at 90,000 Lithuanians, 60,000 Latvians, and 15,000 Estonians.[3] Other estimates vary significantly. Regardless, this level of effort, particularly in Lithuania and Latvia, had the practical effect of reducing the available manpower for possible resistance movements.

Military recruitment and conscription

Anyone who tries to invade Russia finds themselves overstretched, and the Germans were no exception. Initially, Germany did not want to use armed locals in places like the Baltic states, Poland, or Ukraine. But as the Nazi military advance continued, they found that they could not secure and police their rear areas, guard prisoners, police occupied territory, massacre the innocent, and safeguard transport routes with their own forces alone. While Hitler had said that nobody west of the Urals should be armed other than Germans, Himmler, head of the SS, contradicted the Führer and started issuing decrees to arm locals.

It was these efforts to use Baltic people for military and paramilitary purposes that have proven the most fertile fodder for later controversy. The exact terminology and the exact chronology of events varies significantly between the three Baltic states, so I will focus on the broader categories. A specific category of self-defence forces and stay-behind teams recruited late in the war is discussed in the next chapter.

Schutzmannschaften

Unlike places such as Denmark, France, and Belgium, where local police largely remained in post after the Germans invaded, the

Soviet Union evacuated its police along with the rest of the regime's forces and officials. The pre-1940 governments had been rapidly dismantled by the Soviets a year earlier. The new occupiers were, simply, caught short in manpower for even a relatively non-punitive occupation, let alone the planned atrocities. For the amount of land Germany was trying to conquer and occupy, the Third Reich found itself being reminded that greater Germany had lost millions of men in the previous war and was, in fact, not manned sufficiently well to take on the Soviet Union while still occupying much of the rest of Europe and still fight in the West. Within weeks of the invasion, Germany switched policies and authorised the recruitment of auxiliaries from the local populace.

The first category was the so-called *Schutzmannschaften*, literally 'guard units'. Eventually, as many as 300,000 *Schutzmannschaften* were recruited or conscripted across Eastern Europe. Many works refer to these as 'auxiliary police'. These units were staffed with German officers, but the rank and file did not wear German insignia, which were reserved for Germans, and so an odd mix of uniforms and equipment was used instead. Arms were generally from captured Soviet stocks.

Schutzmannschaften were used for a variety of purposes ranging from firefighting and local policing of the non-controversial sort, to guarding infrastructure and prisoners, and so-called mobile battalions, some of which became infamous. Mobile units were used in paramilitary operations against Soviet partisans and as part of SS operations against Jews and other targets of the Holocaust. A number of atrocities can be directly attributed to some of these units. Many of these mobile battalions were sent outside of their countries. For example, two Latvian battalions were shipped to Warsaw to guard the Warsaw Ghetto.

The auxiliary police came from many sources. Initial 'recruits' were co-opted from partisan units that had been set up during the 1941 uprisings. Criminals and deserters from the Soviet military joined seeking to avoid Nazi concentration camps. Other people wanted wages and food. Some saw the opportunity for plunder. Many were simply avoiding forced labour. There were ideological recruits, seeking to continue the fight against Communism, but these appear to have been rare. As with the Soviet *istrebiteli* units before and after the German occupation, some of these battalion members could be described as the dregs of society. As the war progressed, the Germans resorted to conscription to fill these units. Desertion was rampant. A significant effort was devoted to propaganda and indoctrination in these units, and much of this effort was devoted to deliberately conflating Judaism and Soviet Communism.[4]

Recruiting differed slightly in each of the three Baltic countries. Estonian auxiliary units were originally provisionally organised around the 'self-defence' Omakaitse unit that cropped up in the first month of the war. Eventually, twenty-six *Schutzmannschaften* battalions were recruited in Estonia.[5] In Latvia, there were similar developments, with nationalist formations and former Latvian soldiers being co-opted or recruited into a handful of so-called 'police' units, several of which were shipped quickly to the front for military duties. It should be noted that thousands of ethnic Russians served in the Latvian battalions as well as Latvians. Lithuanian auxiliary police units had their genesis in the provisional units set up rapidly during the 1941 uprising. Around 13,000 Lithuanians served in twenty-six battalions.

The Germans used these battalions for a wide variety of duties. Some of them were assigned to help carry out the Holocaust, one of the most infamous being the Latvian Arājs Kommando, which massacred many Jews. Its personnel were transferred into the Latvian Legion. Others were assigned to fight Soviet partisans or guard supply lines, and a few were also used in combat roles at or near the front. Many police auxiliaries served in largely innocuous roles as rural police. Desertion was common.

National legions

A different group of units were conventional 'legions' of troops that were not disguised as 'police' units. These were combat formations used in military operations. The military forces of Nazi Germany did not just include the traditional army, the Wehrmacht. The armed combatant wing of the SS—the so-called Waffen SS— evolved as another entire army that fought alongside the traditional German military. The Waffen SS, once strictly ethnically German, became the administrative mechanism for having foreigners fight for Germany. It became, in effect, Germany's foreign legions. These units contained both volunteers and conscripts.

The Germans managed to form 'legions' in both Estonia and Latvia. These legions were recruited under false pretence and coercion. The word 'volunteer' was used as a dodge to avoid the appearance of violating the 1907 Hague Convention, which bans conscription of the inhabitants of occupied countries. Such recruitment efforts that did occur were heavily doused in anti-Soviet, anti-Russian, and anti-Communist propaganda that would find fertile ground in countries that had been hard hit by Stalinist occupation only a few years earlier. In some cases, existing police units were simply rebranded. Many were given a direct choice of prison, forced labour, or service in a legion unit. Around 20,000 Estonians ended up serving in the Estonian SS Legion. In Latvia, perhaps 57,000 Latvians served in legion units, although estimates vary. Only 15 to 20 per cent of the Latvian Legion are believed to have been volunteers.[6]

Both the Estonian and Latvian Legions saw very arduous combat service. A shortage of German officers meant that Estonians and Latvians could often serve as junior officers, and some rose to command battalions or occasionally even a regiment. This gave rise to situations where Latvians and Estonians fought under Latvian and Estonian officers against a Soviet enemy. Even many German officers saw through this, seeing that these Latvians and Estonians were really wanting to fight for their own country, merely viewing Germany as the lesser of two evils. Because they fought on the side of the Germans, and were badged as part of the SS, these legions are seen by many outside the Baltic states as highly problematic. However, as they were formed to fight at the front, and not as part of the state apparatus of oppression, the legions played less of a role in war crimes than some of the police battalions.

The legions are significant in that they fought against one of the two oppressors and became a source of combat veterans and arms for the Forest Brotherhood after the war. Nonetheless, the Latvian and Estonian SS Legions are a controversial subject to this day. While some people clearly did bad things, others simply fought at the front after being conscripted. It is difficult to figure out exactly where to draw the line before one engages in excessive guilt by association. I grapple with this question more fully in Chapter 14.[7]

Efforts to recruit a legion in Lithuania, on the other hand, were a complete failure. The various Lithuanian nationalist movements and local governments worked rather effectively to mount a boycott of such recruiting efforts. This effort is discussed later in this chapter.

A different kind of collaboration

Any discussion of Baltic collaboration with the Nazis needs some balance. Widespread instances of Baltic men serving German military and police units are more than offset by the large number of Estonians, Latvians, and Lithuanians who served in Soviet forces during the war. The Red Army raised entire divisions from ethnic Balts who had evacuated or retreated in 1941 or who were already resident in the Soviet Union. Many were conscripts. Some were let out of detention or internal exile to join, while others were volunteers. Although many desertions happened from the Red Army units that had been the pre-war Baltic armies, after 1942 there were few desertions or defections. These Soviet Army formations composed of Baltic men saw hard combat service at the front, unlike many of the German auxiliary units used more often for rear-area security. A Soviet Lithuanian division was noted for its bravery at the battle of Kursk. The 249th Rifle Division and the 308th Latvian Rifle Division were awarded the Order of the Red Banner. The 201st Latvian Rifle Division, which was majority volunteers, not conscripts, was awarded the title of Guards Division in 1942. Around 50,000 Balts died in Soviet service in the war. By March 1945, nearly 100,000 Lithuanians were in Soviet service, well over twice the number that had been in German-sponsored battalions.[8] These statistics muddy the waters of the claim that the Baltic countries were German collaborators. If we are going to use the word 'collaborator', we ought to use it fairly and apply it to those who collaborated with the Soviet occupier, seeing how neither the Soviets nor the Nazis ever legitimately ruled the three countries.

The Holocaust

Before the war, there was a significant Jewish population in the region. Tragically, this was not the case once the war ended. The old 'Pale of Settlement' in which Jews were allowed to live in the Russian Empire extended into most of present-day Lithuania and some parts of Latvia. The Jewish population in Estonia was relatively small due to it having been outside of the general footprint of historic Jewish settlement.

The history of the Holocaust is well documented. During 1941–3, the Jewish population was largely deported or exterminated in the region. Early on, *Einsatzgruppen* massacred Jews (and others) with impunity. Gradually, in Riga, Kaunas, Vilnius, and Daugavpils, ghettos were formed as de facto prisons. Over time, ghetto inhabitants were deported to camps, some of which were in the Baltic states, or to concentration and extermination camps elsewhere.

The death toll from the Holocaust in the Baltic states was truly horrific. In Estonia, nearly the entire Jewish population, between 950 and 1,000 people, were killed. Fewer than a dozen Estonian Jews survived the war.[9] In Latvia, the Holocaust started with the burning of Riga's synagogues in July 1941. Exact figures vary, but around 70,000 Latvian Jews, out of a pre-war number of about 93,000, went to their deaths. Several thousand Latvian Jews, including a significant number of Jewish business and community leaders, avoided the Holocaust simply because they had been deported to the Gulag by the Soviets in 1940–1.

In Lithuania, given the size and tenure of the Jewish population, the toll of the Holocaust was staggering. There were about 208,000 Jews in Lithuania in 1941, a number that had greatly increased after Vilnius was returned from Polish control. Various calculations of the grim death toll exist, but the figure of 195,000 to 196,000 Lithuanian Jews murdered is well sourced.[10] Given the surnames and location of some of my ancestors, it is a near certainty that relatives of mine were among these fatalities. The impact on Vilnius was particularly stark. It had been a great centre of Jewish life and learning for centuries. All this was lost. Vilnius was hollowed out.

In addition to these grim figures, various concentration camps were sited on Baltic soil, and Jews and other victims from other conquered territories were imprisoned and killed in the Baltic states. Latvian, Lithuanian, Czech, and German Jews died in camps in Estonia, as one example.

Other groups were also subjected to the full horror of the Nazi regime. Although far smaller in number than Jews, Romany Gypsies in the Baltic region were oppressed with similar vigour. At least 500 Roma were massacred in Lithuania, perhaps one third of the pre-1940 population. A total of 243 were killed in Estonia. Nazi massacres of Roma occurred in Pravieniškės and Švenčionys.[11] Others ended up in Auschwitz alongside Jews. Perhaps half of Latvia's Roma met a similar fate, and the relatively small Estonian Roma population was also heavily affected. Some of the other groups that were oppressed by Nazis, including disabled people, Jehovah's Witnesses, Seventh Day Adventists, and Freemasons, were not to be found in great number but were arrested wherever found by the Nazi authorities. As elsewhere, wherever they went in Europe the Nazis had both willing and conscripted helpers among the local population. This is a story that runs alongside that of the Forest Brotherhood and must inform our understanding of events in the Baltic states.

Anti-German resistance

The Second World War was not a tale solely of collaboration with Nazis or collaboration with Soviets. Collaboration, cooperation, and resistance of various types happened all over occupied Europe. No country was all resistance and no collaboration during this period. And no country was all collaboration and no resistance, not even Germany itself. As with every country, most people were just trying to get by and were neither collaborators nor resisters. Some people even had a foot in both camps. Baltic resistance to German occupation was diverse but generally one of subterfuge and passive resistance rather than armed partisan units taking up armed struggle. This is often cited as evidence of the Baltic states being somehow allied with the Germans, but the overall theme was the development of organisations that could represent national interests once the war was over, whichever way the war went.

Estonia

As Estonians were higher than Latvians and Lithuanians in the Nazi racial hierarchy, German rule was generally less harsh there, and German brutality rarely impacted regular Estonians. Estonian resistance to the Germans remained non-violent.[12]

Anti-German resistance in Estonia was aided by its coastline. Various Estonians were in exile in Sweden and Finland, and with luck and skill, these could be reached by small boat under the eyes of the Germans. Many Estonians, in fact, sought refuge in Finland. As a result, Estonians could keep in touch with exile groups that had already formed in places like Stockholm.

The National Committee of the Republic of Estonia (Eesti Vabariigi Rahvuskomitee—EVRK) gradually evolved as the umbrella movement operating in Estonia, with some exiles helping from neutral Sweden. Their prime motive was to be in a position to declare a provisional government when the war ended. Perhaps they were thinking of the First World War, when both Germany and Russia collapsed and left voids throughout the region. Jüri Uluots, the last pre-war prime minister who had refused to help the German directorate, became the leader of the EVRK. A poorly documented 'Green Legion' armed group was operating in southern Estonia in 1942, but it was relatively minor and contained Communists.[13]

Latvia

The Latvians formed a seven-person Latvian Central Council (Latvijas Centrālā Padome—LCP) representing the four centre-left to centre-right parties but not the quasi-fascist Pērkonkrusts. This group largely operated within Latvia, although it had a few supporters in exile. Like the EVRK in Estonia, its members operated under the optimistic hope that the war would leave both Germany and the Soviet Union seriously weakened, thus providing an opportunity to rise up and declare independence. The LCP elected Konstantīns Čakste, a law professor, as its leader.

The LCP engaged in a lot of covert activity. It developed a military arm, under General Jānis Kurelis, to plan for the defence of a new provisional government, who convinced the Germans that he could form a military unit in Riga to guard property. As we will see in the next chapter, Kurelis and his cadre played a role in the rise of armed resistance at the end of the war. The LCP also engaged in underground publishing, which is discussed in greater length in a later chapter. They kept in touch with Latvian exiles in Sweden and elsewhere. In an act of pan-Baltic solidarity, they also held coordinating meetings with Estonian and Lithuanian resistance movements. These attempts at liaison, however, ended up exposing the Latvians to much danger, as they were often discovered.

Perhaps one of the most prominent LCP efforts was the rescue boats. It is not that far from the coast of Latvia to the Swedish island of Gotland, and a handful of boats had smuggled people to Sweden in 1943. In 1944, the LCP, working with a committee formed in Sweden, set up a more organised effort. In the summer of 1944, many boat journeys were made. After September 1944, conditions, both military and meteorological, got worse, so fewer voyages were made. The Latvian coast was the last part of the Baltic states to be reoccupied by Soviet troops at the end of the war, so these journeys did continue when possible until June 1945. Over 4,000 Latvians escaped both Nazi and Soviet tyranny this way. It had been hoped that some Jews might also be rescued by boat. A few were, but by the time this route of escape opened, most of the Jews had been imprisoned or killed.

Lithuania

In Lithuania, resistance to German rule resulted in several different groups springing up in 1942 and 1943, including the National Council (Tautos Taryba), a pro-Catholic group operating within the country. The other major group was the Supreme Committee of Lithuanians (Vyriausiasis Lietuvos Išlaisvinimo Komitetas—VLIK), which was an umbrella group of various non-religious groups. VLIK started in Lithuania and sent emissaries to Sweden and Finland. But its leadership ended up fleeing west ahead of the Soviet return to Lithuania. Both were active in passive resistance and published underground newspapers. There was even a clandestine radio station for a brief period.

The most significant result of Lithuanian resistance during the war was the boycott of an SS Legion. As the most populous of the three Baltic states, the Germans reckoned that they could recruit or conscript at least as many Lithuanians as Latvians or Estonians. The

Germans ordered a former Lithuanian colonel, Antanas Rėklaitis, to form the '1st Lithuanian SS Regiment' and offered him a large feudal estate in post-war Ukraine as an inducement. He refused. Starting in early 1943, a recruiting office opened in Kaunas. The underground press was uniformly opposed to the recruiting effort, and very few Lithuanians turned up at recruiting offices. In retaliation, the Germans arrested forty-six prominent Lithuanians and sent them to Stutthof concentration camp in Prussia. The Germans eventually gave up, considering the Lithuanians morally weak[14] and instead focused on conscription for forced labour.

Why so little fighting?

Why was there so little armed resistance against the Germans? While there was, indeed, a fair amount of organisation-building and much passive resistance, such as underground publishing and resistance to conscription, there was comparatively little armed partisan resistance against the Germans aside from the Jewish and Soviet partisans mentioned earlier. This has often been weaponised by those wishing to portray the Baltic states as collaborators or even allies of the Germans. As we have seen, there were various forms of collaboration, of active, passive, and coerced. There were also active, passive, and coerced forms of collaboration with the Soviet occupation both before and after the Nazi occupation. But collaboration and resistance happened alongside each other in many countries during the war. So, why was there not so much armed resistance against the Germans?

One reason for the lack of a widespread, armed resistance is that there was a brief 'honeymoon' period of relief because the 1940–1 Soviet occupation was so bad for Estonia, Latvia, and Lithuania that anything, even a German occupation, seemed preferable. Older people remembered the German occupation in the First World War, particularly in Lithuania, as not being particularly worse than being ruled by the tsar. In some ways, it had been better than tsarist rule. It took months for the reality to set in that the Nazi occupation was also bad, even though in some ways it was less harsh than Soviet occupation. All of this delayed the formation of armed resistance.

Another factor is that a lot of resistance activity had been flushed into the daylight during the uprisings as the Soviets left, particularly in Lithuania but also, to a lesser extent, in Latvia and Estonia. The newly arriving German occupiers then knew who these people were. In many cases, the uprisings' leaders went to the Germans and introduced themselves, wrongly thinking that the Germans would eventually allow them to regain their independence. It is not really accurate to say that the Germans ignored them: they dismissed them and kept a list of their names.

This fed into the next factor. The Germans were good at running a police state. By 1941, they knew that resistance would emerge in the countries they conquered. The German security apparatus did a lot to keep an eye on Baltic nationalists and possible troublemakers. At various points, possible resistance leaders were locked up, while others were closely monitored. Military officers from the independence era were viewed with particular suspicion.

The Nazis were also good propagandists. They branded their war against the Soviet Union as a crusade against Bolshevism. Because of this, many people who might have taken up arms against the Germans were co-opted, coerced, hoodwinked, or conscripted into military and paramilitary units under the guise of fighting Communism. Many people who might have been recruited into partisan units were stuck at the front. In addition, the conscription of people for labour in Germany took a lot of fighting-age males to Germany, where they worked in factories and farms and were thus simply not available for resistance work.

Pragmatism was likely the most important factor. It did not take too much time before there was a strong realisation among many Baltic patriots and nationalists that Germany's military crusade against the Soviet Union was a doomed affair. The Nazi defeat at Stalingrad in early 1943 was seen by some as an omen. We should not forget that we are talking about a relatively compressed timeline. There was less than four years between Operation Barbarossa and the German surrender. In the war in the East, Germany was only on the ascendant for around a year and a half of that time, and it can take a year or two for a partisan resistance movement to coalesce under harsh conditions.

By the time some groups got themselves organised, the war in the East was not going Germany's way. Some potential resisters clearly felt it would be better to let their enemies fight each other before making their own presence felt. Others held the similar belief, borne out as correct, that the eventual defeat of the Germans by the Soviets would bring an even more vicious Stalinist occupation. Germany's fear of the Soviet advances was palpable and visible to Balts, as the German occupier would hardly have begun recruiting from among the occupied population and handing out weapons if it believed it was winning the war.

All of this combined to create a situation where resistance took the form of watching and waiting. Every Soviet soldier that fell was going to be one fewer to occupy the Baltics. Every month that the front did not reach Baltic soil was another month to plan, prepare, and steal weapons and ammunition.

Assisting the Jews

Another form of resistance involved helping Jews to survive, hide, and escape the Holocaust. Well over 1,000 people from the Baltic states are officially recognised as 'The Righteous among the Nations' by the Yad Vashem memorial in Israel for having helped or saved Jews during the Holocaust.

In Estonia, there are relatively few individuals that are known to have helped the Jews, but it should be noted that the pre-war Jewish community there was miniscule. One notable figure, however, is Uko Masing, a poet, folklorist, and philosopher. A true polyglot— he was conversant in as many as sixty-five languages and could effectively translate twenty languages into Estonian—Masing and his wife Eha spent the German occupation salvaging and protecting Jewish cultural and religious objects. They also hid, fed, and supplied forged documents to one of Masing's pre-war students, the Jewish folklorist and theologian Isidor Levin, who survived the war.

Yad Vashem's archives list 138 names of the righteous in Latvia. Two of them were Paul and Charlotte Schiemann. Paul was Baltic German by descent and had been a minor politician and editor in the interwar era. In Riga, during the German occupation, although he was seriously unwell with tuberculosis, he and his wife hid a Jew named Valentīna Freimane, who survived the war and went on to become one of Latvia's leading cinema and theatre scholars during the second Soviet occupation. Roberts Seduls, a boxer and former seaman in Liepaja, along with his wife Johanna, saved eleven Jews by hiding them in a cellar. Sadly, Roberts was killed by an artillery shell near the end of the war.[15] Jānis Lipke was a dockworker in Riga. He became a contractor for the Luftwaffe but used that role to smuggle at least forty Jews out of the Riga Ghetto, saving them from certain death.[16] His deeds are commemorated in a 2018 film called *Tēvs Nakts*.

The Yad Vashem list names 918 in Lithuania. A few examples suffice to give a glimpse of the heroism involved. Elena Kutorgienė was an ophthalmologist who helped a number of Jewish children escape doom by hiding them with non-Jewish families who could claim them as their own children if questioned.[17] She also bought firearms to smuggle into the Kaunas ghetto and managed to save the diary of Chaim Yellin, a theatre reviewer and one of the Jewish partisan leaders of the Kaunas Ghetto.

Another Lithuanian example is Father Bronislovas Paukštys, a Catholic priest.[18] He had several religious posts in Kaunas and forged baptismal records and birth certificates for Jews from the Kaunas Ghetto. He also hid twenty-five Jews in churches until they could be smuggled out to the countryside. It is estimated that he helped about 200 people. After the war, he was arrested and sent to the Gulag for helping Lithuanian partisans.

Another hero was Mother Bertranda, née Janina Siestrzewitowska. She was the prioress of a Roman Catholic convent of Dominican nuns. As well as hiding Jews, Mother Bertranda set up a network to acquire weapons and ammunition and smuggle them to the Jewish resistance in the ghetto. Dressed in a disguise, Bertranda also delivered baskets of grenades herself. She was eventually arrested by the Germans but survived her imprisonment and lived quietly in Poland under the name Anna Borkowska. In 1984, she was rightly recognised by Yad Vashem as one of the Righteous among the Nations.[19]

No account of this period is complete without mention of two non-Lithuanians in Lithuania who saved many Jews. Chiune Sugihara was the Japanese vice consul in Kaunas. Between 1940 and 1941, he issued thousands of visas that allowed Jews, many of whom had fled from Poland, to transit through the Soviet Union elsewhere. Another diplomat, Jan Zwartendijk, was a Dutch part-time acting consul in Kaunas. In 1940, before the Soviet occupiers shut down the Dutch embassy, Zwartendijk granted visas that allowed Jews to go to the Dutch colony of Curaçao in the Caribbean.

Jewish resistance

It is important that we do not forget a particular, albeit literally segregated, strain of partisan resistance. One of the more pernicious anti-Semitic tropes is that Jews went to their deaths without putting up any resistance. Serious armed resistance was more rare than various types of passive resistance, but the same could be said across all of Europe. Some of the more famous incidents of armed Jewish resistance occurred in Belarus, not far from the regions covered by this book. Two armed resistance movements of note also arose within the Baltic states. One was in the Vilnius Ghetto and the other was in the Kaunas Ghetto. Many sources refer to these under other spellings, so one often encounters reference to Vilna and Kovno.[20]

In the Vilnius ghetto, the United Partisan Organisation (UPO) was formed, which was one of the earliest armed Jewish resistance movements in Europe. Some of its members were brave and talented heroes. One was the poet Abba Kovner whose manifesto 'Let Us Not Go Like Lambs to the Slaughter' is a salutary riposte to the idea that Jews meekly went to their deaths. Kovner had escaped capture by hiding in a Catholic convent, returned to the Vilnius ghetto, and organised the UPO. Kovner worked with other partisan leaders in Vilnius. One was Yitzhak Wittenberg, who had been a Communist. Another leader was Josef Glanzman, who had served in the Lithuanian Army before the war. Accounts vary, but at least 100 people were members of the UPO.

Unfortunately, this resistance came to little. Wittenberg was betrayed to the Germans, and others had to flee rather than stage a full revolt. Kovner broke out of the ghetto with others and formed a partisan band named 'The Avengers', which attacked Germans until the Soviets turned up. Kovner survived the war and ended up in Israel, after having been involved in a group that was seeking revenge killings on Germans. Kovner later testified at top Nazi official Adolf Eichmann's trial in Israel in 1961 and lived until 1987. Glanzman died in 1943, fighting Germans to the end. The Vilnius ghetto was liquidated by the SS in a series of deportations over the course of 1943. By 1943, the Jews of the ghetto had been killed or sent to camps.

Several armed resistance groups were also formed in the Kaunas ghetto. The largest was the 'General Jewish Fighting Organisation', which unified several smaller groups. One of the leaders was Chaim Yellin, mentioned earlier. He established contacts with some non-Jewish resistance group outside the ghetto. He evidently escaped from the ghetto and received weeks of training somewhere in eastern Lithuania, possibly from Soviet Partisans, and returned into the Kaunas ghetto. Eventually, he was betrayed by a German informer after the liquidation of the ghetto in the autumn of 1943. Another member was Sara Ginaite, a rare example of a female armed Jewish partisan. She escaped the liquidation of the ghetto and formed a small Jewish partisan cell called 'Death to the Occupiers', survived the war, and became an economics professor in Vilnius. In retirement, she managed to move to the West, and died in 2018 at the age of ninety-four in Canada, having written extensively about her experience.

Soviet Partisans

No work on this subject would be complete without discussing the partisans who actually used the word 'partisan' in their title. The Soviet Union organised and supported large partisan formations to fight guerrilla actions against German occupation. I refer to these as 'Soviet Partisans' to differentiate them from Baltic nationalist partisans. The scattered and confused nature of the Red Army's retreat left many small units and individuals cut off from the main forces. Invading Germans captured many thousands of Soviet soldiers, but in the early days the German Army's efforts to handle such numbers were inadequate, and many prisoners escaped only to find that the front line was now far away. Communist officials or family members who were not able to retreat in time found themselves in hiding lest the Germans arrest them. In many cases, these various populations founded partisan groups. Gradually, as a more coordinated war effort coalesced in the USSR, special operations were mounted to infiltrate Red Army personnel behind the lines to set up partisan operations or join existing ones. In addition, some of the Jewish partisan groups that escaped liquidation in the ghettos did establish contacts with the Soviet Partisan groups and operated alongside them.

On closer examination, it is clear that the Soviet Partisan units were created from the top down rather than being a grassroots movement with widespread popular support .They contained relatively few Estonians, Latvians, and Lithuanians. These were not traditional resistance movements that sprang out of the local population, and it would be wrong to categorise them in the same fashion as local units. Individuals did join these units, and such examples should not be ignored. However, Soviet-era historiography greatly overstates the size and effect of these forces and sometimes misrepresents them as indigenous forces. They were far more militarily significant in other parts of the Eastern Front, and this reputation is sometimes disingenuously retrofitted on to Baltic history by post-war historical accounts.

It does not take much investigation before the concept of Soviet irregular forces leading a partisan resistance in the Baltic states starts to fall apart. Archival records from the Red Army's Central Partisan Headquarters, examined by Canadian historian Alexander Statiev, reveal a less impressive account.[21] Reports show that in 1944, 1,633 Soviet Partisans were operating in Lithuania and 856 were operating in Latvia. Only 234 were operating in Estonia. These are derisory figures considering that tens of thousands of Soviet Partisans were fighting in Belarus and Russia. In Estonia, the reports show that the number of native Estonians in these 'partisan' units was, stunningly, zero. The percentage of ethnic Russians and Belarusians in these Soviet Partisan units was quite high—over half in the case of Lithuania.

Much of this is because, after the harsh repressions of 1940–1, very few people in the rural areas supported Soviet policy. Those that did had likely fled in 1941, been killed or imprisoned by Germans, or were already serving in the Red Army. There simply weren't available recruits. These partisans were infiltrated in from Russia. In addition, harsh German reprisals against civilians in areas of Soviet Partisan operations made it difficult for the Soviet Partisans to find support. In one operation, Soviet Partisans ambushed Germans in

Lithuania near the village of Pirčiupiai, in the Varena region not far from my ancestral village. In retaliation, the Germans burnt the village and murdered everyone they could find. In total, 119 residents were killed, including forty-nine children. Most of them were burned alive in their houses.[22] The Germans knew that the local population did not support Soviet Partisans. This was an act of spite and cruelty that serves as a reminder that German rule was not kind.

However, the war was not going the way the Germans had intended. By 1944, the winds had shifted. The Soviets were coming back.

4

THE END OF THE SECOND WORLD WAR. OR NOT?

By the middle of 1944, the war was clearly not going the way of German plans. By the spring of 1944, most of the gains of the war on the Eastern Front were gone. Momentum had long shifted, and a resurgent Red Army had not only recovered from a disastrous first year of the war but had been hardened by epic conflict and seriously reinforced by American hardware. Germany was also under pressure in the Mediterranean, with Italy having folded under Allied invasion. The German heartland was under constant aerial bombardment by American and British bombers day and night, which caused great strain on industry and logistics. An Allied invasion in France was imminent, even if Germany did not know the time or place. Resources were in short supply, particularly fuel. Food and ammunition were also running short.

Military units to stay behind

The Germans had seen the Baltic states as a new province to cleanse for resettlement and as a small but useful reservoir of resources, principally agriculture and labour. With the Red Army reapproaching in 1944, colonial resettlement of civilians from the Fatherland had faded into Nazi dreamland. However, resources could still be extracted in the form of labour deported back to Germany. Other assets could be stripped. From a military perspective, Balts who had not been particularly willing to fight for the Germans could be persuaded to at least fight against the Soviets once the Germans left. A patriotic Estonian, for example, may have refused to fight for the Germans on principle. But if the Germans were to give him a weapon and ammunition on their way out the door, the equation was somewhat different.

The German military staffs could see impending doom on the Eastern Front. The German military, fighting partisan resistance in places like France, Italy, Greece, and Yugoslavia, knew that irregular troops operating in the enemy rear can cause havoc and tie up many resources. A pragmatic viewpoint was that such irregular forces could cause similar havoc among the advancing Soviets.

The Abwehr, the SS, and the Finns (in Estonia) developed various efforts to use local Estonians, Latvians, and Lithuanians as 'stay-behind' intelligence or special operations detachments to cause mayhem in the enemy rear areas. As the Abwehr had spent years infiltrating spies across the front lines on short espionage missions, it had some methodology and experience in training operatives. The SS had less expertise in such operations but trained some small stay-behind units anyway. These groups were small detachments designed to collect intelligence, report back to Germany, and conduct resistance efforts. Many simply disappeared or were captured. Some deserted immediately. Others became part of resistance efforts.

Estonia: help from Finland

Finland played an important role in the establishment of anti-Soviet resistance groups in Estonia. Finns and Estonians are close relations in ethnic and linguistic terms. Both are broadly Lutheran in religion, and both fought to establish their independence in bitter conflict against the Bolsheviks after the Russian Revolutions. Finns had helped Estonia gain its independence after the 1917 Russian Revolutions, and 4,000 Finnish volunteers had intervened at a critical point in Estonia's war for independence. A number of Estonians also crossed over the Baltic Sea in 1939 and 1940 to assist the Finnish defence against the Soviet Union in its Winter War.

After the German invasion of the Soviet Union in 1941, Finland and Germany found themselves as odd allies, fighting the same enemy but for very different reasons. Finland was fighting what it refers to as 'the Continuation War' against the Soviet Union. The full extent of Finnish war aims remains a viable subject for debate, but regaining territory lost in the Winter War was clearly one strong motivation.

Many in Finland saw Estonia as a front that could be used to fight against Soviet Communism, and the existence of anti-Soviet partisans in Estonia served Finnish military interests. There were several major Finnish efforts to help Estonia. The Finnish government had been secretly arming and training some Estonians in Finland since 1940. One unit, known as the Erna Group, operated in Finnish uniform. Part of the group was landed by speedboat on 10 July 1941, and another element of it was parachuted in on 28 July. They started operating in the Kautla marshes south-east of Tallinn.[1] These marshes were giving refuge to both nascent Forest Brothers and hapless civilians fleeing Soviet deportation. When *istrebiteli* battalions attacked the swamps to try to crack down on the displaced people, the Erna group intervened, broke the siege of the swamp, and let many refugees escape.[2] Various individuals who had received training in the Erna group later became partisans.

The next major effort was a special operations 'stay-behind' unit. This was the so-called Haukka group. The Haukka group was named after the location in Finland where it trained. The Haukka men were led by an Erna veteran, Leo Talgre. Their role was reconnaissance, intelligence collection, and reporting back to Finland. Radio communications and encryption was a significant part of their work. Their official mission was to report on Soviet activity in Estonia as the Soviets returned. Finland's German allies were suspicious of Haukka and were correct in their suspicions, as Haukka also had a secret mission of monitoring the German retreat. Some Haukka men were put under German control. However, the EVRK was highly effective in infiltrating Haukka, and a number of the Haukka men used their radio sets to communicate with Estonian exiles instead of their putative German masters. Some individual Haukka men later became active in the Forest Brotherhood.

The other main Finnish effort was known as JR200. In 1943, as conscription efforts in German-occupied Estonia increased, some young Estonians wanted to fight the Russians but not serve their occupier. They made the often-dangerous journey across the Gulf of Finland to join the Finnish military instead of serving the Germans. Volunteer Erna veterans in speedboats helped to smuggle

Estonians into Finland. Sufficient Estonian volunteers made it to Finland to form a mostly Estonian regiment in the Finnish Army. Infantry Regiment 200 (Jalaväerügement 200 or JR200 in Estonian-language sources) was formed with about 2,300 Estonians and several hundred Finns.[3] In addition, hundreds of Estonians served in the Finnish Navy, and some individual Estonians were scattered around in other units. Some Estonian mechanics worked in maintenance depots. JR200 fought against the Soviets for months in 1944. A number of JR200 members became prominent later in their careers. Several writers, a historian, a physicist, an artist, and a Catholic priest were all JR200 veterans.

JR200's legacy after combat was more important than its short tour of battlefield duty. In the summer of 1944, the German Army was withdrawing from Estonia. Finland was looking to exit the war and negotiate a ceasefire with the Soviets. With the Germans cynically leaving Estonians to fight rearguard actions to cover their own retreat, prominent Estonians were calling on Finland for help. Estonians serving in Finland were agitating to be released to go back to Estonia to fight the Soviets there. The EVRK, which was practically a shadow government in the brief void left by the German retreat, sent a telegram to Finland on 2 August 1944 asking for Estonians to return home to fight. All of these factors added up, and the large majority of JR200's Estonian soldiers were eventually infiltrated across the gulf back to Estonia. Some of them ended up in the Forest Brotherhood. Others managed to flee to the West, often via Sweden. Many more ended up as Soviet prisoners.

Other Estonian units were mobilised for sacrificial battles to cover the German retreat. Many Estonians had already joined or been conscripted into the Estonian SS Legion. Various self-defence battalions were set up in 1944. As with efforts elsewhere, this was viewed rather cynically by everyone. The message was, informally, 'Your German occupiers are leaving, so here are some weapons for you to harry the incoming Russians', and Estonians joining such units should be viewed more as defending their homeland rather than as active Nazi collaborators. The Estonians who had most closely collaborated with the Nazis tended to flee rather than stay and fight.

One group of note was the 'Admiral Pitka Group'. Admiral Johan Pitka, born in 1872, was one of the oldest Estonians to fight the Soviets. He had been a merchant sailor before the First World War and had founded the Estonian Navy. He had spent the Second World War in exile in Finland but returned and set up a volunteer battalion in the summer of 1944 to defend Tallinn after the German retreat. Many of his men were deserters from German units. They fought bitter battles against the arriving Soviets, giving a few weeks of breathing room for the EVRK to attempt to organise a government. Eventually, like all the other improvised self-defence units, Pitka's battalion was crushed, and the elderly Pitka fell in battle, although at least one account claims he committed suicide instead of being captured.

Latvia: the Kurelieši

As previously discussed, the Germans in Latvia had already mobilised the Latvian Legion. But the approach of the Soviets gave impetus for mobilising more forces. The most significant of these was the Kurelis group. The Kurelis group, the Kurelieši, was so-named after its leader, General Jānis Kurelis. Kurelis' life would be worthy of a biography in itself. Born in Latvia under the Russian Empire, he served with distinction in the Russian Army in the 1904—5 Russo-Japanese war and the entire length of the First World War, earning many medals. He then helped Latvia build up its military during its two decades of independence. He had the good fortune to have retired just before the Soviet occupation in 1940, and the Soviets had yet to begin rounding up retired officers.

General Kurelis maintained a low profile early in the German occupation, but when the war started turning against the Germans, he approached the occupation authorities and asked to set up a 'Guards' organisation to protect buildings in the Riga region. This group, separate from the Latvian Legion, evolved into the Kurelieši. But, importantly, Kurelis was secretly liaising with the Central Council of Latvia, the key underground resistance body. The Kurelis group secretly assisted boat operations to smuggle people to Sweden.

The existence of the Kurelis group proved to be a morale and retention problem to the Germans. Latvians were leaving the Latvian Legion in droves and hiding in the forests with the Kurelieši. The prospect of fighting under a Latvian command, for Latvia, against the Soviets was viewed by some as more patriotic than fighting in what had become just another wing of the German Army. Eventually, German forces, including significant numbers of Latvians, were cut off from the rest of Germany's forces in western Latvia as part of what became known as the 'Courland Pocket'. In November 1944, rumours started circulating that the Latvian Legion's 19th Division would be pulled out of Latvia and sent to Germany. The legion's Latvians had mostly signed up to fight for Latvia, not to desert Latvia in its time of need.

As part of his agreement with the Germans, Kurelis was not supposed to solicit deserters from the legion. With the Kurelieši numbering as many as 3,000 in the Courland Pocket, Kurelis was now viewed as a threat. A full battalion under one of Kurelis' officers, Lt Roberts Rubenis, numbered at least 400. Another 600 or so were at Kurelis' headquarters. These were the kinds of numbers that would make the Germans nervous. The SS police chief in Courland was a cruel man named Obergruppenführer Friedrich Jeckeln. One of his previous misdeeds was the Babi Yar massacre, an infamous mass execution of Jews in September 1941 in Kyiv, Ukraine. Either on his own authority or based on an order from above, Jeckeln began to crack down on the Kurelieši in November 1944.

Jeckeln's SS troops surrounded Kurelis' headquarters. Some resisted, but most were captured. A number of Kurelis' officers were court-martialled and shot. About 450 men were shipped off to Stutthof concentration camp, where many died. A few who weren't deserters were scattered around other German units. The fate of the Rubenis battalion was even worse. Jeckeln ordered them to surrender or face death. Rubenis refused. A battle ensued from 18 November to 9 December 1944, with the spectacle of Luftwaffe air strikes behind their own German lines. Some of Rubenis' men counterattacked and seized Jeckeln's headquarters. Jeckeln had to call in an air strike on his own office as well as regular army reinforcements off the front line to help him, surely an embarrassment for a German SS commander. Some Latvians in a German Army construction battalion even joined the Rubenis group. But eventually the Latvians were crushed. About 160 were killed, including Rubenis himself. About 300 Germans were killed. After the uprising was crushed, the Germans retaliated against Latvian civilians in the vicinity, ruthlessly murdering women and children.[4]

Kurelis himself was taken to Germany. Imprisoned, he ended up surviving the war and died as an exile in the United States. Some of his officers were executed. As an official 'stay-behind' force, the Kurelieši were over. However, many of the Kurelieši managed to evade capture and melted into the forests. Exact figures are scant, but many hundreds of them became part of the Latvian Forest Brotherhood.

Lithuanian Territorial Defence Force

German attempts to mobilise Lithuanian military volunteers and conscripts for a Lithuanian SS Legion had failed miserably due to resistance efforts and a mass national boycott in 1943. However, the Red Army's impending return led to a change in policy on the part of the German occupiers. Sending Lithuanians out of Lithuania had been an impossible sales pitch. But the front would soon be in Lithuania.

The Germans gave off the faint odour of panic, and Lithuanian underground organisations took great advantage of the situation. A Lithuanian general, Povilas Plechavičius, sprang into action. By 1944, he was fifty-four years old and one of the most senior Lithuanian military officers left in the country. He had served as a cavalry officer in the tsar's army, fought in the war of independence, and served in the interwar Lithuanian Army. He was heavily involved in the 1926 coup, but by 1929 he had been forced into reserve status. General Plechavičius convinced the Germans that a Territorial Defence Force could be raised. The agreement with the Germans was that the volunteers for this new force would only serve in Lithuania. The various underground organisations secretly supported this development as it would be a way for Lithuanians to arm themselves.

Plechavičius was allowed to make a national announcement, and he did so on 16 February 1944, Lithuanian Independence Day. He called for recruits. Eventually, thirteen battalions of volunteers were raised. They were armed and allowed to wear Lithuanian insignia on German uniforms. Between 20,000 and 30,000 Lithuanians enlisted. However, desertion was not uncommon, as was multiple enlistment—some people joined several times merely to desert with a uniform and a rifle. The active but covert involvement of resistance organisations helped to promote the Territorial Defence Force as a tool to prepare for the inevitable Soviet re-occupation.

The success of this recruitment drive, in contrast to the failure of previous ones, made the Germans suspicious. Among other things, it absorbed manpower that parts of the German apparatus wanted to conscript as factory labour. Within months, the Germans felt that the effort had got out of control, and they started to crack down on it. The Germans kept trying to insert German officers into the units, and the SS kept trying to rewrite the enlistment oath to include a reference to loyalty to Hitler. Unsurprisingly, swearing-in ceremonies with the new oath were permanently rescheduled and mostly did not occur. Germans started delaying shipments of arms and transportation to the new units.

Although some of these Territorial Defence Forces fought in operations against Soviet partisans and even against Polish Home Army units, these operations did not last long. The Germans started plotting to force a national mobilisation and incorporate the Territorial Defence Forces into the Germany military or the SS. Jeckeln, the notorious SS commander, tried to force the units near Vilnius to swear personal loyalty to himself, wear SS uniforms, and use the 'Heil Hitler' salute. Eventually, the whole effort collapsed. Plechavičius started presiding over the disbandment of the force, and many units fled with their weapons to the forests to become the basis of later resistance. Many Territorial Defence Force personnel were arrested, and some were executed. Others were imprisoned or sent to work as slave labour in German factories. About 3,500 were forcibly conscripted and went either to the Eastern Front or to Germany to guard airbases. General Plechavičius himself was imprisoned. He ended up escaping to the West, aided the CIA during the Cold War, and died in Chicago in 1973.

The Polish Home Army

An easy error for casual observers to make is to use current political boundaries to try to understand what was going on in 1939 and

1940. But it is important to remember that for two decades, the border between Lithuania and Poland had been in dispute. The region around Vilnius (Wilno in Polish) had been part of Poland until the German invasion of 1939. Both Poland and Lithuania claimed the region, and a brief war had been fought in 1919–20 over border issues. Despite the dispute and despite being declared Lithuania's capital, Vilnius and its surrounding territory spent the interwar years as a Polish province, with Lithuania forced to declare Kaunas as its provisional capital. It was only after the German and Soviet conquest of Poland that the Vilnius region was under Lithuanian rule, and even then, only for less than a year, as the Soviets annexed Lithuania in 1940. It should be noted that historical and political grievances between Poles and Lithuanians have a history going back centuries, well beyond the scope of this book.

No account of the wartime era in Lithuania should ignore the fact that Polish resistance was active in an area now defined as Lithuania. The primary Polish resistance group was the Home Army, although there were a number of other underground resistance groups. The Home Army was particularly active in the region around Vilnius. The principal Polish resistance group in the region was the Home Army's 5th Brigade, reputed to have around 500 members in the Vilnius region.

Polish accounts of this period firmly refer to the area as Polish, while Lithuanian accounts refer to it as Lithuanian, and there are accounts of clashes between Lithuanian and Polish resistance fighters having taken place in 1944. Lithuanian and Polish historical interpretations of this period vary significantly as old grievances are still resolving themselves.

Soviet return

As the Germans left the Baltic states, they left behind three countries that had been traumatised by back-to-back Soviet and Nazi occupations. Much of their material wealth had been denuded. The various slapdash military units of various types were left to resist the Germans, and they either fought, melted away into the woods, or a bit of both. In all cases, they provided training, experience, equipment, and personnel for armed partisan resistance. Particularly in Latvia and Estonia, defence efforts provided brief periods where people could escape to Finland and Sweden.

As the summer of 1944 ended, the Soviet Union gradually started reoccupying the Baltic states. The arriving Soviet military, which also contained many soldiers of Baltic nationality, behaved less like liberators and more like rapacious conquerors. Red Army units scavenged, foraged, pillaged, and committed rapes, assaults, and murders. They were followed by the security forces of the NKVD, which operated in a more systematic fashion, reintroducing the Stalinist security state in the conquered areas. The Soviet Union considered the Baltic states to be part of the Soviet Union and attempted to conscript as many military-age males as it could into the Soviet military. Conditions were ripe for resistance.

PART 2

THE PARTISAN WAR BEGINS IN EARNEST

PROFILE OF A PARTISAN

The true heart of the era of partisan resistance began when the Soviet Union reoccupied the Baltic countries. The longest and most active period of violent anti-Soviet resistance started in 1944 or 1945, depending on the region, as the return of Soviet forces was gradual. Some parts of Latvia, for example, were not reoccupied by the Soviets until May 1945. Because of this, there is no one day in history that historians can point to as the beginning of the second anti-Soviet phase of partisan resistance.

Individuals and groups who had been, both literally and figuratively, keeping their powder dry and letting their enemies fight each other now had a second Soviet occupation to contend with. They had seen the repressive, totalitarian nature of the Stalinist regime in action in 1940 and 1941, and few were under any delusion that it would somehow be a liberation to have the Soviets back. And the Soviet occupiers, even if they did not openly say that they considered every Balt to be a Nazi collaborator, used tactics that suggested that they did. There was, indeed, much collaboration and cooperation, both active and passive. The Soviet occupiers not only picked up where they had left off in 1941 but also, formally and informally, sought revenge on real or perceived collaborators with the Germans.

While there were some links between the partisan movements in the three countries, it is important to treat the movements separately. It is not uncommon in Western Europe and America to confuse one with another or to conflate the region as 'The Baltic(s)'. I will attempt to undo some of this damage, and there are separate chapters to follow on each of the armed resistance movements.

This chapter focuses on commonalities in the movements across the region. Individual histories, specific episodes, and some notable people are described in the three chapters that follow.[1]

Despite the differences explored in later chapters, much of the daily reality of the struggle was very similar across the region. Similar types of people fought similar battles and lived for years in ways that were quite similar across the three Baltic states.

Demographics: who were the Forest Brothers?

Numerous types of men (and women) joined the Forest Brotherhood. As was the case in other movements in that era, the Forest Brothers were mostly but not completely male. While no full census exists of Baltic partisans, the movement contained people who joined from a variety of sources and for many different reasons. These included, in no particular order, the following overlapping categories:

- Military deserters of every type, including from both German and Soviet units. Some had, in fact, served in both.
- Escaped Soviet prisoners of war, some of whom were of Baltic nationality.
- Members, both voluntary and conscripted, of German military and paramilitary units.
- Members of German or Finnish 'stay-behind' units deliberately sent to cause disruption in Soviet rear areas.
- People considered 'class enemies' by the Soviet Union (such as members of various political parties, clergy, prosperous farmers).
- People of partial Baltic German ancestry.
- Youths evading conscription (first into the German forces, then into the Soviet military).
- Veterans of the Estonian, Latvian, or Lithuanian military from the interwar era.
- Former members of organisations banned by the Soviet state, such as political parties, religious youth movements, the Lithuanian Riflemen, or the Scout movement.
- People seeking revenge for atrocities and misdeeds committed by the Soviet occupier.

- Student radicals.
- Devout Christians, including clergy and lay employees of churches.
- People with reason to fear Soviet reprisal (sometimes real reasons, sometimes not).
- Relatives of partisans (the Soviets would deport the family of a partisan).
- Actual fascists and other far-right types.
- Farmers and farmworkers facing dispossession through collectivisation.
- Individuals and small groups at loose ends hiding in the countryside who needed to band together for survival.

There are examples of a single person who could simultaneously fit into at least five of the above categories. There is little evidence of many actual fascists, although we can certainly point to a handful of specific examples. The question of who was and was not a 'Nazi' or a 'fascist' is discussed in detail in Chapter 15. The largest single category was farmers facing expropriation of their property.

In some ways, the Forest Brothers were a cross-section of society. But when subjected to latter-day scrutiny, the Forest Brothers were not an evenly distributed cross-section. Being a Forest Brother (or Sister) meant living a cold, damp, harsh life in the forests and swamps through all four seasons and somehow not starving to death. This meant that people who were used to rural life and had relevant outdoor skills and experience were better represented in the movement than city-dwellers. Former Scouts were prominent in the Forest Brotherhood, as were members of the various pre-war paramilitary auxiliary organisations. Intellectuals, professionals, and office workers were under-represented but by no means absent in the movement. The latter were heavily represented in urban, non-violent resistance movements.

Leadership within the partisans was largely meritocratic and organically grown. Although some partisan leaders were officers from the pre-war Baltic militaries, most of the higher-ranking officers—large numbers of whom had been deported, ended up in prison camps (both Soviet and German), or fled—were not available. Many of the leaders who came to prominence either had little military training before the war or had been of relatively low rank during their military service.

The ethnic composition of the Forest Brotherhood was largely indigenous, but this was not by any means universal. Some accounts mention individual Germans, Russians, and Poles serving in units, particularly in the early phase of the conflict. There were non-Baltic deserters from both German and Soviet forces. Aside from the occasional Latvian in a Lithuanian unit or similar situations in border areas, the movements tended not to let foreigners ascend through the ranks. Local knowledge and knowing local people were, perhaps, the most prized traits for a Forest Brother, and foreigners, however sincere in motivation, did not have these traits. Juozas Lukša, a famous Lithuanian Forest Brother discussed in Chapter 8, claimed that foreign fighters were often persuaded to go home to start or support local movements. Lukša wrote that reports of some of these partisans using their position to loot, as well as fear of infiltration, led to bans on foreign members in Lithuania.[2]

The social and occupational background of the partisans was, at least partly, recorded by the Soviets for ideological reasons consistent with Marxist–Leninist notions of class and society. Based on these records, Statiev's research shows that in the Vidzeme region of Latvia, 85.3 per cent of the captured or killed partisans were former farmers. In Lithuania, a Soviet document looked at the social profile of partisans who were put on trial in 1944–6. The composition was 79.7 per cent farmers. The Soviets made rigid distinctions between different types of farmers in order to identify 'kulaks' (the Soviet term for a prosperous farmer, held to be a class enemy) and aid with plans for collectivisation. The Soviets also deported family members of partisans and kept statistics on how prosperous the deported farming families were. This leads to the conclusion, at least in Lithuania, that prosperous farmers, owning larger properties and thus targets for collectivisation and possible punishment, were better represented in the Forest Brotherhood than poor smallholders or landless peasants.[3]

Particularly in the early stages of the active conflict, there were a number of people who were simply hiding out in the woods rather than being actual partisans. Some were just trying to lay low and survive. Gradually, the Soviet authorities considered such conduct illegal, and it became progressively difficult to normalise one's status. There was ample fluidity between the categories, and it is genuinely hard to draw a firm dividing line. A person might have been in hiding in 1945 but have joined a partisan group in 1946, wandered off as his group reduced in numbers later that year, and laid low in 1947 merely foraging for food before joining a partisan group again in a neighbouring district in the following year.

Forest Sisters/Daughters: women in the movement

Although the movements were largely male, they were not entirely without women. Women appear in many photos of small partisan groups. There are numerous individual accounts of women who were active combatants in the partisan resistance across all three Baltic states.

There are several reasons why women joined the movement, not least their treatment by the invading and occupying troops: rape by German and Soviet invaders was commonplace, even well after the war was over, and some women hid in partisan detachments to avoid being the victims of such crimes. Many were wives, girlfriends, sisters, or mothers of male partisans. Others were avoiding arrest or deportation for the same sorts of reasons as their male colleagues. Although very few women in the movement had any pre-war experience with weaponry, a number of them did serve as active combatants. The Lithuanian scholar Enrika Kripienė estimates that there were about 250 female partisans in the Lithuanian movement.[4] The Latvian scholar Sanita Reinsone has thoroughly studied the phenomenon and gives a rough estimate of 500 women living with the Latvian partisans, most of them as non-combatants. Reinsone uses the apt phrase 'Forest Daughters' to refer to the women who were part of or worked alongside the partisan movement.

The dynamics of the struggle being what they were, simply hiding with Forest Brothers did not last long, and women became useful contributors, both as auxiliaries and in very necessary roles as full members of the struggle. Many women clearly took up roles that were usually gender-defined in the broader Baltic societies of the time, taking charge of cooking and cleaning. Others took up vital roles including looking after the sick and wounded. Many others served as liaison officers, as couriers, whose role is described later in this chapter. A few were even useful spies, taking jobs that could give them access to useful information or the ability to perform valuable tasks like issuing documents. Some were valued writers and editors of underground publications (underground publishing is discussed further in Chapter 10).[5] Accounts of individual women involved in operations in Estonia exist, but I was unable to find an overall estimate of numbers.

Size of units

Early in the active phase of the conflict (circa 1944–5), there are instances of platoon (20+ combatants) and even company (90+) sized partisan units. Such sizes of operational units proved impractical for partisan warfare. The size of the encampments for such groups meant they were more easily discovered by the Soviets. Larger groups also proved harder to support logistically. As Soviet security forces cracked down on obvious encampments, a number of vicious battles ensued, but partisans gradually learned the lesson of dispersal.

For the most part, after the initial 1944–5 period, the Forest Brothers started to operate in smaller units. A group of three to ten partisans could hide easily enough without having to go to great lengths to do so. Such a group could support itself without having to go great distances and could live on the quantities of food that could be gathered from a few small farms. A group of fifty would easily deplete both the food stocks and goodwill of small farms, but a group of five could more realistically glean at least a minimal amount of food from nearby farms.

Arms and equipment

Partisan memoirs are full of detail about equipment. Many hundreds of photographs of Forest Brothers also exist, and we can examine the equipment in the photos. Partisans worried about weapons, food, clothing, radios, and publishing equipment in that approximate order. Weapons were a motley mix of small arms. Rifles, submachine guns, pistols, and some machine guns were widely noted.

These weapons largely came from three sources. First, there were weapons left over from before the war. These came from the relatively modest Estonian, Latvian, and Lithuanian militaries or their various auxiliary paramilitary arms. This category would also include some number of sporting and hunting firearms, as such arms were far from rare in rural areas in the 1930s. The second category was German weapons, some of which were available in great quantities at the end of the war in parts of the Baltic states. In Latvia, a lot of German units had surrendered at the end of the war, leaving many arms in the Courland Pocket. There was also a small quantity of Finnish weapons, at least in Estonia, that had been sent across the strait from Finland. Across the region, many had joined German-sponsored military formations with either primary or secondary motives to acquire weapons and other equipment, so that they would be able to desert and become partisans. The final category was Soviet armaments, generally gained through theft or capture.

Although a comprehensive study or quantitative figures are not possible, it appears that submachine guns and pistols were the preferred weapons. Both could more easily be concealed under clothing and were useful at close range, with a higher rate of fire than the longer rifles that were still very much the military standard issue at the time in conventional forces. Most engagements happened at close range, often in darkness or thick vegetation, somewhat negating the longer-range and higher-penetrating power of long rifles. In some respects, the Forest Brothers learned the same lessons that would be learned by insurgents in South East Asia in the 1960s.

Hand grenades were particularly favoured. Grenades seemed to have reasonable shelf life in adverse conditions and were not particularly hard to use. They could also be turned into booby traps and were silent when thrown, thus having the benefit of not giving away a partisan's location. Grenades were also a last-ditch weapon when faced with capture, torture, and the inevitable reprisals against a partisan's family. There are numerous accounts of Baltic partisans committing suicide with a grenade rather than surrendering. In doing so, their face and fingerprints were obliterated, making identification impossible. To this day, grenades continue to be recovered in the Baltic states, some of which were doubtless from the period of partisan struggle.[6] Individual examples of forgotten military ordnance have occasionally been discovered in the modern era buried in farmyards, under floorboards, or in similar hiding places.

Weapons larger than light machine guns were rare. There are various anecdotal reports of individual anti-tank guns, anti-aircraft guns, and mortars being in possession of small partisan groups. There are also isolated and generally unconfirmed reports of such weapons being used in the earlier phases. However, moving, hiding, operating, and stocking ammunition for heavier weapons was burdensome on Forest Brother units. Soviet reports show that in Lithuania nine artillery pieces, thirty-one anti-tank guns, and thirty-two mortars were seized from partisans between 1944 and 1953. In comparison, however, over 3,000 machine guns and 39,433 small arms—rifles, pistols, and submachine guns—were seized in the same period.[7]

Ammunition was a particular concern. German ammunition from early in the war or before was made of brass and would last for decades if kept dry. Much German rifle and machine gun ammunition produced later in the war was made with steel cartridge cases as copper ran short as a raw material. Such ammunition degraded over the course of several years in field conditions. Despite the multiplicity of German weapons available across the region, they became less useful over time because of ammunition degradation. Ammunition compatibility was also a serious issue. Partisan accounts contain complaints about having six or eight different calibres of weapons, with many rounds for one particular pistol but practically none for a dozen rifles, or vice-versa.

Arms and ammunition were simultaneously a motivator for operations and a limiting factor. The relatively slow operational tempo of Baltic partisan warfare was dictated in part by the scarcity of ammunition supplies, as frequent or protracted operations could not be supported by scant stocks of ammunition. However, ammunition and arms shortages were also serious motivators to conduct raids on Soviet forces in order to obtain additional stocks.

Food, health, and welfare

Access to food was a major constraint on the Forest Brothers' activities. As discussed, subsistence concerns, as well as security, dictated the size of partisan detachments. The various first-hand accounts from Forest Brothers contain numerous complaints about the quantity and variety of food available to the partisans, with widespread accounts of living on apples, foraged mushrooms, and buckets of milk from local farms. In a diary entry from April 1949, the Lithuanian partisan leader Lionginas Baliukevičius mentions tiring of a diet of buckwheat and rancid bacon.[8]

In many instances, the local authorities adopted policies designed to limit the consumption of alcohol, although locally brewed beer was often rightly considered part of essential nutrition. It is not so much that the Forest Brothers were temperance enthusiasts but more that local and regional leaders viewed alcohol as troublesome. Drunken mistakes could cost lives. Moreover, the occupying Soviets were—largely correctly—portrayed as having serious problems with drink. Soviet security forces and their auxiliaries and collaborators were at their cruellest when drunk. Drunk Soviet troops and police were easier targets, but this also served to remind the partisans of the dangers they could be placed in if they were drunk. Furthermore, the crops most used for homemade spirits were rye and potatoes, both needed for subsistence. Lukša reports a local edict against partisans accepting alcohol from farmers in 1946 in the Tauras partisan district (modern Suvalkija) in Lithuania.

Poor diet and the sanitary limitations of an outdoor life in all-weather took a toll on the movement. Diseases like pneumonia are mentioned in accounts, particularly in winter as damp and cold took their toll. Typhus and other diseases were not unheard of. Fleas and lice were problematic. Some partisans described visiting a farm to take a bath as an annual event. Combat injuries also occurred, and though there were medical professionals among the resistance movement, including doctors, nurses, medical students, dentists, and veterinarians, they were rare, and their ability to help the sick and injured was usually severely constrained by lack of medicine and equipment. Physicians and surgeons were sometimes summoned, at great risk to their own lives and liberty, to sneak out to help wounded partisans. A former Lithuanian Army doctor, Antanas Povilonis, served bravely not only as a doctor but as chief of staff of the Algimantas partisan district until his death.[9] Women serving largely as untrained or poorly trained nurses shouldered much of the burden of medical care in the forests.[10]

Shelter

Early in the movement, partisans hid wherever they could. They often lived in barns, tents, and sheds. Short nights and mild summers meant that many could sleep in the open. As the struggle moved on, cold weather forced many people indoors. After many battles and skirmishes in 1945, partisans needed to make more efforts to hide.

The forest provided the best refuge. From 1946 onward, the typical strategy was to build and inhabit structures variously described as bunkers or dugouts in the forest, at least for part of the year. In Laar's book, Estonian partisan Meinhard Leetma[11] describes the Brothers' selection criteria for such refuges. They needed to be close enough to a village or farm, so that food could be had, but far enough way for people visiting the farm not to notice and to avoid the risk of a farmer's dog giving away their location. Drinking water needed to be nearby. Leetma had a preference for berry bushes or heather to surround the bunker so that obvious paths to it were not seen.

Olaf Tammark, who was the first Forest Brother this author met, had different criteria, which he lists in his detailed appendix, also in Laar's book,[12] backed up by sketches he showed me in 1991. Tammark felt that logging roads would be useful, as there would be footprints around such a road, thus not giving away a dugout. Although there are numerous variants along the same theme stretching from Narva to the Suwałki gap, these bunkers were constructed broadly along the same lines. Contemporaneous accounts from partisans in Latvia and Lithuania describe similar bunkers in the two countries.

These bunkers and dugouts played an important role in the resistance. They provided warmth and refuge in the winter. They were relatively well insulated, if not necessarily well ventilated. A relatively small amount of fuel could keep a partisan warm. Tammark's detailed account describes a tactic of erecting a chimney pipe up a tree trunk, thus dispersing smoke in the treetops. Lukša refers to well-dried oak as being preferable as a clean-burning fuel. None of these bunkers were particularly large—Laar claims that even the largest bunkers could only accommodate two dozen partisans.[13]

Most importantly, partisan bunkers provided concealment. They were designed to be almost undiscoverable. Numerous incidents occurred wherein partisans hid in their bunkers while Soviet forces literally trod over the top of them, not discovering the hidden entrances. Once again, a Forest Brother tactic thus presaged developments from a later guerrilla conflict, the elaborate tunnel complexes of the Viet Cong in South Vietnam.

Clothing and appearance

Existing photographs of the era show partisans in a wide variety of attire. Most partisans viewed themselves as representing the Estonian, Latvian, or Lithuanian state and considered themselves military combatants. Where possible, Forest Brothers preferred to use military uniforms from the pre-war Baltic militaries. Others went to great lengths to modify German, Soviet, or even Finnish uniforms to closely resemble Baltic uniforms. Also, as a practical matter, field uniforms were not bad for military operations, and thick wool military greatcoats were essential to survival in harsh Baltic winters.

It could also be helpful to impersonate local farmers. Particularly early in the struggle when even legitimate farmers did not yet have Soviet papers, it was easy to pretend to be a local farmer if confronted by police or security forces. As the struggle progressed, it became more difficult to do so, especially as conscription rules were being enforced for military-age males. A common defence was some sort of forged document showing that they had already done their service or had some exemption.

It was not unknown for men to let their hair grow long and dress in ways that could suggest they were women, at least when seen from a distance. Soviet authorities often stopped men, thinking that they could be conscripted into the military, but women were often ignored on such conscription drives.

Partisan operations

Operational tempo

Modern military doctrine in the West occasionally uses the phrase 'low intensity conflict'. In many senses, the Forest Brothers embody the concept. Compared to other examples of partisan and guerrilla warfare, the Forest Brothers' resistance campaign was a war in slow motion. This is not a conflict where there was daily or even weekly combat. Unless they had done a raid or won a skirmish and restocked on ammunition, most partisan detachments simply did not have the ammunition to conduct frequent operations. Every bullet and every grenade was precious, and a reserve needed to be held to defend a group's hiding spot if it were discovered.

Partisan operations involving armed violence would also attract the attention of security forces, who would then conduct search operations to try to find partisan hideaways. If partisans did engage in an armed operation near their hideout, they would have to carefully lie low, in the most literal sense, by laying quite still and silent in their bunkers, often for days and occasionally for weeks, thus hindering their ability to forage for food or distribute underground literature.

As a result, it was not uncommon for small bands of Forest Brothers to lay low and conduct no actual warfare activity for months at a stretch. Many partisans viewed active armed engagements as only part of their role. Particularly early on, but even into the 1950s, Forest Brothers widely believed that a conflict between the West and the Soviet Union was inevitable. Waiting for this conflict and then being able to rise up and present some sort of patriotic presence was seen as the likely road to the restoration of independence. Merely surviving and being outside the control of the Soviet state was an objective in itself. Indeed, the failure of the Korean war in 1950 to spill over into a NATO versus USSR conflict did much to reduce morale and motivation among the remaining Forest Brothers.

The Forest Brothers generally understood that numbers and attrition were not on their side. Losses incurred by Soviet security forces, both in terms of personnel and resources, could easily be replaced. Partisan losses could only be replaced with difficulty. In most locations and most periods of the struggle, partisans were greatly outnumbered by their Soviet enemy. Direct confrontations were to be avoided except on terms dictated by the partisans. Partisan strategy was less about holding territory and more about denying free movement to the enemy. As a result, Forest Brothers rarely initiated major attacks unless they could be sure that the local odds were in their favour. Some of the largest engagements occurred when Soviet forces had surrounded a partisan group's hiding location and there was no easy method of escape. The Soviets almost universally won such engagements through strength of numbers and firepower. Such incidents taught the Forest Brothers to avoid these kinds of engagements at all costs.

Who were the targets?

The Soviets were not just tyrants; they were also petty bureaucrats. If a partisan shot a Soviet official, it was likely to be recorded. Due to excellent archival research by Lithuanian scholar Arvydas Anušauskas (who at time of writing in 2023 serves as Lithuania's defence minister), statistics are now available on who and what were the targets and casualties of partisan actions in Estonia, Latvia, and Lithuania during key periods of the armed struggle. Table 5.1 analyses targets of partisan attacks during 1946.[14]

Analysis of Forest Brother Attacks in 1946

Target of attack	Estonia	%	Latvia	%	Lithuania	%
Red Army	18	6.7%	15	2.2%	35	1.9%
MVD/NKVD Troops	7	2.6%	24	3.4%	64	3.5%
Istribiteli reprisal squads	14	5.2%	60	8.6%	101	5.5%
Communist Party activists	60	22.2%	98	14.1%	350	19.0%
Local residents (including local police and collaborators)	102	37.8%	336	48.3%	1047	56.9%

Target of attack	Estonia	%	Latvia	%	Lithuania	%
State enterprises attacked	54	20.0%	117	16.8%	38	2.1%
Govt offices attacked	4	1.5%	16	2.3%	78	4.2%
Sabotage acts'	6	2.2%	16	2.3%	24	1.3%
Proclamations posted on military sites	5	1.9%	14	2.0%	103	5.6%

Source: Arvydas Anušauskas, 'A Comparison of the Armed Struggles for Independence in the Baltic States and Western Ukraine', in *Anti-Soviet Resistance in the Baltic States*, edited by Arvydas Anušauskas. Vilnius: Genocide and Resistance Research Centre of Lithuania, 2006, 63–70.

What do these figures tell us? Well, they are a snapshot in time, and the years before and after were not exactly the same. Also, there is probably scope for under-reporting in some of the categories. The categories 'sabotage' and 'attack on state enterprise' are a bit vague. The category 'attacks on state enterprises' could also include raids to gather food or supplies to print underground publications. Is a rock through a window being captured in the data? Being a victim of sabotage or having partisan proclamations plastered around one's base reflected poorly on security practices, and it is easy to envisage local officials not reporting all such incidents if they could be covered up. But people dead and wounded from armed violence are harder to conceal.

Local police and secret police informants, who were numerous, are listed as 'local residents', so this information should not be taken at face value as evidence of atrocities against civilians. Anušauskas points out that most of the civilian casualties in the 1946–7 period in Estonia and Latvia were accidental, a category that might include inadvertent casualties during Soviet attacks as well as partisan ones.[15] This archival data does not enumerate incidents where partisans themselves were attacked, and thus defended themselves, yet we know numerous such incidents occurred that year.

The figures do give us a sense of targeting. Wherever possible, it seems that Forest Brothers avoided initiating attacks on the harder targets—Red Army and NKVD/MVD internal security troops. In 1946, the year of this data, such troops were still highly likely to have a high percentage of hardened combat veterans. There were more attacks on *istrebiteli*—much-hated local goon squads of auxiliaries designed for the dirty work of oppression who were less well trained and less well armed. (The various types of Soviet security forces are discussed in more detail in Chapter 9.) The largest categories of targets were Communist officials and activists, local police, and collaborators. While many of these were armed, some were not.

Tactics and operational practices

Throughout history, ambushes and raids have been a core tactic of irregular forces in asymmetric warfare. Ambushes are typically surprise attacks where the attacker waits in hiding for a moving enemy to reach a particular engagement area or target zone. Raids are short-term violent attacks designed to strike a target for a specific reason but then to depart shortly thereafter instead of trying to occupy and hold a position. Some raids and ambushes were intended strictly for military purposes in order to inflict damage on the enemy forces. But such raids were a minority of partisan actions. Other forms of attack included bombings, which were rare due to lack of suitable explosives and expertise, targeted assassinations, and miscellaneous armed violence. Rather than try to classify Forest Brotherhood activity by these categories, it is perhaps more constructive to examine partisan activity by objective.

Gathering supplies

The Forest Brothers had very little material support from outside. What little support they had will be discussed in Chapter 11. A partisan movement often exists on the goodwill of a population, and much material support was gathered from the population in terms of food, information, and recruits. But there were many things that rural farms or liaison with resistance groups in the cities simply could not supply in quantity. Many Forest Brother attacks were raids intended to obtain resources such as food, arms, ammunition, medical supplies, money, documents, or supplies for printing operations. Such was the perceived value of information operations that more than one Forest Brother martyred himself for ink and paper. As pre-war ammunition was used up and Second World War-era German ammunition started to corrode, theft or robbery of ammunition, and by necessity the arms that used the new types and calibres of ammunition, became an operational necessity.

Did Forest Brothers rob farmers for food or property? This was a common allegation made by the Soviet authorities, which also allowed them to depict Forest Brother groups as bandits. Some incidents of theft or robbery clearly did occur. Particularly early in the post-war era, much of the Baltic theatre of operations was a wild place, and opportunist deserters and criminals, as well as looting German and Soviet units, were as commonplace as, or even more common than, nationalist partisans. The overall situation is murky, but it seems improbable that no theft or robbery occurred. To further complicate the situation, it was far safer for a farmer to report a pig stolen than to admit that he slaughtered it and gave ham and bacon to partisans. The Soviet penal code would consider picking a single apple in the dark of night to be theft of state assets, even if the person who picked it was the son of the farmer who had grown up there. For such reasons, accusations of theft and thievery, either cotemporaneous or retrospective, must be viewed with some scepticism.

As the struggle crystalised from 1946 onward, rules and regulations were implemented in many groups, and an ethos of protecting the population became more prominent. Some partisan operations were intended to redistribute assets back to the people. Food was to be stolen from the Soviet authorities, not the farmers. In many cases, food that had been ruthlessly requisitioned from farms was secretly returned to farms, with partisans taking a portion of it. Farmers who were collaborators with the Soviets, however, were considered fair targets for theft of food. There were also raids and robberies to take payroll cash from state enterprises or tax authorities.

Protecting the populace from repression

Many partisan actions were intended to protect the population from repression. Early in the period of armed struggle, both formal and informal efforts were made to resist looting and attacks on civilians. Many Forest Brothers could trace their history as partisan resisters to a point where they had to flee or hide because they had resisted German or Soviet looting or attacks on their family. Much of this looting and pillaging happened early in the struggle, before many partisan groups had coalesced. But there were also many instances of Soviet officials, conscripts, police, or especially the *istrebiteli* militia squads taking liberties with persons and property. Many partisan actions were direct responses to either stop such attacks and confiscations or to retaliate against units and individuals that had conducted depredations. Particularly as the partisan struggle evolved, and more so in Lithuania, where the movement had more of a national hierarchy, some Forest Brothers and some segments of the population felt that the Forest Brotherhood was the legitimate embodiment of statehood and that the movement's members could be appealed to for protecting public order.

When waves of mass arrests and deportations occurred, Forest Brother units tried to slow or resist these crimes against humanity. Overall, such resistance was not successful, as the vast numbers of people sent to labour camps and exile settlements can attest. Was the deportation of some people delayed or deferred? This is almost certainly true. Were some deportation operations disrupted in ways that allowed some people to flee and become partisans themselves? There are instances of such occurrences, and the late 1940s waves of deportations and attempted deportations were actually the last great wave of recruits to the movement.

Delaying Sovietisation of the countryside

Part of the overall Soviet plan for the Baltic states was to turn the entire economy into an arm of the state. While the partisan movement could not effectively resist the nationalisation of heavy industry or the Sovietisation of the urban economy, Forest Brothers could act in ways to directly and indirectly hinder the Sovietisation of agriculture. It took several years for effective collectivisation of agriculture to happen in the Baltic states. Because of the proliferation of smallholdings, it took a lot of effort and planning to simply inventory the agricultural sector and determine who lived where and who farmed what. In some places, the activists and officials who were undertaking the ground-level work for collectivisation took their lives into their own hands if they went out to survey fields or count livestock. Harassment of the collectivisation effort ranged from relatively petty acts such as letting air out of tyres or concealing chickens all the way through lethal ambushes and arson attacks on barns that had been left abandoned due to the deportation of their owners.

Liberating prisoners

Some of the more flamboyant Forest Brother exploits were efforts to free prisoners, whether the prisoners were themselves captured partisans or simply civilians detained for imprisonment or deportation. Some of the simpler efforts were ambushes on routes out of rural areas, where convoys of deportees would be taken. More elaborate raids on jails and prisons also occurred. Multiple sources describe undated and unsuccessful raids on prisons in Tartu and Pärnu, Estonia. Laar describes several Estonian Forest Brother actions to liberate captives. One of these was an action in July 1945 in Saue, near Tallinn, where a farmer, Jaan Arujärve, had been arrested. Partisans killed an NKVD officer and a local policeman and wounded the local police brigadier in the course of liberating the farmer.[16]

Resisting conscription

As the Soviet Union considered the Baltic states to be integral parts of the USSR and their occupants to be Soviet citizens, young men in the three countries were subject to years of conscription. Soviet officials literally dragooned people off the street for years of military service in distant parts of the USSR, where Baltic conscripts were treated badly as part of the harsh *dedovshchina*— abusive hazing—that has long been commonplace in Russian and Soviet military units.

At times, disrupting Soviet conscription efforts became an integral part of partisan operations. It was a way of protecting the local populace, as the partisans almost universally considered their countries to be occupied territories, not part of the USSR. As such, conscription was illegal in their eyes. The conditions of service were harsh, so being drafted into an infantry unit stationed in, say, the Urals, was not necessarily viewed as preferable to deportation. Saving young men from conscription also served as a recruitment stream for the partisan movement. Someone liberated from a truck convoy full of involuntary conscripts could hardly go back home to where he'd been grabbed. Many felt that they had the choice between military service or taking their chances as free men in the resistance movement.

Reprisal or retaliation against collaborators

Other actions involved reprisals and acts of revenge against collaborators. Individual Soviets or collaborators who had committed crimes or who were particularly threatening could face the threat of assassination. Some of the great exploits of the Forest Brotherhood movement were reprisals against secret policemen, notorious collaborators, informants, or Communist Party officials.

Reprisal and retaliation sometimes initiated a vicious cycle, and it was a disproportionate struggle. The Soviets had more resources and an infinite reservoir of repressive measures at their disposal. In a tit-for-tat cycle of vendetta, the Soviets would eventually win based on their vastly greater resources. But there was some operational and strategic value in reprisals. First, it meant that some individual Soviet officials would face justice for their actions, which would never have happened had Forest Brothers not taken matters into their own hands. But more importantly, the threat of a partisan's bullet or grenade discouraged excessive zeal in the pursuit of Soviet policy. Lazy officials were thus encouraged in their laziness. After all, sticking your neck out might get you shot by a partisan. Officials keen to do their job were forced to be more cautious, and more resources were tied up in security for them. Both served to slow down the campaign of repression and Sovietisation.

Interference with elections

Elections in the Soviet Union were a completely undemocratic sham, with single-candidate ballots and coerced voting. Everyone in the Baltic states had experienced the 1940 sham elections that had resulted in the illegitimate assemblies that later requested annexation by the Soviet Union. There was plenty of bad feeling about this and widespread sentiment that fraudulent elections would be used to further justify occupation of the three countries.

Once again, the accounts left by Lukša[17] and the compilations put together by Laar contain valuable accounts of resistance against these fake elections. Forest Brother actions against elections typically took the form of encouraging abstention from voting, attacking or intimidating the infrastructure of the elections, and physically attacking the ballots themselves. Partisans circulated among the citizenry and temporarily confiscated Soviet internal passports from voters, so that they could not prove their identity at the polling station. Some partisans harassed Soviet cadres for days prior to the election, keeping them awake all night with gunshots, thus ensuring they were too exhausted to spend the day canvassing for votes. Lukša speaks of roadblocks to keep Soviet authorities from visiting rural villages. Furthermore, villagers could play both sides and claim that 'bandits' (i.e. Forest Brothers) had kept them from voting. Many partisan sources claim to have suppressed the turnout in rural areas.

In Estonia, Laar describes one group attempting to put flammable chemicals into ballot boxes. He also describes local partisans taking down Communist Party posters and handing out handbills during the 1946 Supreme Soviet elections.[18]

It is unclear what actual effect these acts had. The elections occurred. The authorities were going to report that their candidates won, as they were literally the only candidates. Most Estonians, Latvians, and Lithuanians knew that these were not legitimate elections. These actions served to make elections more difficult logistically, but their practical value is open to question. Soviet authorities could even claim that partisan activity was anti-democratic by suppressing the vote.

Symbolic acts

Many acts of partisan resistance were symbolic and merely intended to remind the population and the occupier that the Forest Brothers were still present and active. These acts generally involved raising the national flags, particularly on days of national importance and at places of public prominence. Flags are powerful symbols, and the pre-war flags of Estonia, Latvia, and Lithuania were banned. To wake in the morning and see the Estonian flag on one of the highest towers, Pikk Hermann, in Tallinn, is a symbol stronger than an ambush in a distant rural parish, word of which was easily quashed. Flying these flags was a form of resistance that lasted much longer than the Forest Brotherhood movement itself. It was genuinely moving to see how many pre-war flags emerged from hiding in the 1980s, having been carefully hidden for decades.

Other symbolic acts included issuing and posting pronouncements and edicts. Forest Brotherhood groups often viewed themselves as the last remaining official voice of the pre-war state, so they would issue proclamations and try to post them as leaflets, fliers, and— where printing was possible—posters in public places.

It should be noted that some of these acts were by civilian sympathisers, not actual Forest Brother partisans. However, the Soviet state often didn't make that distinction. If you were caught raising a Latvian flag on a public building, you were likely to be branded a partisan by the Soviets and punished as such.

Information operations

The Soviet state maintained its authority, in part, by keeping a monopoly on information. Moscow and its local proxies tried to control the entire public narrative and worked hard to filter not just news, but every form of information through their lens. Fighting against Soviet domination meant contesting this monopoly on information. A partisan struggle is, in part, information warfare. A very large part of the partisan movement was involved in writing, publishing, and distributing printed materials. These operations are discussed at some length in Chapter 10.

Liaison and communication

As mentioned, the Forest Brothers eventually realised that it was more effective to live and operate in small units. This greatly aided their long-term survival prospects. However, it also hindered their ability to conduct coordinated operations or amass larger forces for operations. The dispersed nature of the movement meant that higher levels of command would have difficulty passing orders or information to subordinate units. A normal military of the era would make great use of radio and wire communications, which were largely unavailable to the Forest Brothers.

The movement evolved to make great use of liaison officers, many of whom were women and young people from the local areas. These liaison officers would often memorise information but carry nothing incriminating, conveying messages between partisan groups and information and orders up and down the chain of command, where one existed. Or, if a written message was to be conveyed, it was written down at the last minute and secreted in a dead-drop. The liaison officers did so at great risk. Many were caught, captured, and imprisoned or executed after torture. In many cases, the messages they memorised were coded and meaningless to their captors, even under torture. Much of this work did not capture the glory and glamour of the Forest Brotherhood, but it was vital to the movement nonetheless. Many of these liaison couriers lived in the community, not with partisans, so they often escaped the tragic fate of partisans at the end of the conflict. How many people served as liaison members of the Forest Brotherhood remains unknown, and many such people are not always included in estimated numbers of partisans.

Response to amnesties

A common Soviet tactic, discussed further in Chapter 9, involved declaring an amnesty. As the war dragged on, not every Forest Brother wanted or was able to continue the struggle. Indeed, older, sick, or injured partisans could be a burden on a partisan cell. Although some amnesties were basically traps to arrest and imprison partisans, many amnesties were at least partially genuine as they were indeed intended to drain manpower from resistance movements.

Partisans, both individually and collectively, had to figure out how to deal with amnesties. On the one hand, an amnestied prisoner was likely to be interrogated and could give up valuable intelligence. On the other hand, someone who was a liability to a group or who was not motivated enough to continue the struggle, for whatever reason, probably needed to leave the movement. Some partisan groups developed tactics to allow members to take advantage of amnesties. As the Soviet authorities did not believe a person to be a partisan if they were unarmed, quitting partisans were given the oldest and poorest weapons. Partisans to be amnestied were usually quarantined for a time, often several months, so that their unit could move their bunker to another location. The partisans leaving the group may even have been told that they could lead the security services to their old bunker site to prove their bona fides, as the unit would by then have moved to a new location.

6

ESTONIA

THE METSAVENNAD

Chapter 5 discussed the partisan war in an overall sense. Many things were quite similar. But across the three Baltic states, the exact development and fate of the partisan movements differed. Starting in the north with Estonia and working our way south, the next three chapters will discuss the post-war anti-Soviet partisan movements in each country.

Over the course of 1944, the Soviets reconquered Estonia. The German retreat left Estonians to fend for themselves. Remembering the 1940–1 occupation, few viewed the arriving Soviets as 'liberators'. There was a brief period of battlefield resistance, made by a mixed bag of regular and irregular forces left behind by the Germans. This armed resistance was crushed by arriving Soviets, but it also provided a source of arms and manpower for what became known as the Metsavennad—the Forest Brothers.

Much of what we know about the Estonian partisan resistance comes from former Estonian Prime Minister Mart Laar. In the last years of the USSR, Laar and other members of the Estonian Heritage Society assembled oral history and memoirs from survivors of the movement. After 1991, some archival documents from the Soviet Union's state agencies also became available.

German retreat

The German retreat from Estonia and the arrival of Soviet occupiers provided a brief interregnum between a fully staffed German

109

occupation and a fully functional Soviet reoccupation, which allowed for the development of an Estonian resistance framework. To simplify somewhat, the Germans left, temporarily, an Estonia full of Estonians poorly equipped and in inadequate number to face the Soviet onslaught.

The Germans had months of bad military news on the Eastern Front to foresee this retreat. Germans armed and trained various units as 'stay-behind' elements. Some of these were special operations units designed to foment partisan resistance. But more significantly, they conscripted and recruited various conventional Estonian units and left them behind to fight off the Soviets, covering the German retreat. This was both cynical and transparent, and many Estonians joined this last-minute effort in order to obtain weapons to resist the returning Soviet occupiers. The actual Nazis and their closest collaborators almost invariably ended up fleeing with the rest of the Germans.

As discussed earlier in the book, a number of so-called 'self-defence' units were set up by the Germans. Given the relatively small size of these units, there was no way they were going to last long without German backup. The early stages of the Soviet re-occupation of Estonia were replete with platoon- and company-sized battles as some of these Estonian units went down fighting. Others, acting more wisely, melted into the woods to become the basis of the Metsavennad.

The German intelligence service, the Abwehr, left a surprise for the arriving Soviets. Even before the shooting stopped, NKVD officials took control of the Abwehr field office in Tallinn. Some files had been left intact. The Abwehr's files on the Estonian nationalists and potential resistance members were left for the Soviets to find, as they had not been taken back to Germany or destroyed. This last-minute omission was either an accident or a spiteful gesture.

The summer of 1944 provided a brief interlude. The Germans had largely retreated, and the Soviets did not arrive in Tallinn until 22 September 1944. The National Committee of the Republic of Estonia (Eesti Vabariigi Rahvuskomitee—EVRK) came out of hiding and declared itself the provisional government of the Republic of Estonia on 1 August. Although he was in poor health, Uluots resumed his old role as acting prime minister. The long-suppressed official state gazette, *Riigi Teataja*, even published proclamations and a cabinet. Uluots ended up handing over to Otto Tief, a lawyer who had been justice minister in the 1920s. Tief's term was brief. Some members of his provisional government fled to Sweden. Tief was arrested by the Soviets and spent a decade in the Gulag in Siberia. Uluots made it to Sweden to establish a proper government in exile but died of cancer soon after.

This period during the summer of 1944 provided a window of opportunity in which thousands fled by sea to Sweden and Finland. There was much resistance activity during this period. Estonia has extensive coastline and a number of islands, as well as a long tradition of fishing and small boats. Estonians who had been fighting with the Finns against the Soviets were able to infiltrate back.

Soviet security forces were aware of people fleeing the country. Gradually, the Soviet Navy started patrolling more aggressively. Fishing villages were strictly controlled by harsh security measures, and many people lost their livelihoods as their boats were confiscated. An entire coastal culture was suppressed in order to prevent people fleeing. Soviet secret police even set up sting operations involving fake escape rings.

Despite these measures, it is estimated that as many as 80,000 Estonians managed to flee to Sweden or Finland during the brief period in 1944 before the Soviets established full control of the country. September 1944 is now remembered and marked in Estonia and elsewhere as 'The Mass Flight of 1944'. Much of the Estonian emigration that served as the collective memory of a free Estonia were people who fled during this period and their descendants. Many were also actively working in various ways in their adopted countries to restore Estonian independence.

The struggle grows

The Soviets returned and, in many ways, picked up where they had left off in 1941. As they reoccupied Estonia, the Soviets recruited *istrebiteli* battalions out of opportunists and criminals, many of whom had performed similar dirty deeds for the Germans. Red Army troops behaved in rapacious and predatory ways as the Soviet forces swept through Estonia in the autumn of 1944. The Soviet authorities announced a national mobilisation and tried to conscript as many military-age men as they could lay their hands on. Many thousands of men, some having been in various military units, others merely trying to escape Soviet conscription or detention, fled to the forests, providing the genesis of the Forest Brotherhood. Some were even deserters from the Soviet Army.

This was a ripe environment for the development of partisan resistance. Armed resistance had sprung up around the country more or less organically in small groups. Much but not all of this effort was based around old Kaitseliit (Defence League) and Omakaitse (self-defence) units, networks, and comrades. At least one unit was formed from former border guards who had hidden their weapons in a dugout in the forest. Early on, the Forest Brothers took many losses because they simply did not know how to practise the stealth and secrecy that a partisan struggle entails. Many were living in sheds and barns and thus were more easily discovered. At first, many partisans were, in fact, part-time fighters. Many tried to help out with the autumn harvest in 1944. This made it easy for *istrebiteli* and NKVD forces to crack down on military-aged men. Perhaps some of the early lack of concealment of partisan efforts was due to the widespread belief that a war between America and the Soviet Union would soon follow the downfall of Germany.

The chaos and confusion of 1945 also made it easy for the Soviets to crack down on the partisan groups that were not taking their security and concealment seriously. Some of the groups would accept recruits with little scrutiny and were easily infiltrated by Soviet agents. Laar describes how an agent using the nickname Metsnik, a former Forest Brother, was used to infiltrate a group north-east of Pärnu. He learned the identity of the group's members, betrayed them to his handlers, and compromised their location. A gunfight resulted in the capture of seven Forest Brothers (including one woman) and the suicide of Herman Lillimäe, who was a trained radio operator. An additional thirteen people from the local area were arrested for helping the group.[1]

Despite Soviet efforts, by the summer of 1945 partisans were striking back in serious fashion across Estonia. Several rural ambushes in July and August 1945 killed a number of Red Army, Soviet Navy, and NKVD officers. A number of early partisan actions were aimed at liberating prisoners. Truck convoys carrying prisoners were also ambushed. The threat of ambush forced the Soviet authorities to devote considerable effort to route planning and security. Other attacks were symbolic, like attacking recently erected Soviet war memorials or raising Estonian flags, often accompanied by signs claiming the flagpoles were mined or booby-trapped. In one case, an obelisk erected as a monument to the Soviets was thrown through the window of a Communist official's apartment.

By 1946, it was clearly apparent that it was no longer safe to hide in barns and outbuildings on farms. The struggle had literally gone underground, as it also did in Latvia and Lithuania. Partisans started operating in smaller groups, with more rigorous security. Forest Brothers adopted the practice of building and living in concealed bunkers in the forest. In 1946, significant efforts were devoted to disrupting the Soviets' plans to hold a clearly rigged election. Posters calling for people to cast blank ballots appeared. In some rural areas, Forest Brothers stole or destroyed voter registers. Some incidents were considerably bloodier, with assassinations of Soviet Communist officials working on the elections.

These early efforts were small and fragmented. Eventually, there was some attempt to organise on a broader scale. Gradually, an organisation called the Relvastatud Võitluse Liit (RVL—'The Union of Armed Struggle', roughly). The RVL gradually started to organise itself to become a national movement. It was active in some counties and not others. It did not manage to achieve the same level of organisation as national groups in Lithuania but was more nationwide, in many respects, than the fragmented groups in Latvia.

The RVL was clearly set up with an ethos of preparing for future struggle, not for immediate conflict or armed resistance except as necessary to protect itself and gather supplies. The RVL's charter stated its objective: 'The organisation is preparing an armed uprising against the Soviet regime at such a time when England and the United States go to war against the Soviet Union, or when a political coup occurs in the Soviet Union.'

The RVL was generally apolitical and, although armed, eschewed direct confrontation in favour of preparation for the battles that the organisation believed would inevitably occur in the future. Unfortunately, the war between the West and the Soviet Union played out in proxy conflicts in places like Korea and South East Asia, and the coup, which did occur, happened in 1991, not 1951.

The existence of the RVL enraged the Soviet occupiers, and significant effort was expended to infiltrate the group and roll up its operations. Around 500 RVL members were captured or killed in the late 1940s. The RVL tried to maintain a central command structure and a hierarchy, but this was exploited by the Soviet authorities. A courier with knowledge of several cells was captured and forced to divulge the location of a number of secret bunkers. In another blow, Soviet secret agents set up a phantom RVL, using the same name, and collected information on possible recruits, who were then arrested. By 1950, the RVL was largely a spent force.

City Brothers (and Sisters)

Several accounts of the Estonian Forest Brothers refer to urban resistance groups that supported their comrades in the rural areas. There are fewer such records in Latvia and Lithuania. These groups were known as the Linnavennad—'The City Brothers'. Many of these resisters were students. While acts of open armed resistance appear to have been rare in Estonia's cities and large towns, urban resistance members focused on procuring medical supplies and information to pass to their rural brethren. City Brothers also had better access to printing technology and paper and were thus an excellent source of forged documents. In 2020, the Estonian defence minister stated that the City Brothers were active in helping young men avoid Soviet conscription efforts.[2]

The City Brothers also engaged in symbolic acts of resistance. Chief among these were numerous acts of raising the banned Estonian flag. As well as it being illegal to raise the blue, black, and white flag, mere possession of one risked arrest or deportation. Yet for years, particularly on Estonian national holidays, such flags were secretly raised in Tallinn, Tartu, and other places. Some of the flags appeared on iconic buildings and towers, raising much speculation about who heroically scaled such buildings under cover of darkness to raise the flags.

One episode of violent resistance by City Brothers was, in fact, committed by a pair of young City Sisters. In Tallinn, a temporary wooden monument with a large red pentagon on top was erected by the Soviet occupiers on Tõnismägi, a hill in the centre of the city, replacing much-revered pre-war Estonian monuments. During the night of 8 May 1946, on the eve of Soviet victory celebrations, Aili Jürgenson and Ageeda Paavel (aged fourteen and fifteen respectively) destroyed this monument.[3] Not content with merely setting the wooden plinth on fire with petrol, as they easily could have done, they procured some explosives and training from a City Brother named Juhan. Under the eyes of a militia member, who was distracted by flirting with another girl, they planted the explosive and destroyed the monument. Although nearly all of Tallinn heard the explosion, news of this act was suppressed and the monument quickly replaced. Jürgenson and Paavel were arrested and imprisoned in the Gulag, not returning to Estonia for many years. Jürgenson lived well past the demise of the USSR, and both women were honoured by the president of Estonia after independence had been restored.

Characters and exploits

The nature of a dispersed conflict like the Estonian insurgency means that it is very hard to write a chronicle of it in the same way one would write about a conventional military campaign. Nor is it really possible to do justice to the topic in a book of this length. Perhaps the best way to capture the nature of the Estonian struggle is to look at some of the people and incidents that represent the broader conflict.

Richard Saaliste

Richard Saaliste was one of the more famous Forest Brothers. Of middling fame as a Greco-Roman wrestler, he grew up on a farm and had done some military training before the war. He participated in the summer 1941 uprisings but had been seriously wounded in his right hand. This injury left him exempt from German conscription efforts, but he assiduously spent the next few years learning how to use his left arm rather than his right.

Saaliste ended up as a company commander in one of the Estonian military units the Germans used to try to delay the Soviet advance and cover their retreat. His unit, the 1st Border Guard Regiment, fought hard against advancing Soviet troops in the summer of 1944. After being wounded, he escaped from a German hospital on the island of Hiiumaa and helped Estonians escape by boat to Sweden. The Germans arrested him, but he managed to get out of custody by persuading the German commandant to release him. When the Soviets arrived on the island in October, he fled by boat to Sweden.

After a time in internment in Sweden, Saaliste worked with fishermen to bring people in and out of occupied Estonia. If he'd only lasted a few years longer, he might have played a role in Western espionage, as we will see in a later chapter. In a perilous and cold boat journey, he returned to Estonia in late 1946 with several other Estonians and some weapons and a radio transmitter. However, the Soviets were waiting for them at the landing site. In the ensuing gunfight, Richard escaped but lost his radio.

Miraculously, he managed to find his brother Artur in a Forest Brother group and established contacts with other groups. He somehow managed to find one of the Haukka group radio operators, Vambola Oras, who still had his transmitter set and had been living in hiding.[4] Saaliste used Oras and his radio set to keep in contact with Estonian émigrés in Sweden. These radio contacts enraged the Soviets. Various manhunts involving radio direction-finding equipment ensued.

Saaliste became involved with the RVL. Saaliste was in contact with Estonians in Sweden and could verify the bona fides of arriving agents from the West. Some of them were Soviet infiltrators, and Saaliste's efforts helped keep them compartmented away from RVL operations. In 1948, Saaliste made an unsuccessful attempt to escape back to Sweden in which he narrowly survived an ambush. In 1949, he became involved in leading reprisal operations to resist deportations and collectivisation. Eventually, Boris Kumm, the security minister for the Estonian SSR, made Saaliste's demise or capture the highest priority. On 14 December 1949, his bunker was finally discovered. Cornered, he and several other partisans went down fighting.

'Ants the Terrible'

No description of the Estonian Forest Brothers is complete without
the tale of Ants Kaljurand, known as 'Ants the Terrible'. Laar's
book provides several first-hand accounts of Ants the Terrible.[5] This
man was truly the scourge of the Soviet oppressors, as the Soviet
security services amassed a five-volume file on him. Ants was a
farm labourer who worked in the Pärnu region and had served in
the Kaitseliit before the war. In 1941, he helped organise a Forest
Brothers group as part of the improvised uprising alongside the
German invasion. He was later mobilised into German forces (it is
unclear whether this was by enlistment or conscription), but he did
not retreat with the German Army and stayed to fight the returning
Soviets, as was often the case with Estonians in German units. The
returning Soviets captured him and placed him in a prison camp
in Tallinn.

Ants' tale of heroism starts with this escape from the Soviet
prison camp in late 1944. He then returned to the Pärnu region
and founded a Forest Brother unit, eventually becoming the
RVL commander in his district as the RVL evolved. Ants became
something of a specialist in jail breaks, with he and his band
conducting several infamous raids to free prisoners. On at least one
occasion, some prisoners smuggled out a plea for his help. After
receiving this message, Ants mounted a raid and freed the prisoners.

Ants the Terrible made no effort to hide his actual name, which
spread throughout the area, and he became a local hero. At times,
he would operate in disguise. In one episode described in Laar's
book, he sent a letter to the manager of the Baltika restaurant in
Pärnu announcing that he would dine there. Undercover NKVD
operatives surrounded the restaurant and filled the dining room.
Dressed as a senior Red Army officer, Ants drove up in a Pobeda staff
car with army registration plates, promenaded into the restaurant,
and dined in high style. He left a note with a generous tip and left,
unmolested by the room full of secret policemen. Allegedly, the
note read: 'Thank you very much for the lunch. Ants the Terrible.'[6]

Country stores were robbed of vodka, right under the nose of
NKVD guards. State money transfers were robbed, based on inside
tips passed to Ants. Kaljurand dodged death many times. Betrayed by
an informant, he dodged a shootout at a village dance. On Christmas

Eve, 1948, his hideout in a barn was discovered, but he managed to turn the Soviet attack into an ambush, creating a deadly kill zone in the farmyard with overlapping machine gun fire, massacring the Soviet attackers and fleeing in the chaos of the aftermath.

On top of all this, Ants was a capable RVL leader and directed the activities of several detachments in the Pärnu region. Although his nickname was Ants the Terrible, he absolutely refused to risk the bloodshed of innocents. He passed up an opportunity to assassinate a local Communist Party official at yet another village dance for fear of hitting innocents. We can infer from this that he was a bit of dancer. He was actually quite good looking, a trait not all partisans shared. Some of his exploits were symbolic, like raising Estonian flags in positions that would embarrass the Soviets and sending threatening letters to terrorise Soviet officials.

Ants had one of the longest runs of any of the Estonian Forest Brothers. But the Soviets eventually caught up with him. He was captured in June 1949, allegedly after being knocked out by poisoned vodka. After much torture and over a year in captivity, he was executed by the Soviets in early 1951.

'Captain Pargas'

Another swashbuckling hero emerged in the Viru region. Heino Lipp was the son of a forester, and the forests were his natural environment. Sporting a hipster beard long before the word 'hipster' entered the popular vocabulary, he gained the nickname 'Pargas', roughly meaning 'bearded log rafter' in local slang. During the war, Pargas had served with the Omakaitse, but the character of his service is not well documented. He became a Forest Brother when the Soviets returned in 1944.

Pargas built up a small team of Forest Brothers, numbering perhaps only five men. But his reputation for flamboyance built up quickly, and he entered local folklore. Laar reports that he was ambidextrous as a pistol marksman, keeping pistols in both pockets, and smoked 'Tallinn' brand cigarettes. Pargas became known for taunting the Soviet occupiers. He placed recruitment signs advertising for volunteers to enlist in his band, and the local authorities were too scared to pull the signs down. In one incident, near the town of Tapa, Pargas erected a sign demanding a delivery of boots for his men from the Soviet state and specifying a time and place for the delivery. When NKVD troops went to ambush the delivery site at the appointed time, Pargas ambushed the ambushers. Later, a pair of bloody boots and a Russian cap was left alongside another sign thanking Stalin for the boots.[7]

In one incident, Pargas liberated food supplies from a local store and handed a bottle of vodka to each of the customers before making a toast to his health. Clerks viewed being robbed by Pargas as an honour. Just exactly where and when Pargas came to his end seems to be a matter of dispute in the literature, but it was either in 1949 or 1951, when his bunker was surrounded by Soviet security forces and he was shot to death. The date of 1949 appears in the more recent, authoritative sources.

Battle of Viru-Kudina

In 1946, an entire Soviet battalion descended upon a small detachment of Forest Brothers in the Viru-Kudina area of Virumaa. The partisans, however, had had time to prepare. As a rank of attackers was drawn into an open field, they were mown down by partisan gunfire. In the ensuing confusion, the partisans shifted their positions and thence engaged the Soviets from different angles of fire. After killing at least fifty Soviets, the Forest Brothers managed to escape.[8]

Battle of Määritsa Farm

On 31 March 1946, Soviet forces in Võrumaa received reports of partisans holed up at a farm in the village of Osula. Red Army, NKVD, and *istrebiteli* surrounded the farm. A raging gunfight ensued as seven besieged partisans held off at least 200 Soviets well into the next day. It is not known how many of the attackers fell, but the Soviets eventually set fire to the farm, killing the partisans and the family that lived at the farm. Years later, in 2012, the remains of six of the fallen partisans were identified and interred in the local cemetery.[9]

Robin Hood operations

Some groups of Estonian Forest Brothers practised a form of Robin Hood-style redistribution of assets. A variety of acts were directed at taking property and money that had been seized by Soviet authorities and finding ways to give it back to people who had been subject to Soviet depredations. Cash was distributed anonymously, sometimes being tossed into villagers' yards in potato baskets at night. Partisans evidently went to great lengths to respect private property and only take from the Soviet occupiers. Laar reports an incident in the Pärnu region where partisans stole the payroll cash from a forestry plant and discovered that a pencil was in the cash. The pencil was returned, with compensation and an explanatory note that the Forest Brothers respected private property. Partisans often had inside informants and were able to rob payroll cash in transit without a shot. Soviet memos of the time record the severity of these incidents.[10]

Some of the more famous 'Robin Hood' exploits involved train robberies. On 1 December 1948, a band of partisans led by one Johannes Heeska stopped a train in Võrumaa. Two of his men had been on the train and threw the emergency brakes. They held up the mail car, which had bags of cash collected as taxes, and made off with 152,000 roubles.[11] Despite a large manhunt, Heeska's men escaped into the nearby swamps. Several other groups also conducted train robberies to take cash for redistribution. On 5 December 1951, one of the last remaining RVL units, under Eerich Järlet, robbed a train on the Tallinn–Pärnu route, taking 200,000 roubles from Soviet officials.[12]

The bloody toll

The Soviets kept data on the insurgency in Estonia. Statistics show that, between 1944 and 1953, the Soviets killed 1,495 Estonian partisans and arrested a further 8,708, mostly before the end of 1947. However, this is almost certainly an undercount as these figures report barely any deaths or arrests in 1944; partisans at that point are likely counted differently as the war was still ongoing. During this same period, the figures show 512 Soviet deaths and 497 civilian deaths.[13] Many of those civilians may have been collaborators. This nevertheless provides an idea of the size and intensity of the conflict in Estonia. The RVL's ethos of quietly waiting until they could hold an uprising under the right conditions may have served to keep some violence under wraps.

Some people might draw a few uncomfortable conclusions about some of the Estonian Forest Brothers. Rather a lot of the more flamboyant characters did serve in some capacity with the Germans, thus leaving them open to the charge of collaborating with the Nazis. Many of the better-known actions of Estonian partisans were acts that could be characterised as thefts or robberies, even if it was the Soviet state that was the victim. Such acts make it easier to propagandise that the Forest Brothers were lawless bandits, not freedom fighters. However, while the partisan resistance can, and probably always will be viewed from different angles, such accusations must be tempered by the reality that the actual bandits, consisting of petty criminals and opportunists, were generally on the side of the Soviet occupier.

7

LATVIA

THE MEŽABRĀĻI

The strategy and tactics of the Latvian Forest Brothers evolved in similar ways to those of their Estonian and Lithuanian brethren, with recruits drawn from a wide variety of sources. Because of more successful efforts at recruitment and conscription by the Germans—the line is often blurred between the two in the Baltics—a lot of Latvian men were under arms and could desert to join partisan formations rather than retreat or surrender.[1]

The end of the Second World War in Latvia

The last year of Nazi Germany's war on the Eastern Front was plagued by Hitler's personal meddling in strategy and tactics. Hitler's various orders against retreating and the successful advances of the Red Army resulted in a significant German force being cut off in western Latvia. In July 1944, the remnants of the Nazi Army Group North became entrapped on the Courland Peninsula, the forested westernmost part of Latvia that became known as the Courland Pocket. Soviet attempts to reduce this pocket were at best a secondary effort as the primary energy was devoted to the march on Berlin. But roughly 200,000 soldiers, including around 14,000 Latvians, were contained here right up until Germany surrendered in May 1945 and thus were unable to contribute to the Nazi war effort. The surrender of troops in the Courland Pocket also meant that a large number of weapons and other equipment were left lying around, which soon became useful for the partisans.

However, many of the partisans were in other parts of the country, not the Courland Pocket.

Resistance and fragmentation

Unlike Lithuania, a truly national-level organisation did not emerge in Latvia, as we will see in Chapter 8. One reason for this is that the Germans were able to crack down on the nascent Latvian provisional government-in-waiting, the Latvian Central Council— 'Latvijas Centrālā Padome' (LCP). In 1944, liaison couriers had been captured, revealing information about Latvian underground organisations. From April 1944 onward, the Gestapo arrested several prominent members of the LCP, including several successive chairmen. General Kurelis, head of the military wing of the LCP, was arrested in the Courland Pocket in November 1944 and taken to imprisonment in Germany. Being sent back to Germany to camps meant that several of the LCP leaders actually survived the war, but they were then in exile, unable to lead operations in Latvia.

The situation on the ground in Latvia varied quite significantly. Eastern Latvia was occupied by the Soviets a long time before the Kurzeme region in the west of Latvia was finally occupied. In the east of Latvia, Daugavpils, Latvia's second largest city, fell under Soviet control in late July 1944, and Riga fell in October 1944. The seaports of Ventspils and Liepāja, in the Courland Pocket, only fell into Soviet hands on VE Day, 9 May 1945. This phased reoccupation of Latvia over the course of nine months left the resistance in different situations in different parts of the country. The active front line between Germans and Soviets was difficult to cross and made nationwide coordination difficult.

Latvia has several different regions, and there was a distinct character to the Forest Brothers in each of them. Different groups sprang up at different points, with different members. This was very much a dispersed rural conflict.[2]

Recruitment came from broadly similar sources as in Estonia and Lithuania. However, due to the Courland Pocket, there appears to have been an influx of Forest Brothers directly from German units at the end of the war. This phenomenon provokes some of the less nuanced allegations that Forest Brothers were merely Nazi fighters.

Their initial use of German uniforms and weapons, usually for lack of any alternatives, has helped feed such narratives. However, it is important to keep in mind that many of these Latvians in German units were either conscripts or recruited through propaganda and false pretences who knew that severe punishment in the Gulag was likely for surrendered soldiers. A large percentage of the Latvian men between sixteen and sixty years old in the Courland Pocket ended up in 'internal exile' or imprisonment. Around 4,000 Latvians from the Courland Pocket are believed to have joined partisan groups.

Groups and movements

At its peak, an estimated 10,000 to 15,000 partisans were active in the Latvian Forest Brotherhood. Because of the degradation of national-level movements and the regional variations in conditions, a bewildering array of organisations emerged instead. Some of them had aspirational names implying that they were trying to be national, but none of them truly had a nationwide footprint. Many groups started out as close-knit family groups, with fathers, sons, and brothers working together.

Different groups evolved in the various regions of Latvia. In the Courland area, two groups sprang up. One was the 'Hawks of the Fatherland' and the other was the Organisation of Latvian National Partisans. In eastern Latvia, the Latvian Homeland Guard Union was led by a Roman Catholic priest, Father Antons Juhnēvičs, who was later executed by the Soviets. In northern Latvia, the most prominent local group was the Latvian National Partisan Union.

The Latvian movement also included dozens if not hundreds of smaller partisan detachments that were only loosely affiliated or unaffiliated with the larger groups.

As Latvia sat in the middle of the Baltic states, cross-border cooperation was not unheard of in border regions. The Sēlija (Selonia) region in the south of Latvia saw some close cooperation with Lithuanian partisans. For a period in 1945, around 100 Lithuanian forest brothers temporarily formed a company in the local Latvian Forest Brother regiment.

One group, called 'Latvian Self Defence', distributed an underground newspaper. The group was led by one Kārlis Plaudis, who had served in the Latvian Army. He had worked as a policeman under the German occupation but had been secretly organising resistance and deserted rather than retreating with the Germans, as ordered. In an area called Ērgli parish, a force of over 400 NKVD soldiers, supported by at least one armoured vehicle, attacked this group. It was one of the larger actions of the period. Several partisans were killed, and at least 130 people from the local area were arrested. Plaudis escaped, but he later made the mistake of venturing into Riga, where he was arrested and executed.[3]

A small group of the Polish Home Army was also operating in the region around the city of Daugavpils, where there has long been a significant Polish minority population. A small part of this region had bordered on Poland in the interwar period.

Heroes and deeds

An easier way to examine the Latvian Forest Brothers is through some of their more prominent deeds and characters.

The Battle of Stompak Marsh

Pēteris Supe, a young agronomist who knew the local countryside, was the catalyst for partisan resistance in the Abrene area in the far north-east of Latvia. Supe was one of the German 'wildcat' operatives recruited and trained to set up 'stay-behind' operations.[4] He was parachuted into Latgale, the easternmost part of Latvia, in October 1944 and requested arms to be airdropped by the Germans. The Germans refused, so he went his own way and recruited local Latvians, including deserters from the Red Army. As previously discussed, these 'wildcat' efforts by the Germans were cynically exploited by both sides and do not necessarily imply any political motivation.

Supe founded the Latvian National Partisan Union at a meeting on 10 December 1944 in Abrene, in the far north-east of Latvia. The group had 123 members but grew throughout 1945 to a membership of about 1,000.[5] The group adopted a broadly anti-Communist, pro-independence, and pro-democracy manifesto at its founding. In January 1945, Supe's group hid out in the Stompak marshes on an island, fortifying it and building bunkers, a chapel, a bakery, stables for thirty horses, and a field hospital. Supe was assisted by a local forty-year-old Catholic priest, Father Ludvigs Štagars, rector of Šķilbēni parish. This priest had to go underground lest he be arrested and likely deported to the Gulag. Father Štagars played an important role in recruiting among local Catholics.

As partisans up and down the Baltic states discovered during this period, large partisan units of hundreds are difficult to support and hide. In early March 1945, the NKVD discovered the encampment. The clash became known as the Battle of Stompak Marsh, and it was one of the biggest partisan engagements of the conflict. On the morning of 2 March, 483 Soviet soldiers from the 143rd NKVD rifle regiment surrounded the island base. The Soviets only expected thirty to forty partisans, not 300. The two sides fought bitterly all day and long into the following night. During the night, due to darkness and heavy snowfall, most of the partisans managed to escape, although they had to abandon their supplies. Twenty-eight partisans died, as did forty-six of the NKVD attackers. The Soviets displayed nineteen of the dead partisans in the village of Viļaka in order to terrorise the population. This horrific practice was commonly used throughout the Baltic states.

The NKVD was clearly aware that Father Štagars was involved with the Brotherhood. Several Catholic families in his parish were murdered, including seven children. The NKVD openly blamed partisans but made no effort to investigate the murders, leaving the community widely suspecting that the NKVD had perpetrated the crime.[6] However, all of the Supe group forces had not been concentrated in that one island in the swamp, and they shifted to hiding and operating in smaller groups. Father Štagars was eventually caught and twice imprisoned in the Gulag. He died in Latvia in 1973 after being released from his second period of imprisonment, a broken man and martyr to his faith.

The Bear Hunters

A number of partisan resistance acts involved assassinations of Soviet officials. One of the first incidents was the assassination of Mikhail Kodalyev, a Communist Party activist, at his wedding on 17 April 1945. He was assassinated by the Krēmers family, a family of partisans in the Vidzeme region.[7]

One group of partisans that came to be known as the 'Bear Hunters' set about plotting the most high-profile assassination that could be managed in Latvia in the 1940s by twice attempting to kill Vilis Lācsis, the chairman of the Council of Ministers of the Latvian Soviet Socialist Republic. In the minds of many, he was the most senior Latvian collaborator with the Soviets.

The Bear Hunters was a small nucleus of partisans founded by Tālrīts Krastiņš, who survived a period of imprisonment in the Gulag and lived until 2008. He managed to tell the story of the Bear Hunters after Latvia regained independence.[8] Krastiņš was part of a group of sixteen Latvian Legion soldiers who had refused to surrender in the Courland Pocket. Like many others, his group fled to the forests. This particular group came up with the idea of assassinating Communist officials. They started to operate differently from most of the Forest Brothers. Krastiņš got a job as an accountant for a dairy collective, a role that, by his own admission, he was hilariously unqualified for. Unlike other groups, they avoided contact with locals or their relatives, obtained an apartment in Riga to operate from, and stole some vehicles, which gave them mobility. The Bear Hunters stole money from the Soviets and bribed an official to get legitimately issued documents in false names.

Seemingly bored with lesser officials, the Bear Hunters set their sights on killing Lācsis, thus giving the group its nickname (*lācsis* means 'bear' in Latvian). The group started surveillance and recruiting informants. They took close interest in Lācsis' movements and started plotting attacks. The group befriended a Russian woman who worked in the Supreme Council building, who gave information on Lācsis' movements and vehicles. The Bear Hunters set up an ambush on the road from Riga to Jūrmala, the nearby beach town where the Latvian Communists had houses. They hid beside the road with German machine guns. One of the Bear Hunters, on a fast German motorcycle, scouted out Lācsis' car and sped ahead to alert the killers. They shot up the car, but the car continued, and the attackers escaped into the forest. It later transpired that either Lācsis was not in the car or had not been hit.

The next attack was plotted in Riga. The idea was simple: they would scout out Lācsis' house on Elizabeth Street in Riga, and Krastiņš would speed by at the appointed moment on the team's motorcycle and shoot Lācsis. Alas, by this point the Bear Hunters had been infiltrated by two Soviet agents. The night before the planned attack, the NKVD rounded up the Bears. Krastiņš tried to escape the interrogation room by attacking his interrogator with a water jug and fleeing down a lift shaft, but he did not get out of the building. He was sentenced to twenty-five years in the Gulag in 1948, where he participated in an uprising in a camp in Norilsk. After a decade, well after Stalin's death, he was let out and settled in Estonia for a time. He died in 2008.

Battle of Īle

One of the last major battles of the Latvian Forest Brothers was the Battle of Īle, a village in south-west Latvia. A mixed group of twenty-seven Latvian and Lithuanian Forest Brothers had constructed a hidden bunker in the forests, under the leadership of Visvaldis Brizga. It is not certain how the Soviets discovered this unit, but it could have been traditional reconnaissance, an informant, or even just pure luck. On 17 March 1949, a very large force of 760 NKVD troops surrounded the bunker, and a fierce battle ensued in which the Soviets used smoke grenades to defeat the partisans. An unknown number of Soviet soldiers died. The partisans suffered fifteen dead; nine others were captured, all of whom went to Gulag camps. Three of the partisans, including Brizga, escaped. Brizga fell a year later in a shootout.

The Battle of Īle figures well in national memory because one of the survivors who was sent to the Gulag was Modris Zihmanis. He participated in Gulag uprisings (see Chapter 13) and later in life became well known as a poet and novelist. His accounts formed part of the research for a film about the Battle of Īle.[9] The bunker, which he helped build, has since been reconstructed.

The overall toll

Archival documents from the KGB and its predecessor agencies provide some useful statistics on the size of the Latvian armed struggle. The bureaucrats of the security state kept records of whom they shot and arrested. This material provides the basis for Latvian scholar Zigmārs Turčinskis's figures for this period, according to which 2,420 Latvian partisans were killed or committed suicide to prevent capture. Another 5,489 were arrested, of whom 498 were sentenced to death. Given Soviet jurisprudence at the time, the number acquitted was likely zero. Some 4,341 partisans took advantage of various amnesties, although some of them were eventually deported in 1949. While some of those arrested were likely to have been innocent people rather than partisans, these are nonetheless interesting figures. Turčinskis estimates that the Latvian armed resistance numbered around 12,250 people in total.[10]

The historian Heinrichs Strods has compiled similar statistics on the Soviet casualties during the July 1944 to October 1953 period. These show 2,208 Soviet dead and 1,035 wounded, which is not an insignificant figure in a small country. This was a real conflict, not just some banditry in the woods. South of Latvia, as we will see in the next chapter, the struggle was even more intense.

8

LITHUANIA

THE MIŠKO BROLIAI OR ŽALIUKAI

With its larger and more rural population, Lithuania's partisan movement was bigger than those in Estonia and Latvia and, arguably, better organised.

Although the Forest Brotherhood was a broad movement, the environment brought about by the Second World War and the ongoing rigors of life in the wilderness affected its composition. About half had served in the Lithuanian Army in the interwar period, but given the levels of active or reserve military service in that period, this is not unusual. Partisan leaders were often lower-ranking officers from the old army, as a high percentage of the higher ranks had been detained by the Soviets. Schoolteachers, students, and former policemen also rate in the partisan leadership.[1] Members of the intelligentsia were under-represented, as they were early targets of both Soviet and Nazi oppression.

Some work has been done on the composition of the Lithuanian Forest Brotherhood. The historian Dainius Noreika has dug into the background of 1,000 partisans[2] and notes the prevalence of familial ties, with many brothers and cousins serving together. Members who had previously been in the Riflemen's Union were particularly numerous. Noreika also notes that, in the units he studied most closely, few of the members were parents. Familial responsibilities may have kept fathers and mothers from joining partisan units, although many were supporters of the movement in other ways. Many were sons of people who fought in the war of independence (1918–20).

The Lithuanian partisan struggle can be divided into several phases. The overall trajectory was for larger local groups early on but with little coordination. This was followed by a period of adjustment, as Forest Brother detachments divided into smaller groups and literally went to ground in bunkers to hide. These fractionated groups then started to coordinate with each other, gradually building up a national structure. All the while, the Soviet authorities ground the groups down. The final phase, the 1950s, was a long, slow decline as the last of the Forest Brothers were rounded up.

Large actions

The 1944–5 period was one of larger partisan groups in which groups exceeding twenty members were commonplace in various parts of the country. Some partisan groups were organised in groups into the hundreds. These large groups were easy to locate and hard to sustain from a logistical perspective, as the Soviets could identify large encampments from the air and bring large forces to bear on groups of partisans. This resulted in heroic acts of defiance but also led to serious losses of partisan personnel, arms, and ammunition that proved difficult to replace.

This period gives us early examples of battles that may not have been spectacular or large from the viewpoint of the Second World War but that were significant in terms of the partisan movement. One of the first occurred in Pušynė forest, near Kėdainiai, in the centre of Lithuania on 14 December 1944; fourteen partisans were killed. In Troškūnai forest, near Panevėžys, sixty-eight partisans died on 9 February 1945. On 27 March 1945, a battle in the Ažagų forest near the Panevėžys district saw the death of seventy-five more Forest Brothers.[3] A particularly epic battle in the Alytus region is described in more detail below. Records show other such battles with double digit figures of partisan losses. Although many Soviet security forces also fell in these battles, this rate of attrition would doom the Forest Brotherhood movement. An enemy that could bring literally thousands of troops to bear to surround an entire rural district, resupply with ample ammunition, move troops rapidly by truck, and employ aircraft, mortars, and artillery on an encampment was not easy for irregulars to confront.

The lessons of this period were hard learned but were incorporated into practice by partisan leaders. Both the ease of discovery of larger groups and encampments and food supply issues bore down on the groups. Food supply, plentiful early on, would diminish with the presence of Soviet security forces. In 1944, a group of 100 could forage from farmers with impunity, but by 1946, farmers were being arrested for supplying food. As a result, the partisan movement had to shrink to smaller groups. As discussed in Chapter 5, bunkers and dugouts became the main means of shelter, as these afforded a great deal of concealment. But also, for practical reasons, such bunkers could only handle smaller groups.

Changing tactics

Moving to smaller units required a change in tactics. Many groups felt that their most important mission was to be able to rise up in a general uprising under the right conditions. Forest Brotherhood operations from 1946 onward focused on survival and information operations above other objectives. As discussed in Chapter 10, producing and disseminating underground publications were a large part of the operation.

Partisan units started counterattacking the Soviet authorities and trying to undermine their operations, but Forest Brothers sought to do so in ways that were not as dangerous as the larger confrontations of the early period of resistance. One particular line of work was sending threats to Soviet officials and known collaborators. Offensive actions were generally ambushes and raids, either against specific officials or to gain supplies. Actual combat operations were to be avoided at all costs, and effort went into planning raids and ambushes so that a minimal amount of ammunition could be expended. If a raid or ambush could be done at gunpoint without firing a shot, so much the better, as ammunition was scarce. Resisting elections and destroying Soviet documentation, such as tax registers, were also common activities.

Collaborators were specifically targeted, especially the locally recruited *istrebiteli*. The Lithuanian slang for them was *stribai*— meaning 'freaks'—and they were a particular source of hatred. People suspected of being informants, local residents assisting collectivisation, and ethnic Lithuanians who were members of the police or the Communist Party were also targets. As collectivisation continued, some non-Lithuanians from various parts of the Soviet Union were moved in as colonists to take over farmsteads. The usual practice was to issue a warning to collaborators and colonial arrivals. In some instances, collaborators or arriving colonists were merely warned to leave a particular district and instead go to the towns and cities. One partisan publication was even printed in Russian to help spread the warnings. It should also be noted that the Soviet occupiers recruited local people to do all kinds of things, so there were ample opportunities for partisans and their supporters to actually infiltrate the Soviet regime.

Between 1946 and 1948, the number of active partisans dropped through attrition. All of the various counterinsurgency tactics discussed in Chapter 9 chipped away at the strength of the movement. A study in 1996 estimated 4,500 active partisans in 1946 and 2,300 in 1948.[4] New recruits would trickle in each year as young men reached conscription age, and waves of collectivisation or deportation brought people seeking refuge or revenge, or who joined the movement simply because they no longer had a farm to go back to. But as the movement became smaller, and Soviet tactics, including infiltration and double agents, improved, it became increasingly difficult for people to join the partisans.

Organising nationally

A different arc to the story of the Lithuanian Forest Brotherhood is that, after initial fragmentation, the movement started to organise itself regionally and then nationally. There were both advantages and disadvantages to broader, national organisations.

Some advantages came from organising on a broader front. Adjacent groups could coordinate operations. If a local bunker was compromised, Forest Brothers could take refuge with nearby units with which they had contacts. Information was shared, such as intelligence and lessons learned. Broader networks could distribute underground publications more widely. Scarce resources, such as food, ammunition, radio receivers, and printing supplies, could be shared around. Training could be established.

All of this happened to a greater or lesser extent in Lithuania at various points.

But there were also some disadvantages. One disadvantage of organising a chain of command that ranged from a single remote cell all the way up to the national level is that a lot of resources got taken up simply by communicating. Large numbers of couriers and liaison agents were needed. There were a lot of meetings and a lot of people moving around carrying messages.

The effort in staff and liaison work led to the other key disadvantage, namely that such efforts made the broader movement more vulnerable to infiltration and counterinsurgency measures. You can't have local, regional, and national levels of organisation without various interactions between people and groups. These interactions were vulnerabilities, and considerable damage was done to the Lithuanian Forest Brothers at various points because networks were compromised and infiltrated. A decentralised movement that adhered rigidly to a cell structure would have been harder to infiltrate.

The LLA

Quite early on, individuals and small units started to organise above the level of an individual cell. As we have seen, some national organisation had already occurred in the 1940–1 period. Some further organising happened during the German period, and the Lithuanians started organising even more as Soviet forces crept towards the Lithuanian border. The first of these national organisations was the Lithuanian Liberation Army (Lietuvos Laisvės Armija—LLA). The LLA was a broad tent movement that tried to distance itself from political groups and political factions. The LLA had started organising during the German occupation. It did not support VLIK (the Supreme Committee for the Liberation of Lithuania, which went into exile) and did not support the creation of the Territorial Defence Force. LLA prohibited its members from leaving Lithuania in an attempt to weed out people who might retreat with the Germans. (Many did flee to Germany regardless.)

One of the key founders was Kazys Veverskis, a law student with some military training who had been a reservist in the interwar era. His deputy was Adolfas Eidimtas, who had been a cavalryman before the war. While the LLA was broadly anti-German, Eidimtas' record was not pristine. He had served as mayor of the town of Radviliškis during the German occupation, which makes his record somewhat problematic.

One general operational concept of the LLA was similar to the 1941 LAF in that it recruited and organised for a general offensive to coincide with a German retreat and Soviet advance. A dozen colonels from the old pre-war Lithuanian Army that had somehow survived death, captivity, or being co-opted by the Germans were recruited as commanders. Many rank-and-file members had been members of the Riflemen's Union, and a number were veterans of the 1941 uprising. Deserters from German-sponsored units were common. However, some LLA recruits had served in German police battalions, and some of those were truly brutal units.

The LLA was organised into cells of three people. Members with weapons and the ability to survive in the forest were called 'Hawks' and told to hide. Others were meant to support the armed members. Multiple sources credit the LLA with 10,000 members, but this has been disputed by other sources, which consider that to be an inflated claim. Secrecy, rampant use of easily repeated pseudonyms, and a cell structure, as well as potential issues like double counting, double reporting, and various other flaws, could have easily distorted reports of the group's size.

The Soviet military advance across Lithuania did not allow the LLA to fully develop a regional structure. Many LLA members fled to the West and became refugees in displaced persons camps. Among those who stayed to fight, Soviet crackdowns in occupied areas hit the LLA hard. Veverskis was killed in an ambush in late 1944 while couriering underground publications. His successor, Eidimtas, was arrested and interrogated by the NKVD in early 1945 and eventually executed. The LLA was a spent force by the end of 1945, demonstrating many of the disadvantages of a highly centralised movement.

Partisan regions

Many lower-level LLA members survived crackdowns and kept organising. One of the key reasons why the Lithuanian movement eventually did become a national organisation was that the practical work of organising from bottom up was far more successful than the other way around. Local units started liaising with the units around them. People with common sense understood the need for a chain of command, so that someone would be in charge if a leader fell or was captured. Even relatively untrained partisans understood the need to know who their neighbouring partisans were and how to get in touch with them. Despite everything written about organisations with grand titles and 'supreme committees' and such, it seems that the heavy lifting was done from the ground up.

The first region or 'military district' to form was the 'Vytis' district in central Lithuania. The Vytis is the ancient national symbol of Lithuania, the coat of arms showing a white knight on horseback, generally on a red background. This also started a tradition of naming these partisan districts along heroic and poetic lines. The Vytis district started functioning collectively in December 1944, about the same time as the LLA was falling apart. It lasted all the way until its final demise in January 1953.

From late 1944 to 1948, a total of nine partisan districts were organised, covering the entire country. The others were named Didžioji Kova ('Great Battle'), Vytautas (after Grand Duke Vytautas the Great), Algimantas (another grand duke), Dainava (roughly 'the area of the singers'—the far south of Lithuania), Tauras (a common name in Lithuanian, not easy to translate), Kęstutis (yet another grand duke), Prisikėlimas ('resurrection'), and Žemaičiai (the Lithuanian name of the Samogitian area in the north-west of the country). Each of these units had several tiers of sub-units below them. The partisan districts survived as viable entities into the 1950s, with the last of them ceasing to operate as a functional unit in the summer of 1953 due to deaths and capture of partisans.

BDPS

The next attempt at national organisation was the United Democratic Resistance Movement (Bendras demokratinio pasipriešinimo sąjūdis—BDPS), which was established in 1946. One of the leaders of the Tauras district was Antanas Baltūsis ('Žveijys'— The Fisherman), who was instrumental in bringing the BDPS into existence. Baltūsis started to knit together a national organisation out of the various partisan districts that were emerging across the

137

country. However, he is one of the more problematic figures in the Forest Brotherhood movement, as he served with German police units and commanded a company of them. For those who wish to point to Nazi collaborators, Baltūsis is often the one they point at.

The BDPS was plagued by Soviet infiltrators. One of its leaders was Juozas Markulis ('Erelis'—The Eagle). Markulis was a former reserve lieutenant of the Lithuanian Army and had worked at the anatomy department of Vilnius University. He had been active in the LLA, but when the LLA was rolled up by the NKVD, he was captured, interrogated, and became a double agent. Markulis did considerable damage to the movement and riddled the BDPS with people who were, in fact, Soviet agents.

Much of the BDPS's work was wrecked. Markulis started transferring partisans from armed work in the countryside to passive resistance roles in cities and towns. In such places, they were more easily watched by the authorities and agents and were caught in various traps and arrested. However, the movement's cellular nature prevented its utter destruction. Baltūsis gradually learned of Markulis' perfidy with the help of Juozas Lukša. Several partisan districts started to distance themselves from the BDPS central structures. Baltūsis ordered a crackdown on Markulis. With the aid of his handlers, Markulis fled Lithuania in 1948 and was given a laboratory job in Leningrad. He returned to Lithuania after the suppression of the partisan movement and ended up having a career in forensic pathology, dying a few years before Lithuania regained its independence.

Baltūsis did manage some organisational work. His key achievement was to have sent some agents to the West to establish contact with Western governments and diaspora movements. Because of that mission to the West, much material about the movement is now known to us. However, in early 1948 Baltūsis was betrayed by Soviet double agents. His bunker was surrounded, and he, along with two other partisans, committed suicide to avoid capture.

LLKS

Eventually, partisans working from the ground up to expand regional organisations will reach critical mass, possibly picking up some other efforts at national organisation. This is how the LLKS—Lietuvos Laisvės Kovos Sąjūdis (the Union of Lithuanian Freedom Fighters)—was formed.

The LLKS was founded in early 1949 out of the ashes of the BDPS. On 10 February 1949, a summit meeting of partisan commanders from around the country met in a partisan bunker near the village of Minaičiai, in central Lithuania. Fortunately, it appears that the infiltrators who had riddled the BDPS had been rooted out of the movement, as this meeting was not compromised. The new LLKS adopted a national structure and elected a leader, effectively declaring itself the political and military leadership of an underground state, not dissimilar to what the Polish underground movement did during the Second World War.

The LLKS elected Jonas Žemaitis ('Vytautas'—after Lithuania's most famous grand duke) as the leader of the movement and Lithuania's de facto underground president—a role confirmed posthumously by the Lithuanian parliament after the restoration of independence. Žemaitis, unlike Baltūsis, is untainted by accusations of wartime collaboration with the Germans. By 1949, he was one of the most senior remaining officers from the former Lithuanian Army left in partisan service. He had trained and served as an artillery officer in the pre-war period and had even trained at the French artillery school in Fontainebleau. He got dragged into Soviet service with the annexation of the Lithuanian Army but surrendered to the Germans rather than retreat to Russia. He spent the war in civilian employment, first extracting peat and then managing an agricultural cooperative. Žemaitis spent some time during the war distributing anti-German underground publications. When Plechavičius set up the territorial forces to resist the arriving Soviets in 1944, Žemaitis joined but then fled to the forests two months later once armed.

Žemaitis became a Forest Brother in early 1945 and took his oath as a member of the LLA. His reputation as a combat leader was cemented early on in a bitter battle in Virtukai woods near Raseiniai, a town between Šiauliai and Kaunas. Tipped off by an informant, the Soviets surrounded the partisan encampment in the forest on 22 July 1945 and advanced on the Forest Brothers. However, possibly due to Žemaitis' skill and knowledge, the partisan camp was well fortified with trenches, entrenched fighting positions, and overlapping sectors of fire. The partisans were greatly outnumbered—some accounts say that over 1,000 Soviet soldiers were pitted against perhaps fifty or so partisans. However, the partisans were very well armed—six machine guns, twenty-four submachine guns, and four automatic rifles as well as traditional rifles, pistols, and grenades.[5] The battle dragged on for hours. Most of the partisans escaped, and over forty Soviets fell. Žemaitis' reputation was made. He went on to lead several other actions and ascended through the ranks. He developed local and regional structures, which became part of the LLKS.

As well as providing national and regional command, the LLKS worked to function as an army. It had ranks and published regulations and developed training courses for junior and senior leaders. There was an effort to spread knowledge among the remaining partisan units and to share lessons learned. Lukša's account tells of several of these training courses.

The LLKS was also active in publishing, including one of the longer-running partisan publications, the newspaper *Prie rymančio Rūpintojėlio* (roughly, 'The Caring Caretaker'). This newspaper had a run of twenty issues, with between 200 and 1,000 copies per issue that were printed in a series of bunkers between 1949 and 1954. The partisan Juozas Šibaila, a former schoolteacher whose entire family had been deported to Siberia, was the publication's primary editor.

Anecdotes, exploits, and heroes

The length of this book prohibits me from an encyclopaedic listing of all of the known exploits of the Lithuanian Forest Brothers. While many heroic deeds languish in obscurity, others now form part of a popular folklore culture in Lithuania. They give some flavour and texture to the story. Given the nature of the struggle, some of it makes for gruesome reading.

A partisan movement such as this one does not happen without some courage and dynamism. The Lithuanian Forest Brotherhood contained a number of truly heroic people. Many of them are lost to us, having died out of public sight in the forests. But no account of the partisan war in Lithuania is complete without talking about two heroic characters, Adolfas Ramanauskas ('Vanagas'—The Hawk) and Juozas Lukša (pseudonym 'Daumantas'). Much of the granular detail about life in the Forest Brotherhood comes from their memoirs.

Ramanauskas

Adolfas Ramanauskas was born in New Britain, Connecticut, in 1918, making him both chronologically and geographically a close contemporary of my own Lithuanian immigrant grandparents. He was a citizen of both America and Lithuania. His parents had emigrated to America, like many others, during the era of tsarist rule. When he was still only three years old, his parents moved back to newly restored Lithuania and bought farmland in Dzūkija, the heavily forested south of Lithuania.

After finishing school, Ramanauskas went to Klaipėda to train as a teacher before enrolling in the Kaunas Military School, where he trained as an army officer and was commissioned as a reservist. He was in the last class to graduate in 1940 before the Soviet occupation. In September 1940, the Soviets redrew Lithuania's boundaries, and the area around the spa town of Druskininkai, formerly under Polish control, became part of the Lithuania SSR. Ramanauskas went to the village of Krivonys just outside Druskininkai and took up a teaching job.

Ramanauskas took part in the 1941 uprising in Druskininkai, which happened as a small part of broader uprisings across the country immediately after the 1941 German invasion, although that was very much a backwater of the 1941 revolt.[6] During the German occupation, Ramanauskas kept his head down and served as a well-regarded teacher in the small city of Alytus, teaching Lithuanian, mathematics, and physical fitness. The German occupiers largely left schools alone. In 1945, with the return of the Soviets, Ramanauskas went to the forest to become a Forest Brother and was almost immediately elected leader of his small band of partisans. As was the style in the partisans, he took a codename and selected Vanagas ('The Hawk') as his name.

Vanagas is a good example of the grassroots organising that later became such a useful feature of the movement. He started liaising with the groups on each side of his own platoon. Whether it was natural leadership, fostered by his military training, or his ability as a teacher, aided by education and teaching experience, he appeared to be the natural leader every time he met with another group. People who knew him seemed to respect him highly as a person. He became one of the main forces, possibly even the primary one, behind the organisation of the Dainava partisan district. He commanded the district for over a year, in 1947 and 1948, having ascended up the ranks. His wife, Birutė (codenamed 'Vanda'), was also a partisan, and their daughter was born while they were serving as partisans.

Vanagas became the scourge of the Soviet occupier in the Dainava area of southern Lithuania. He was part of the famous raid that temporarily occupied the town of Merkinė. Possibly of greater importance, Vanagas and his network of partisan groups became the Forest Brother equivalent of a publishing empire. His daughter's account identifies no fewer than six newspapers that Vanagas published, edited, and distributed in southern Lithuania between 1945 and 1952.[7] When Žemaitis became ill, Vanagas was the de facto leader of the movement.

Vanagas' memoir details many deeds.[8] Some of these stand out. He details efforts by his partisans near Marcinkonys to sabotage railway lines. The partisan movement almost always lacked explosives, so they resorted to creative techniques to block railway lines used by the timber industry. The Forest Brothers seized and sabotaged a locomotive, thus blocking the line. This led the Soviets to deploy rail cars with improvised fortifications on them, effectively bunkers on wheels, in order to fight back against the partisans. In turn, Vanagas' men dug under the rails and inserted logs to raise the rails and derail the trains,[9] likely causing considerable disruption to the area's timber industry. Chasing down Vanagas became the symbolic denouement of the partisan struggle, and he was the one of the last to get caught. Large manhunts, sometimes involving hundreds of Soviet security forces, combed forests and chased down Vanagas' men. Hundreds of informants were tasked with finding information on him. His downfall is described in Chapter 14.

Juozas Lukša—'Daumantas'

Juozas Lukša is a name that comes up a lot in the accounts of the Forest Brotherhood. He was born into a large farming family in 1921 in Juodbūdis, near Kaunas. He went to high school in Kaunas and was active in a Catholic youth organisation before entering the university in Kaunas as an architecture student. He got involved in the early organisational efforts of the LAF and was locked up by the NKVD in Kaunas just before the 1941 invasion and uprising. Lukša managed to keep his head down during the war and continue his studies as best he could, although the capacity of the university was greatly reduced. He also helped on his farm.

The return of the Soviets interfered with his ability to continue his studies. Eventually, he had to withdraw from student life and made the difficult decision to become a partisan. His codename, Daumantas, is drawn from the name of one of the pre-Christian dukes of Lithuania. Other members of his family became Forest Brothers too. Three of his brothers, Jurgis ('Piršlys'—Matchmaker), Antanas ('Arūnas'), and Stasys ('Juodvarnis'—Blackbird), were partisans. Jurgis and Stasys both fell in combat in 1947. Antanas was arrested, harshly interrogated, and sent to Siberia. Yet another brother, Vinca, was exiled to Siberia for helping partisans.

Daumantas served loyally and effectively as a partisan, and he spent considerable time harassing the illegitimate Soviet elections. It is clear from his memoirs that he was particularly skilled at networking, connecting various bands of Forest Brothers. He appears to have been a good judge of who was and was not a trustworthy partisan. He was quite lucky, too, as this was a period of much penetration of the scattered movement by both willing and coerced Soviet agents. His account tells of a number of near misses and lucky escapes. Daumantas appears to have had that great combination rarely found in an irregular military leader—he was both lucky and good.

Like Vanagas and others, Daumantas spent a considerable amount of his time developing, producing, and distributing underground literature. The effort he clearly devoted to this part of the struggle gives some idea of how important underground publication was to the movement. The rotary printer was easily as important as a dozen or more machine guns.

As the partisan movement got simultaneously smaller through attrition and more organised, Daumantas showed skills in intelligence and counterintelligence. He helped to reveal that Markulis was a Soviet infiltrator and helped move the venue due to be attended by a large gathering of partisan leaders that Markulis had tried to organise on 17 January 1947. If it were not for his actions, the leadership of the Forest Brotherhood might have been captured at that meeting. Daumantas may very well have saved the movement. He became the intelligence chief of the Tauras district.

Although it did not yield the results that were hoped for, the Forest Brotherhood movement desperately sought to establish communications with both Western governments and the Lithuanian diaspora, such as VLIK. Daumantas was part of this effort. Daumantas' greatest exploit was escaping Lithuania. He managed to sneak across the iron curtain. During this interlude in Western Europe, Daumantas was able to provide information on the existence and exploits of the partisan struggle. He left significant written material in the form of his memoir and a short book that was, in effect, an appeal for help.[10]

For reasons that remain unclear, it was the French intelligence services that initially took the most interest in Daumantas. He was trained first by the French and then the American CIA, with an emphasis on communications skills and intelligence collection. During his stay in the West, he also married a Lithuanian exile, Nijolė Bražėnaitė, a doctor who survived him by many decades.

Daumantas was parachuted back into Lithuania along with two other Forest Brothers in October 1950. An unmarked American C-47 cargo plane, flown by two Czech veterans of the British RAF, delivered the three parachutists from a base in Wiesbaden, Germany.[11] (The Western intelligence operations that conducted such missions are discussed in Chapter 12.) The return of Daumantas, and his promotion to the higher rank of major in the movement, caused panic among the Soviets. Literally thousands of Soviet security forces were detailed to search for him. As we have later learned, the Western intelligence operations were heavily compromised by infiltrators from Soviet intelligence. But these infiltrators also knew that Daumantas was, in fact, the real thing, a partisan leader. He was eventually killed by Soviet security forces in a village south of Kaunas in 1951, having been betrayed by an informer. He is considered a national hero in Lithuania.

Kalniškės forest—the Lithuanian Alamo

An early but legendary battle between Forest Brothers and Soviets happened very early in the struggle. In the south of Lithuania, west of Alytus, a band of Forest Brothers had gathered around a local leader, Jonas Neifalta ('Lakūnas'—The Flier). Lakūnas had served as a non-commissioned officer in Lithuania's elite Ulonai. His wife, Albina, also served in the partisan unit as a machine gunner. The pair had gone into hiding after Lakūnas had been shot at and detained by Soviet soldiers in late 1944. He escaped a guarded hospital ward and took up the partisan life.

On 16 May 1945, Lakūnas and his wife had gathered between ninety and 120 partisans in the area west of Alytus. As this and similar engagements taught the Forest Brothers, it was difficult if not possible to hide such a force. Although they had moved several times, eventually the NKVD caught up with the unit in Kalniškė forest. The 220th NKVD regiment, which greatly outnumbered the partisan detachment, surrounded the Forest Brothers' encampment on Meškakalnis hill. Unbeknownst to the NKVD attackers, the Forest Brothers had dug entrenchments and fighting positions, under supervision of their leader and several other of the Forest Brothers who had military experience.[12]

To conserve ammunition, the defenders waited until the approaching Soviet troops were within 60 to 70 metres. Automatic gunfire, including Albina on a machine gun, combined with grenades being rolled down the hill, devastated the attacking NKVD troops. The battle dragged on and became a meat-grinder for the NKVD troops, who eventually overcame the partisans through sheer numbers, though a number of them were able to escape. The eventual toll was forty-five to sixty-five partisan dead and around 400 NKVD dead. The dead included Albina Neifaltienė ('Pušelė'— roughly 'Little Pine'), felled by a sniper shot in the battle. As valiant as this battle was, the partisan movement could not survive too many such engagements against such a numerous enemy. The partisan dead were buried in a mass grave excavated by an aircraft bomb. After independence, the heroic dead were exhumed and reburied with honours.

Lakūnas managed to escape but fell in another battle on 20 November 1945. Surrounded, he shot himself rather than face capture and torture. His mutilated body was dumped in the centre of a local town for some days in order to intimidate the population.

The Battle of Merkinė

It was generally unheard of for the Forest Brothers to attempt to seize territory. But in late 1945, Forest Brothers in the far south of Lithuania came close to doing so. Merkinė is an ancient town in the far south of Lithuania. Soviet oppression was bitter there. Soviet authorities had burned down forty-eight farmsteads in the vicinity, killed thirty-seven local residents, and arrested 120 others.[13] In response, the local Forest Brothers, under their already rising leader Vanagas, described above, felt that they had to respond.

On 15 December 1945, in one of the largest partisan actions of this struggle, around 200 Forest Brothers under Vanagas raided and occupied Merkinė. The Soviet military post and some administrative buildings were taken by surprise. Weapons, ammunition, documents, and typewriters were seized. The Soviet forces took refuge in the town's Catholic and Orthodox churches, from which they fired upon the Forest Brothers. The partisans were reluctant to shoot at their own churches, so the Soviets managed to hold out until reinforcements arrived. Eventually, the partisans retreated. Five partisans lost their lives that day, but seventeen Soviets fell in the action. The battle cemented Vanagas as a brave and credible leader. Once again, though, it was not the sort of ratio that a partisan movement could easily maintain.

Burning the Studebakers

Lukša's memoir tells of an operation to inhibit illegitimate elections near Prienai, north of Alytus. The partisan leader Kazimieras Pinkvarta ('Dešinys'—roughly, Right-Hander), set up an ambush operation to interdict election officials. Two partisans wearing Soviet uniforms set up a fake checkpoint to stop official vehicles. Partisans with machine guns hiding in the forest alongside the road would disarm the Soviets at gunpoint.

This went on all day. Seven captured cars and trucks were rolled into the forest and hidden. These include a number of American Studebakers and a Ford, both having been given to the Soviets through Lend Lease. At the end of the day, the Forest Brothers had amassed a group of prisoners and captured weapons. The election materials were destroyed. Here's Lukša's account:

> The inferior confiscated weapons were tossed onto the partisans' campfire and burned. The superior weapons were appropriated by the partisans. After that, the partisans separated the Communist Party members from the regular Russians [i.e. conscripts]. They lined up the Communist Party members. After they were lined up, Dešinys gave the order to shoot. The first Communist Party member in the line was handed a weapon and told to shoot his comrades. As the executions took place, the regular Russians stood by, rubbing their hands with glee. 'For once, the bastards got what they deserved,' one of them said. The regular Russians were given three of the confiscated vehicles and sent on their way.[14]

The remaining vehicles, three Studebakers and a Ford, were torched. This episode was drenched in both revenge and mercy. Dešinys continued to lead partisans until he went to his death in 1949.

The Queen of the Pancake Ball

Some of the Lithuanian partisans' exploits are the sorts of things that legends are made of. Anelė Senkutė's day job was as an accountant in the municipal government in Marijampolė district. But she was also secretly a liaison to the local Forest Brothers. Several local Soviet officials were infamous as oppressors of the local area, and a decision was made to assassinate them. In February 1947, Senkutė staged a fake engagement party on Shrove Tuesday. The lure of a fine spread of Shrovetide pancakes and ample vodka was used as leverage. She invited a number of local Communist officials. But these pancakes were to be fatal ones.

One problem with this scheme was that Senkutė did not actually have a fiancée and needed to find one. The legendary partisan Kazimieras Pyplys, code-named 'Mažytis' ('The Little One'), was recruited for the task. An unusually tall man, even in a country known for producing tall people, Mažytis was already a famous fighter. A former medical student, he was a boxer and master of several martial arts. Mažytis was also known for his skill as a marksman with many different firearms. Importantly, he also had a forged set of papers saying he had already done his Soviet military service, which allowed him some degree of freedom at a point when people of his age were routinely locked up on suspicion of draft evasion. The plan was originally to put poison in the food and drink, such as cyanide or strychnine. Mažytis travelled to Kaunas to look for poison but could find none.

Part of the problem with the plan was finding a set of decent clothing that could actually fit the improbably tall Mažytis. But a suit was eventually found, and the party started. Mažytis ate an improbable amount of pork fat to line his stomach so that he could match the Soviet guests shot for shot with the vodka. Senkutė and Mažytis kept up the cover story long enough and enough of the targets turned up for the, evidently, excellent pancakes. After much revelry, our accountant and the tall boxer produced pistols and shot dead the first secretary of the provincial Communist Party, the chair of the district executive committee, a Soviet police officer, and three other local Communist 'activists'. Although Senkutė was wounded by returning gunfire, she and the others fled. Her cover now blown, Senkutė had to go to the forest and join the partisans; she died later in the year when her bunker was attacked by Soviet security forces. She has been nicknamed 'blynų baliaus karalienė'— The Queen of the Pancake Ball.[15]

Mažytis went on to greater fame in the movement. He managed to sneak out of Lithuania with Daumantas (one of the reasons we know his stories is through the Daumantas memoir). In 1949, he was smuggled back into Lithuania from Sweden and became a leader in Dzukija, in the south of Lithuania, under the legendary Vanagas. He died in September 1949, cornered by the Soviets, near Alytus.

The Lions of Raišupis

In July 1947, six partisans had been chased from one area to another for days. They had been dashing around, trying to keep one step ahead of the Soviet security forces as they spread warning of imminent deportations. People would flee into the woods, warned by this small band of Forest Brothers under the command of Juozas

Stanaitis ('Liūtas'—The Lion). He was thirty-five years old and had served in the Lithuanian Army before the war. His squad were known as the Lions. On the morning of 30 July, they took refuge in a farmstead.

By midday, however, the Soviet forces had discovered the partisans. The Lions attempted to flee but discovered a vastly superior force had the farmstead surrounded. Liūtas and his comrades holed up in a stone barn that gave good cover against gunfire. The Lions were known as keen marksmen. Their precision gunfire felled several dozen Soviet soldiers around the periphery of the farm. Gradually, more firepower was brought to bear, and the Lions started running out of ammunition. Several of them were hit. At least one partisan bravely sallied out of the barn under covering fire to salvage arms and ammunition from dead Soviets in the farmyard. Eventually, the Soviets won. All six partisans fell, but several of them detonated grenades in acts of suicide. Lukša gives a toll of sixty-seven Soviet dead.[16]

The butcher's bill

The Soviet occupiers kept precise statistics. During the period of 1944 to 1953, Soviet records show that 20,103 partisans were killed in action in Lithuania, while 12,921 Soviet security forces fell. Another 2,619 civilian fatalities are recorded, many of whom were Communist Party officials and collaborators, as well as unfortunate people caught up in battles.[17] There were a small number of fatalities after 1953. Records show 4,461 Lithuanian partisans captured in 1946 and 3,679 in 1947.[18] These were certainly not the only people arrested, as many arrests occurred before and after that point. Thousands of people were sent to the Gulag as either partisans or supporters of partisans.

These are not insignificant figures. Given the size of Lithuania, this is an intensity of conflict greater than that of the Northern Ireland 'Troubles', if measured in terms of numbers killed. Somewhat over 3,500 people died in armed violence in Northern Ireland between the late 1960s and 1998 on all sides of the conflict, a much longer period of time, in a place only slightly smaller in size and population.

The armed struggle faded out, but other struggles continued. Non-violent struggle, including underground publishing, continued all the way until independence was regained. Some people continued the struggle behind the wire in Gulag camps, as we shall see in a later chapter.

PART 3

HELPING AND HINDERING
ARMED RESISTANCE

9

THE SOVIET SIDE OF THE EQUATION

There is always more than one side in any conflict. To understand the partisan war in the Baltic states, we should also discuss and analyse the opponents of the Forest Brothers. Who were they and how did they fight? The same archival sources that give us information about the Forest Brotherhood also give us significant information about the Soviet military, paramilitary forces, police, and civilians who were part of the effort to conquer and occupy the region. While some Soviet-era memoirs exist, such as secret policeman Pavel Sudoplatov's book,[1] they are short on specifics and often mention the Baltic states only in passing.

The Soviets worked hard to incorporate the Baltic states into the Soviet Union and went to great lengths to imprint a Soviet economy and society on to Estonia, Latvia, and Lithuania. Soviet power, and Stalinism in particular, had to appear monolithic. Resistance of any kind, let alone armed partisan movements, was viewed as a serious threat and, for the true ideologues of Marxism–Leninism, an obstacle to the inevitable progress of mankind.

As the tactics and techniques used by the Soviet state were generally the same across the region, this is an area where it is possible to make some region-wide generalisations. Where applicable, regional differences and nuances will be pointed out, but this chapter looks at the three countries as a whole. Most of this chapter could easily also apply to Belarus, Ukraine, and parts of Poland, where similar conflicts were also underway.

Who were the combatants?

The Soviet security forces were composed of a variety of different types of people and units, including soldiers of both the Red Army and the internal security forces, secret police, local police, and a variety of armed auxiliaries.

Internal troops: NKVD/NKGB/MGB/MVD soldiers

The primary Soviet combatants in the Baltic conflict were the internal security troops of the secret police. The internal security arm of the state took on a number of different names over the course of the Soviet Union's existence. During the Stalin era, the names changed a fair bit, but the general structure and purpose did not. At the beginning of the period covered by this book, the security services were under the aegis of the Soviet interior ministry, known as the NKVD (People's Commissariat for Internal Affairs). But by the end, the interior ministry had split into the MVD (Ministry of Internal Affairs) and the KGB (Committee for State Security), with the latter taking on responsibility for secret police work (after a brief spell in which it was known as the MGB, or Ministry for State Security).

Regardless of the title of the day, the Soviet Union had a large structure of troops, equipped as if they were the army, for the purposes of 'internal security'. Some of their duties were to protect infrastructure, railroads, prisoners, and borders. They were the paramilitary backup to the police and the secret police services. The internal troops of the Soviet Union had evolved into a separate army outside the control of the military. These troops of the NKVD had mushroomed during the Second World War, and there were numerous regiments and divisions of NKVD internal troops. Although they were not originally intended for frontline combat, many such regiments and divisions ended up fighting the Germans on the front due to the exigencies of the war. Hundreds of thousands of Soviet citizens—if not over a million—served in such units during the war.

Many sources casually refer to Soviet 'internal troops' as paramilitary, but they were paramilitary only in the sense that they were not under the control of the army or defence ministry. These units were staffed with conscripts doing their national service and were mostly trained and equipped as infantry units, with weapons all the way up to mortars and light artillery. In many ways, they combined the worst features of both army and police. These units had arrest authority but were not under the discipline of the army chain of command and were answerable only to the secret police. It should be noted that people from Baltic nations did serve in the internal troops but almost never in the Baltic region, as it was general Soviet policy that ethnic minority conscripts would never be stationed in their home area. An Estonian conscript, for example, would serve his time in somewhere like Kazan or Novosibirsk.

The border guard units of the Soviet Union were similarly trained, equipped, and organised. Border guard units were prominent in the conflict as well. All three Baltic states had coastlines, and Lithuania has a land frontier with Poland and East Prussia, now Kaliningrad. Strong control of the borders kept people from fleeing and also inhibited external efforts to help the Forest Brothers.

Regular military forces: the Red Army

The Red Army itself was also a combatant in the struggle with Baltic partisans. The Red Army was most prominent in the 1944–5 period, when the front with the Germans passed through the Baltic states. There were a number of clashes between Forest Brothers and Red Army troops in 1944 and 1945. But as the front moved further west, so did the Red Army for the most part. The Soviet Army was composed of conscripts. As a rule, Baltic conscripts would be sent elsewhere in the Soviet Union for their service.

Generally, pacification of Forest Brothers, enforcing public order, and establishing the iron grip of Soviet rule in the Baltic states was the job of the security services, not the army. As the Red Army chased the German military further west, the role of rear-area security, pacification, and Sovietisation fell to the NKVD interior troops who advanced alongside and right behind the army.

Forest Brothers tried to avoid direct conflict with and attacks upon regular army units. Baltic partisans rightly felt that drawing Red Army units into the conflict would be an error. Some even felt sympathy for the conscript troops that made up these units.

Raids to gain arms and ammunition were possible, but direct confrontations were viewed to be largely unfavourable due to the abject imbalance of numbers and firepower. After 1945, conflict between Forest Brothers and the regular army was mostly limited to a number of instances when Red Army troops were called in to reinforce internal security troops.

Regular and secret police

You cannot run a police state without police. The Soviet Union established a full infrastructure of uniformed police—confusingly referred to as 'militia'—and secret police in the occupied Baltic states. In order to avoid confusion, the term 'police' is used in this book instead of the Soviet term 'militia'. Generally, the Soviet authorities distrusted local police left over from previous regimes. Some were considered collaborators, as indeed some were. Many low-ranking police in non-political roles managed to keep their jobs in the new system, but thousands of ethnic Russian policemen were also sent to the area. Additional local staff were recruited. Both uniformed police and plainclothes secret police were combatants in this war. Both were also frequent targets for action by partisans.

The brute squads: 'Destruction Battalions'

Just like the Nazis, the Soviet occupiers relied on collaborators for some of the grassroots-level work of occupation. The Soviet authorities recruited, trained, and armed local people to help with counterinsurgency work just as the Nazis did. Known as 'Destruction Battalions' and often referred to as *istrebiteli* ('destroyers' in Russian), these units had originally been recruited in 1941 from people too old, too young, or otherwise unfit to fight in the regular forces to help with defence against the attacking Germans. By 1944, though, the same name was being used to refer to irregular and auxiliary units recruited in and around 'liberated' areas to fight nationalist partisans and secure rear areas from attack.

Istrebiteli were initially recruited in the Baltic states by offering exemption from military duty. At first, people did not know what they were signing up for, and once they found that they were to fight fellow Baltic people, desertions were rampant and recruitment was more difficult. Partisan groups hindered recruitment. Eventually, only the desperate and the outcasts of society joined these 'battalions', which were rarely, if ever, anything close in size to a military battalion. Lukša, the Lithuanian Forest Brother who left a memoir, disparagingly refers to them as 'human trash'.[2] In some cases, ethnic minorities such as Poles joined the *istrebiteli*, as the Soviets used ethnic differences as leverage. In 1946, the strength of these units was reported as over 8,000 in Lithuania, over 15,000 in Latvia, and nearly 6,000 in Estonia.[3] They were a much larger phenomenon further south in Belarus and Ukraine, where similar struggles were also taking place.

These units were often poorly armed and poorly trained. The training curriculum survives in the archives and was only sixty-four hours in length, with only four hours of shooting practice and six hours of counterinsurgency tactics. Weapons varied widely, and ammunition was sometimes unavailable. Some *istrebiteli* units initially only had enough weapons for part of their unit. Uniforms were inconsistent, and working conditions varied significantly. Some *istrebiteli* clearly enhanced their existence by foraging and scavenging off the local population they were meant to defend. It is truly ironic that Soviet sources referred to partisans as 'bandits', but the closest thing to actual bandits were these *istrebiteli*.

The Destruction Battalions were often considered the worst enemy of the partisans. As well as being viewed as turncoats, some of the worst atrocities of the period were perpetrated by *istrebiteli*. They were full of actual criminals, drunkards, and opportunists. Many of these units engaged in predatory behaviour, which is not surprising given the recruiting base from which they were drawn. Soviet authorities often turned a blind eye to the excesses committed by these units. Pay was often sporadic early on, and at times the units stole from farmers and villagers to survive. Rape and arson were not unknown. Officers supervising them often had a number of small detachments scattered across a range of villages, so oversight was weak, with a commander often seeing his various detachments once a week or so.

Gradually, more resources had to be poured into these units. Army soldiers demobilised from active duty (often recovering from injury), Communist Party members, and Komsomol (Communist youth movement) members were used to prop up these units.

Eventually, more commissars were appointed to provide closer supervision, and more equipment and training was provided.

The *istrebiteli* units were of questionable military value and usually lost in open conflicts with partisans. Forest Brothers infiltrated the units early on, which was easy to do because of poor recruiting standards. Despite their drawbacks, however, they provided a security force presence across the length and breadth of the countryside, thus making partisan life more difficult. Despite their problems, the Destruction Battalions had local language skills and knowledge of local areas, which was ruthlessly exploited by other arms of the security apparatus. The Soviets viewed these units as having a moderate value that exceeded their shortcomings.

Party cadres

Much of the work of collectivising agriculture and Sovietising the Baltic economy was performed by Communist Party staff. The period literature often refers to them as 'activists'. Routine work of tax collection, surveying property, collectivising farms, and generally dispossessing the peasantry was done by party officials. Because of ubiquitous partisan activity, party officials and offices needed to be armed for their own self-defence. There are few recorded instances of party cadres conducting offensive operations, but there were many recorded incidents where armed party members fired back at partisans. It should be noted that this was not simply arming office workers; most of these party cadres were war veterans who were more than capable of defending themselves.

Counterinsurgency tactics and techniques

The Soviet campaign to vanquish and pacify the Baltic states bears many similarities to later counterinsurgency efforts elsewhere in the Cold War and post-Cold War eras in that it was ruthless and consumed many resources but was ultimately effective. The Soviet Union had a reasonable understanding of partisan tactics, having engaged in partisan warfare itself, but the security services were also capable of learning from mistakes and improving their tactics. The counterinsurgency campaign used a variety of tactics, most of which were not new or innovative but improvements and adaptations of previous knowledge and experience.

Omnipresence

Successful counterinsurgency is often a case of providing enough police, security, and auxiliaries around the area in order to provide situational awareness and secure settlements and property from insurgent activity. To be effective, this needs to be backed up with communications and reinforcements in case smaller outposts are attacked. Gradually, the Soviet authorities tried to establish an armed presence in as many settlements as possible in contested areas, even if the presence was token or sporadic. Eventually, such a strategy proved to be resource-intensive in Lithuania, Latvia, and Estonia, with estimates of twenty-five to thirty security personnel per partisan in areas of active partisan activity. Clearly, such an approach only works when an overwhelming disparity in manpower is available.

Traditional military and paramilitary operations

Traditional Second World War-style force-on-force battles were rare. They did occur, but most battles occurred in 1944 and 1945 rather than later in the struggle. As discussed in Chapter 6, the partisan resistance eventually divided itself into smaller units in order to survive. However, traditional conventional military operations were conducted to suppress the partisan movement. These consisted of classical military operations well known in other counterinsurgency campaigns—checkpoints and patrols on routes of movement combined with identification checks and patting down civilians to check for weapons. Objectives that could be partisan targets were garrisoned for their own protection.

Rural areas were subjected to periodic sweeps and patrols, sometimes involving hundreds or even over 1,000 security force personnel. Soldiers were sent out on listening posts for days, and reconnaissance troops sometimes held farms under surveillance for days or even weeks at a time to detect visits by partisans. Locations that were suspected to be Forest Brother hideouts were searched, sometimes by lines of soldiers an arm's length apart from each other. These were heavy-handed, time-consuming, and labour-intensive tactics. They were usually highly obvious to the observers, but such operations were occasionally successful. Even when they were not successful, they were deterrents to the local population and served to make the partisans far more careful. By forcing the Forest Brothers to exercise much more caution, everyday life became more time consuming. By forcing more lengthy journeys to ever more remote bunkers or requiring a partisan group to reconnoitre a route for hours before travelling, such measures served to make partisan life and partisan operations more difficult.

Human intelligence

An extensive component of counterinsurgency was the use of basic human intelligence collection methods. Classic counterintelligence techniques were critical to the struggle. The secret police set up networks of informants and undercover agents. Work had gone into establishing such networks in the 1940–1 occupation, but that work had largely been undone by warfare and Nazi occupation. By 1944, little was left of those networks, and the secret police started over again.

As would be expected of a secret police infrastructure with decades of experience, there was a degree of rigour and structure to these efforts. This was a vast police state with years of experience from the 1930s Great Terror. There were manuals, processes, and training courses on how to do this sort of work. Chief agents, so-called 'rezidents', supervised intelligence networks, sometimes as many as ten villages. These case officers supervised a variety of types of agents and informants. Simple informers were usually normal residents of a rural area and mostly passed on information they acquired by passive observation. But there were also agents recruited and trained for more than simple observation of their environment. People who had occupational reasons to travel around rural areas, such as postal workers, forestry workers, railway workers, and itinerant traders, were recruited and told to look for signs of partisan activity while doing their daily jobs.[4] By 1951, the Soviets had 27,700 informers in Lithuania,[5] and it is probable a similar level of penetration of society had been achieved in Estonia and Latvia.

These secret police residents also recruited internal penetration agents, often captured and converted partisans, who were used to infiltrate partisan groups. Captured partisans could be offered amnesty and the safety of their families in exchange for returning to the forests to betray their comrades. Sometimes, fake escapes from confinement were staged in order to give the spy a reasonable excuse for returning to his old group. Often, the civilian relatives of the flipped partisan were the conduit for communications. Surviving memoirs from the partisan era often talk of such turncoats.

Informants were recruited by numerous means. Some were clearly opportunists seeking personal gain. Informants were paid, and at a time of scarcity sometimes bordering on famine, money can be a powerful motive. There were other opportunists who were revenge-seekers looking to settle scores. Some would have easily been recruits for the Destruction Battalions but were too young, too old, female, or otherwise unsuited for that work. Fear and coercion were also used. An informant could have military service delayed or cancelled, either for the informant themselves or for a relative. Being a police informant could keep you or your family off a deportation list. In rural areas, a farmer with a larger holding could easily be declared a 'kulak' and sent off to Siberia, and there was a fair amount of discretion at the local level about who was placed on such a list. Being an informant could literally save your family. Every form of coercive leverage available was used at one point or another.[6]

Agents and informers varied in quality. Some might even have been fictional, padding the books of a corrupt officer, as such practices were not unknown across the Soviet Union. Others were simply daft or useless. Some people played both sides of the game and actively double-crossed the Soviet occupiers. People coerced into informing sometimes told the partisans that they were now nominally on the Soviet payroll and then served the partisans by feeding useless or misleading information to the Soviets. Manhunts for fictional partisans were not unknown. Sometimes agents infiltrated into Forest Brother units confessed to the partisans and fed back false information to their handlers. This aspect of the war was fought in both directions. The Soviet secret police fully understood this dynamic and routinely doublechecked on their informants. Suspected traitors were often killed.

Interrogation and torture

Practically every torture technique known to man was employed in the Baltic states at one point or another to break captured partisans. By the time of the Forest Brotherhood movement, the Soviet security forces had decades of experience in breaking people.[7] Practical evidence of many such tactics remains in evidence as grisly exhibits in museums in the Baltic states.

Torture and other harsh interrogation tactics had mixed results. Most prisoners were broken, and many gave up actionable intelligence. Others agreed to become informants or double agents in order to make the torture stop. Although useful intelligence could be extracted through such methods, a lot of useless information could be gathered as well. People can and will say literally anything to make unbearable torture stop. Hundreds of thousands of people in the Soviet Union confessed to deeds they did not do, made up stories, implicated others, and admitted to beliefs that they did not hold because of physical and psychological torture. Everyone knew this sort of thing went on. So torture had a psychological effect. Partisans knew that, despite their best intentions, information could be wrung out of them and that their imprisonment would be highly unpleasant. For this reason, many cornered partisans committed suicide, as has been noted in many instances in previous chapters.

Covert operations, fake partisans, and provocations

The secret police used many tactics to locate and identify Forest Brothers as well as their supporters and potential future supporters. Some of these tactics were simple, and others were more elaborate. At the simple end, known sources of food were placed under surveillance by the NKVD. Clandestine surveillance teams would spend a day or longer viewing a chicken coop or a bucket of milk that had been left out through binoculars or a telescope.

A tactic used to great effect across the Baltic states (and elsewhere, such as Ukraine) was the phenomenon of fake partisans. A fake partisan, or occasionally a former partisan turned informant, would sometimes be used to test the loyalty of suspected Forest

Brotherhood supporters. How would the farmer react when he found a partisan in his barn? Another perfidious tactic was to leak documents. This tactic was documented in Ukraine, but it appears likely to have had more widespread use. Police would visit someone's home and question them but 'accidentally' leave a document naming various known partisans as Soviet informants in the hope that partisans would kill the named informants.

In some more elaborate operations, the NKVD would train and equip small units that looked like and acted like real Forest Brother detachments. In some cases, former Soviet partisans with years of experience fighting the Germans were used for this. Fake partisans took advantage of the fluid nature of partisan warfare. Across the region, there were efforts by the Forest Brothers to organise into broader regional and national groups to coordinate their efforts. This meant that one group in a rural area reaching out tentatively to a neighbouring group was not an unknown occurrence. A fake Forest Brother band could infiltrate larger groups, allowing the NKVD to locate and raid an encampment or roll up a whole network.

Fake Forest Brotherhood units sometimes perpetrated atrocities in order to damage the movement's reputation among the population. Fake Forest Brothers would, for example, rob villagers or ransack a farm to discredit the movement. Rape, murder, and arson, as well as common theft and vandalism, have been reported. Soviet media outlets, keen to promote the idea that partisans were bandits or terrorists, would promote the outrages by fake partisans. To this day, in referring to particular events, people trying to take a Russian- or Soviet-slanted view on the era will quote incidents widely believed to have been perpetrated by fake partisans.

Terror and intimidation

The Soviets fully understood that partisan resistance movements needed the support of the population. Even the best foragers could not find enough to eat in the forests and swamps to support partisan bands. Some Soviet tactics were designed to counter local support of Forest Brothers through terror and intimidation. The most obvious and well-known tactic was to punish any farmer or villager who supported the Forest Brothers. People caught supporting partisans would be deported or imprisoned. This forced partisans and their supporters to be more careful. Forcing farmers and partisans to use stealth and trickery to feed the partisan units had the effect of reducing the size of partisan bands.

Another tactic was to place the dead bodies of partisans in visible public places in towns and villages where family members and friends could see the dead partisans. Schoolchildren were even made to look at the dead bodies. Repressive tactics in the countryside often had the opposite effect to what had been intended. Vicious repressions caused some people to join the partisans to avoid arrest or deportation. Others joined to seek revenge against friends, neighbours, or family members. In response to the abuse of the bodies of dead partisans, some Forest Brothers, predominantly in Lithuania, committed suicide with grenades to literally deface themselves so that their relatives would not see them dead.

Dead partisans were often buried covertly in mass graves to prevent commemoration of the dead. This was considered particularly loathsome by the local residents. Efforts have been made to locate and re-bury the remains of these dead partisans in the decades since independence was re-established.

Amnesties

Even the security forces understood that an 'all stick and no carrot' approach does not always yield the best possible results. A no-quarter policy of pursuing every partisan to their death can end up with a radicalised opposition. Many counterinsurgency campaigns over the decades understood, or eventually learned, that in order to win such a war you must give the rank-and-file members of the enemy forces a pathway out of the insurgent lifestyle. Amnesties had been used earlier, during the Russian Civil War, to some effect.[8]

Amnesties became a potent tool in the Soviet counterinsurgency arsenal. Some of the Forest Brothers were from the poorest of backgrounds, and some Soviet Communists believed that they were simply being exploited by their class enemies and thus that some leniency should be shown to such class allies. Also, there was doubtless some jaded but realistic cynicism among Soviet leaders. Some people had joined the resistance out of desperation. Many Forest Brothers would be cold, tired, hungry, and sick. Such people

Fig. 1: Lithuanian Forest Brother leader Juozas Lukša 'Daumantas'

Fig. 2: Forest Brothers in southern Lithuania in the late 1940s

Fig. 3: Latvian Forest Brothers in the Kabile forest, early September 1946

Fig. 4: A Forest Brother grave in Perloja, Lithuania

Fig. 5: The Forest Brother memorial in Merkinė, Lithuania,
the site of a heated battle in 1945

Fig. 6: A memorial to August Sabbe, the last Estonian Forest Brother.
He drowned while escaping capture by the KGB in 1978

Fig. 7: Estonians taking up arms in 1941

CHAPTER 1.　　　JOINT CIA/SIS INQUIRY INTO SECURITY OF EXISTING

OPERATIONS IN LITHUANIA

1. The object of this inquiry is to present a picture of the security
position of current operations in Lithuania with a view to affording
guidance to those conducting any future joint CIA/SIS operations in
that country. It has been necessary not only to study the developments surrounding the important M.G.B. offensive against networks in
the field (December 1952 - January 1953) and subsequent news thereof,
but also to make a retrospective examination of the security of those
networks in the hope of discovering whether any of them were compromised
before the said offensive took place. This has involved a considerable
exchange of information between the two Services including traffic from
the following:

    (a) DEKSNYS (Swedish and S.I.S. traffic)
    (b) DRAMELIS
    (c) SKRAJUNAS
    (d) JACK

2. Although the inquiry is confined to purely operational questions and
is not aimed in any way at presenting a verdict on the political controversies dividing the different emigre organisations from which
operational staff has been recruited, it has nevertheless been
necessary to study the relations between these organisations and
to determine to what extent they may have affected the security
position in the field. It has also been found necessary to study
the traffic from all the networks in order to consider the possibility,
in the event of hostile control, of the said controversies being exploited
in order to maintain and even exacerbate existing divisions among the
emigre organisations.

3. For the sake of clarity, the present report is divided into chapters
on the four networks referred to in Paragraph 1 above (with appendices
as required), followed by conclusions and recommendations for any
future joint operations.

Fig. 8: Archival CIA documents, now declassified, have revealed
much about Western attempts to liaise with Baltic Forest Brothers

Fig. 9: Many Forest Brothers were imprisoned in Gulag camps. This is one of the last remaining examples, in Perm, Russia

could be persuaded to quit the war. It was believed, with some partial justification, that at least some of the rank and file wanted to give up but felt that they could not.

Several waves of amnesties occurred over the period of the partisan war, with varying degrees of success. What is not clear is how many of the people covered by such amnesties were actual partisans. Rather a high percentage were Red Army deserters, draft evaders, and other fugitives simply hiding out in the countryside, not active partisan fighters. Regardless, all of those categories were the type of people routinely recruited into the Forest Brotherhood. Amnesties thus drained the recruitment pool. In some instances, local Communist authorities authorised the return from exile of families of partisan fighters who took up amnesty offers. In some cases, families of partisans were given written guarantees that they would not be deported if the partisan surrendered. Early waves of amnesties, as well as the hardships of the first two winters, drained the forests of these potential partisan recruits.

Not every amnesty was done in good faith. There are instances when amnestied partisans were later arrested or deported. Tales of amnesties being just clever tricks by the authorities did circulate but were based on local aberrations or, possibly, were hyperbole spread among partisans to improve retention. However, overall, amnesties were a highly effective counterinsurgency tactic. There was guidance from higher up the Soviet chain of command to try to maintain the integrity of amnesties. Where amnestied people were betrayed, it was generally because of local officials defying official policy. However, amnestied partisans were harshly punished if they were found aiding partisans still in hiding, and such arrests were clearly authorised. In addition, people who joined partisan bands after an amnesty was announced were not eligible for amnesty. In some cases, amnestied Forest Brothers ascended through Soviet society, and some even served as police officers.

How big were the amnesties? We can look at an example from Lithuania. Statiev calculates that, between 1944 and 1956, 38,822 fugitives were amnestied in Lithuania, of which 21.5 per cent were considered to be partisans, although even the Soviet authorities agreed that the percentage was likely higher, as some partisans taking advantage of the amnesties claimed to be conscription evaders in order to be treated more leniently.[9] Overall, though, amnesties were one of the most effective counterinsurgency tools.

Collectivisation of agriculture

Starvation played a role in eroding the partisan movement. People have to eat, and the Baltic forests provide only limited foraging opportunities. In all three countries, the partisan movement needed and received support in the form of food from farmers. The gradual collectivisation of agriculture was not, in itself, a weapon of counterinsurgency so much as a broad policy goal of the Soviet state. But it was a de facto weapon in that it did as much to defeat the Forest Brothers as any other tactic. Few farmers wanted to join collective farms, and the Soviets had to resort to widespread coercion. Deportation and imprisonment were used to remove prosperous farmers, deemed as undesirable 'kulaks', and other rural residents seen as an impediment to collectivisation. Deportation operations were specifically intended to break the back of resistance to the formation of collective farms.

Widely dispersed small farmers were a strong source of support to partisans in all three countries. It was difficult for the Soviet authorities to closely supervise farmers or keep them from feeding partisans. Farmers not only actively fed partisans but would also turn a blind eye to them taking a bit of food. Many farmers could easily have an 'agricultural accident' and 'accidentally' leave some potatoes or a bucket of milk lying around somewhere. Farmers were also sources of shelter and information. The relationship was often mutual. Forest Brothers would try to protect farmers, and many a farmer stayed informed about what was going on in the wider world because some nearby partisans had a radio set. Depredations against farmers were sometimes the motive for revenge acts by Forest Brothers, and there are many stories of partisans protecting smallholders.

By aggregating smaller farms into larger collective and state farms, it was easier for the security services to keep an eye on the farmers and the food supply, both directly and indirectly. Police or security staff could keep an eye on things more effectively, but the NKVD could also more easily recruit informants who would be able to inform on possible support to partisans or food going missing. This does not mean that collective farms did not find ways to aid Forest Brothers, but the whole business of doing so became more perilous and difficult, both for freedom fighters and for farmers.

Documentation and administrative control

The Soviet regime was a highly bureaucratic totalitarian state. In order to control a population, the population needed to be counted and documented. In the case of the Baltic states, it took years for this process to occur. The dislocations caused by Soviet and Nazi occupations and the war sweeping through the Baltic states in both directions, compounded by people fleeing the country or heading into the woods, meant nobody knew who was living where. Pre-war records, if they existed, were only of modest use.

Establishing the bureaucracy to count, record, and issue documentation, especially in remote areas where partisan activity was strongest, was a lengthy process.

Because of this situation, pre-war identity documents issued by the Baltic governments were still used and considered valid for some years after the war. Not everyone even had an identity document, and some pre-war identity documents did not even have a photograph. The process of issuing everyone with a Soviet internal passport bearing a photograph gradually became a tool of population control. Partisans hiding in the forests had little opportunity to gain new documentation, except by forgery or subterfuge. But this also offered an opportunity.

Forced migration

The forced removal of a percentage of the population was also a tactic. The logic was simple. People in prison or in exile settlements thousands of miles from home could not support Forest Brothers or become recruits for local partisan units. The 1941 deportations were already described in Chapter 2. From the point of the Soviet return in 1944, deportations were selective and focused on eliminating pockets of resistance. From 1944 to 1947, the deportations were in the thousands of people per year.

The Soviet authorities inflicted a second, larger wave of deportations that hit all three Baltic states, concurrent with the widespread effort to collectivise agriculture in 1948 and 1949. In Lithuania, 'Operation Vesna' was a mass round-up of people in May 1948. Around 40,000 people, a quarter of whom were children, were detained and deported.

'Operation Priboi' happened the following year and affected all three of the Baltic states. Over 75,000 police, activists, *istrebiteli*, and internal troops were assembled for a massive deportation blitzkrieg. Across the three Baltic states, more than 90,000 people were rounded up and deported. The Latvian scholar Heinrichs Strods has laboriously combed archival documents and reports the number of deported in Operation Priboi as 31,917 in Lithuania, 42,149 in Latvia, and 20,713 in Estonia. Most were women (44.3 per cent) and children (28.6 per cent).[10] Some people in their nineties were deported. These efforts broke the back of rural society. Collectivisation progressed quickly after these operations.

Most people who went into exile or imprisonment in the Gulag system survived, and many of them were eventually able to return home. But the countries they returned to were very different. By the time people deported to 'internal exile' or sentenced to the Gulag camps were able to return to the Baltic states after Stalin's death, the partisan war was largely or completely over. Small farms had generally ceased to exist. Many former rural residents went to the cities upon their return, not to their home villages. However, as will be seen in chapter 12, some imprisoned Balts merely opened a new front in the war within the prison camps, and some people, in effect, became Forest Brothers behind the wire.

Conscription

Conscription was another means of controlling the population and reducing the number of available recruits. The Soviets considered the Latvians, Estonians, and Lithuanians to be Soviet citizens, and men were subject to national service. Generally, for the period of this book, conscription was for a three-year period. This was a length of time long enough to have an impact, especially later in the partisan war. Someone who turned eighteen in 1950 would not leave military service until 1953, by which point the partisan war was dwindling. A conscript from 1947 getting out in 1950 might have no farm to go back to due to collectivisation.

Whereas evasion of conscription was a widespread motive for joining the Forest Brothers, conscription itself was a tool of control. Conscripted Balts would serve in places like Murmansk, Armenia, the Chinese border, or provincial towns in Russia far from the Baltic. Desertion back into the partisans, a problem that had plagued the Germans, was geographically improbable. Furthermore, by the time these conscripts were released from service, they were fully administratively processed into the Soviet system. The Soviet system knew they existed and often put them in jobs in factories in towns and cities rather than the countryside. The system was then in a better position to keep an eye on them.

Interfering with the church

The Soviet state was officially atheist. Religion was suppressed throughout the Soviet Union, although in 1943 Stalin had reached something of a settlement with the Russian Orthodox Church out of wartime expediency. Religion of every type had been greatly depredated from 1917 onward. But Estonia, Latvia, and Lithuania were newly occupied territory. At the time, Lithuania was heavily Roman Catholic. Churchgoing Latvians were an approximate 2:1 mix of Lutherans and Catholics. Estonian churchgoers were mostly Lutheran. There was a significant Orthodox minority in all three countries. The latter is important, because the Soviet state could subordinate the Orthodox churches to the Moscow-based patriarch.

Lutherans posed less of an immediate security risk to the Soviets. The Estonian and Latvian Lutherans were standalone churches, not responsible to external hierarchies. Both had been seriously denuded of clergy. Many of the priests in both denominations were Baltic Germans and had fled the Soviet advance. The Estonian Lutheran Church did not support the resistance, as its priests felt the necessity of avoiding additional bloodshed.[11]

Soviets found the Catholic Church to be a vexation. Roman Catholics were problematic to the Soviets as their church was part of a hierarchy that had its head in Rome, outside of Moscow's control, and Catholicism was an ideological rival to Soviet Communism. Catholic priests and sacristans were active in the resistance in both Latvia and Lithuania. The vast majority of Lithuanian Forest Brothers were Catholic, and Catholics were well represented in the Latvian

169

movement. Priests helped print underground publications and even participated in the armed struggle themselves. For example, Father Justinas Lelešius served as a chaplain to Lithuanian Forest Brothers and died in combat in 1947.[12]

The Soviets used both oppression and guile to clamp down on religion. Many priests were imprisoned or exiled, and much church property was confiscated. Not wanting to create martyrs, Baltic clergy were mostly not executed, although there were some exceptions. Priests and bishops were threatened, blackmailed, and otherwise intimidated, if not to actively cooperate with the regime, then to at least not promote insurgency. More insidiously, priests were recruited as agents. Playing a longer game, KGB infiltrators were sent to become clergy, but the effects of that played out later than the period covered in this book.

Eventual victory

The partisan movement gradually ground to a halt and withered away in the 1950s. In some ways, this was inevitable. The vast weight of Soviet occupation, which encompassed all aspects of life and was backed by vastly greater resources, ultimately won out. The ruthlessness of the intelligence and security apparatus of the Soviet state played a part. The passage of time worked in favour of the Soviets.

The tactics and techniques described in this chapter were applied over a period of nine years—1944 to 1953—and achieved a victory by gradual attrition. It took a lot of brute force for the Soviets to win, but they had the resources to do so. Garrisoning rural areas with 20:1 or even 30:1 ratios of security service personnel to partisans was, for the large Soviet Union, logistically sustainable for a long time, in a way that US forces in South Vietnam or French forces in North Africa were never able to do.

The Forest Brothers could not compete with the resources arrayed against them. Partisans died or were captured and were not replaced by new recruits. The occasional wave of ad hoc recruitment, usually based on avoidance of conscription, deportation, or collectivisation, did not keep up with losses. Eventually, if a rifle broke, if a grenade was expended, or a radio battery died, it was not at all clear that it could ever be replaced. If partisans fired a few bullets, they might only be replaced by a dangerous raid in which someone might die. But when the Soviets fired bullets, they were easily replaced.

Ratios shifted at some point in the late 1940s, although the tipping point was different in different locales. As partisan activity reduced to a smaller number of rural districts, the Soviet authorities could increase their concentration of forces in the areas where partisans were still active. In 1946, there might be 100 partisans hiding out in a rural parish, with a few dozen Soviets and their proxies garrisoning a compound and venturing out on occasion. By 1952, the ratio was the other way around. Soviet authority was everywhere, and the partisans were few, venturing out only in disguise or at night.

Another factor in the Soviet victory is that the security services grew quite good at their job. In a rural district of Lithuania in 1946, for example, a few highly trained professional secret policemen were trying to do counterinsurgency work with wartime conscript NKVD interior troops who were war weary and ready to go home, backed up by auxiliary squads consisting of petty criminals and alcoholics recruited from the dregs of local society. By 1952, a more professionalised internal security force, with a higher percentage of skilled career secret policemen in charge, hardened by years of such work, were handling the bulk of the counterinsurgency. They still used conscripts, but they used them more carefully. The partisans who had survived to 1951 or 1952 were both lucky and good, but they were few, and their oppressors and hunters were skilful and plentiful. Both were good at their jobs, but there were more hunters than hunted, and the odds favoured the many over the few.

Did the population get tired of helping the partisans? This is a possibility, but it is a difficult hypothesis to prove or disprove. It certainly became more difficult for the population to help the partisans. Collectivisation of agriculture meant that the Soviet authorities were largely able to control the food supply. Pooling the farmers into state farms and collective farms made it harder to feed the Forest Brothers, and, eventually, the odds of getting caught helping partisans increased. Despite motivations, it became difficult for many people to support the Forest Brothers even if they wanted to. In this battle of the irresistible force versus the immovable object, the irresistible force eventually won. The Soviets won this conflict.

10

UNDERGROUND PRESS

No trip to Vilnius, Lithuania's capital, is complete without a visit to a particular museum. If you head west of the baroque old town on Gedimino prospektas, one of the main shopping streets, you end up passing a large green square on your right. This is Lukiškės Square. There had once been a large wooden mosque and Muslim graveyard, used by Lithuanian Tatars for centuries. Both were desecrated and removed by the Soviets. A statue of Lenin stood in the square for decades. It was removed by a newly independent Lithuania. (If you are nostalgic for it, you can go to Grūtas Park in the deep south of Lithuania and visit it too.) On the south side of Lukiškės Square, there is a large imposing building, dating from 1890 and looking like an imperial Russian courthouse. For that is what it was. Before it was other things. This building now houses the genocide museum.

In Riga, in Latvia, there is a concrete block of a building, built in 1971. It sits prominently in central Riga. It was built by the USSR to commemorate Lenin's birthday, and it had served as a museum to the Latvian Riflemen, whose legacy is, indeed, complex and was co-opted by the Soviet occupiers. It could be argued that this is in the heart of Riga. By the time this book is in print, this building should be open to visitors again.

In Tallinn, Estonia, you can stand and face the front of Toompea Castle, the seat of the Riigikogu. At your back is the odd confection of a Russian Orthodox cathedral named after Alexander Nevsky. Turn left and head down the hill. Past a park, you pass a church on your left. On your right, you see the modest headquarters of the Kaitseliit. The next building is a new glass construction that has replaced the dodgy old building with a Russian flag and odd radio antennae that I remember from my own visit in 1992.

All three of these buildings are commended to the visitor to these fine cities. They are all museums to foreign occupations from 1940 to 1991. Objects from the era of the Forest Brothers, relics from Siberian Gulags, and, in the case of the Vilnius museum, cells untouched from the point at which the KGB fled will give tangible reality to the words of this book. I openly wept the first time I went through the Lukiškės Square museum.

Beyond the smell of the detention cells, the things I remember most starkly from these museums were the yellowing sheets of paper. Usually crudely printed on rotary duplicators, carbon copied, or even manually typed out in multiple copies on aged typewriters, there were newsletters. Flyers. Whole newspapers. The Forest Brotherhood was not just an armed resistance movement. It was a literary phenomenon. Although some of these publications ran to one issue and some print runs ran to, say, ten copies, there were valiant attempts to circulate this underground literature. Some lasted for years and had print runs of hundreds of copies. They exist in these museums because they were carefully preserved as evidence by the Soviet oppressors.

Background

The establishment and maintenance of Soviet rule required at least some of the population to go along with the requests, demands, and beliefs of their new Soviet overlords. This was achieved by many means. Part of the mechanisms and infrastructure of the Soviet approach to totalitarian rule was total control of every information outlet. Books, newspapers, other publications, radio, theatre, film, education, and culture were controlled by the Soviet state and subject to strict censorship and controls. There was a monopoly on printing and broadcasting as part of an attempt to establish a monopoly on thoughts and ideas.

Newspapers, journalists, publishers, writers, radio broadcasts, and educators were early targets of the Soviet regime. They were not ignored by the Nazis either during the 1941–4 Nazi interregnum. Anyone in media or culture who did not follow the approved line faced job loss, imprisonment, or worse. One of the objectives of the Sovietisation of media, culture, and information was to gradually extinguish the very idea of independent Estonia, Latvia, and Lithuania. Another was to constrain public information sources so that the Soviet state was the only source of information on world affairs. Outside sources of information were suspect, frowned upon, and many of them were illegal. People were sent to prison camps for foreign contacts and listening to foreign broadcasts.

Resistance movements in the Baltic states wanted to reverse the Soviet occupation and re-establish independence. While such an objective was impractical most of the time, a secondary objective was to remind people, even informally, of the idea of nationhood. Underground publications were a way to remind people of the idea of freedom and independence. They also played a role in keeping people informed of news from the wider world. Not everyone had a radio receiver, but a partisan with a radio receiver and a rotary printer could multiply the dissemination of foreign news.

Underground publications have a venerable history in the Baltic states, long before 1940. In the tsarist era, the region was subject to a policy of Russification in which publishing in languages other than Russian was restricted, and from 1865 to 1904 no printing in the Latin alphabet was allowed. Underground literature in local languages played a role in the rise of Lithuanian, Latvian, and Estonian national consciousness. In Lithuania, book smugglers were considered heroes. In some ways, partisan-era publishing was a reversion to previous time-honoured habits.

Writing, printing, and disseminating underground publications became a key feature of many but not all partisan groups. Not every group had the wherewithal for publishing, but existing memoirs, particularly in Lithuania, indicate a strong focus on printing. Some partisan raids occurred specifically to support publishing activity. Sometimes, raids would be planned and executed to obtain paper, ink, typewriters, or other supplies to maintain underground publishing. For example, the raid on Merkinė by Lithuanian Forest Brothers mentioned in the previous chapter was partly intended to seize paper for publications.

Types of publications

Underground publishing produced a wide variety of content. Broadly, the Forest Brothers' publishing output can be divided into singular productions and periodicals. One-off singular productions were typically one-page, one-sided leaflets and fliers designed around a specific theme or issue, such as boycotting an election, avoiding conscription, or issuing a proclamation in a particular area. Lithuanian Forest Brothers were particularly keen on proclamations, it seems. The most famous of these was the so-called Lithuanian Partisans' Declaration of 16 February 1949. This declaration was a strong statement of democratic principles, Lithuanian independence, and hopes for living up to the statements in the Atlantic Charter. Lithuanian archivists have uploaded a copy of the original document online.[1] Notably, all eight of its signatories were hunted down and killed.

A wide variety of periodicals were issued. Most of these were multiple-page documents styling themselves as 'newspapers', although examples of broadsheet-sized publications are rare. Most were on letter-sized paper, having been typed out on typewriters. Some were one-off publications, but others aspired to be proper periodicals and lasted for months or years.

The production of fake documents was also an important publishing activity, with such documents occasionally produced on actual printing presses. Over time, as the Soviet bureaucratic apparatus started to control every aspect of life, documents and paperwork were important to everyone. Occasionally, fake documents were helpful in the partisan struggle. Lukša mentions fake conscription-exemption documents, for example. While there is less literature available in English on the Estonian partisans' publishing operations, it is known that the Estonian 'City Brothers' were viewed as useful sources of documents.

It should also be noted that, as part of a broad campaign to disrupt and discredit the Forest Brothers, at various points the Soviets published and distributed fake publications. At least four such publications have been identified in Lithuania, and others may have appeared in Estonia and Latvia.

Production techniques

The techniques used to produce underground publications ranged from the crude to the modern. At the crudest end of the spectrum, partisans literally handwrote publications and copied them laboriously by hand. At the other end, there were attempts to use professional typesetting and printing technology, often in the dark of night, at printers. Nearly every partisan-era publication effort was somewhere between these two extremes. Partisan memoirs detail a range of different printing operations.

The various publications catalogued in modern archives or mentioned in memoirs show that a variety of duplication techniques were used for publishing underground literature. The logistics of oil, ink, paper, and plates are mentioned several times in Lukša's memoirs.

At the very top end, professional printing presses with actual typesetting were used. Some smaller presses had been hidden away at various points during the war and occupation and operated out of barns and sheds. Early on in this period, some people had clearly had the foresight to hide smaller printing presses. In other instances, particularly before the full oppressive hand of the state security services could be felt, larger presses were used at night, with connivance from the printers, who put themselves at great risk. In Lithuania, there are references to linotype typesetting machines being used in the post-partisan era by underground publishers. These might have been around for some time before then, given the age of linotype systems.

The next type of printing mentioned is rotary print. Rotary print devices were commonplace across Europe, and it was also possible to make a rotary duplicator. In Lithuania, one notable underground publication was a 1949 document entitled 'Nurodymai pogrindžio spaudai dauginti tinkamai priemonei—rotatoriui pagaminti ir naudoti',[2] which roughly translates as 'instructions to the underground press to make a rotator printer'. It made the rounds, and partisans actually made their own rotator printers, although technical problems such as bad ink and poor paper plagued such operations.[3]

One type of printing and reproduction technique worthy of mention is the hectograph. Also known as gelatine printing, the hectograph was widespread in the early parts of the twentieth century. It even features in works by P. G. Wodehouse and George Orwell. These worked by copying a text on to a block of gelatine, which would then transfer the print or diagrams back on to a blank piece of paper. While it was difficult to do proper mass production on a hectograph, print runs of dozens or even hundreds of pages were possible if one was careful and had time. A crafty individual could also make a hectograph kit if they knew what they were doing.

A widespread but simpler technique was to produce the publications on typewriters. Carbon paper helped make multiple copies, but there are numerous examples of the tedious practice of typing out dozens of copies of the same document. It should be noted that there was a significant amount of often poignant hand-drawn artwork in various documents and publications.

Estonia

The US Library of Congress has some examples of Estonian underground publishing from the period of German occupation, although it is not a very dense collection. Eight examples of newspaper editions and two leaflets appear in the library's catalogue. In September 1944, the pre-war government's official gazette, *Riigi Teataja*, reappeared for the first time since August 1940. A one-off four-page edition was openly printed in Tallinn and distributed to proclaim the provisional government and issue a few edicts.

There are few examples of partisan publications in Estonia during the post-1945 period of the Forest Brotherhood. There are many reasons for this, not least that the movement was smaller and printing resources may have been more limited. Nonetheless, several Estonian publications can be noted. Leaflets and fliers, as opposed to periodicals, seem to have been the dominant published output in Estonia during this period. From Laar's work, it seems that literature in this period was largely produced and disseminated by City Brothers and students.[4] Underground student and youth groups were known to be publishing and posting fliers and leaflets during the period of partisan resistance, and it may have been more feasible for students at schools and universities to gain access to paper and printing.

Broadly speaking, however, the golden era of Estonian underground publications was later than the period of the Forest Brotherhood.

Latvia

A number of underground publications were active during the Nazi occupation in Latvia. Various self-published leaflets and posters were placed in public spaces on Latvian Independence Day, 18 November 1941. A publication entitled *Tautas Balss* ('People's Voice'), which issued its first copies on 15 February 1942, called on Latvians to disobey Nazi policies and warned against joining police units and other German recruitment efforts. Other smaller publications were also issued during the Nazi period. In April 1942, a journalist named Martins Jansons developed a network of about fifty young people who distributed leaflets around Latvia, urging people not to cooperate with Nazi occupiers and not to believe Nazi promises. The Gestapo and their local proxies periodically cracked down on such publications. Over 100 Latvians were arrested by the Germans for such activities.[5]

Strods identifies ten main underground publications in Latvia in the 1945–8 period, including *Sudrabōta Saule* ('Silver Sun'), which was a newsletter put out by the Forest Brothers in Vidzeme that had a run of forty-eight issues. The same group also produced a monthly political issue called *Tēvzeme un Brīvība* ('Fatherland and Freedom') and a handwritten edition called *Dzimteme* ('Fatherland'). Other Forest Brotherhood groups published periodicals such as *Tēvzeme un Brīvība* (which, despite having the same name, was a different journal from that mentioned previously), *Kurbads*, and *Mūsu Sauksme* ('Our Good News'). Other groups in turn published the *Tēvzemes Sargs* ('Guard of the Fatherland') and the rather excitingly entitled *Vilkaču Sauciens* ('Cry of the Werewolf'). Not to be left out were the *Latgales Partisāns* ('Partisans of Latgale') by the National Army of Latgale and *Vanagi* ('The Hawks') by the Hawks of the Fatherland in southern Kurzeme.

Lithuania

The somewhat larger partisan resistance movement in Lithuania spawned myriad publications. Literally hundreds of different titles appear in the archives, although some were apparently very small or even one-sheet single editions. Lithuanian scholars have identified at least seventy-two periodicals that were produced during this period.[6] The partisan press was larger in Lithuania than in the other two countries, which was in part due to the resistance movement being larger. But additionally, at least anecdotally, it appears that typewriters and rotary duplicators were more commonplace in rural areas, possibly having been provided through schools and churches. Seeing how a tenth of the partisan leaders in Lithuania were schoolteachers, one wonders how many rotary printers had been abstracted from rural schools.

Some periodicals were small typewritten publications, with as few as fifty copies. But some of the Forest Brotherhood had covert access to actual printing presses, and some of their publications had print runs of up to 5,000 copies. Lukša mentions working on several newsletters—*Laisvės Žvalgas* ('Freedom Scout') and *Kovos Kelias* ('The Road to Battle'). The longest running was a newspaper called *Laisvės Varpas* ('The Bell of Freedom'). Its name harkened back to the famous tsarist-era *Varpas*, which was published in Germany for sixteen years and smuggled into Lithuania. *Laisvės Varpas* started in 1941 under Nazi occupation and managed to put out an amazing 215 or 218 issues by the time it ceased publication in 1953.

At least one Lithuanian publication was in Russian: *Svobodnoye Slovo* ('The Free Word') was edited by none other than Vanagas himself and was published in several different locations by rotary press. Up to 1,000 copies were made and about ten issues appeared between 1947 and 1952. Underground press published by partisans (as opposed to non-violent resistance in towns and cities) continued until 1957, when the newsletter *Partizanų Šūvių Aidas* ('The Echo of Partisan Gunfire') ceased publication.

Several well-known poets and authors from the pre-war era were involved in underground publications. Bronius Krivickas, a writer and translator of Goethe into Lithuanian, edited and published *Aukštaičių Kova* (roughly, 'Voice of the Highlanders') out of a bunker but was betrayed by a double agent and committed suicide in September 1952. Konstantinas Bajerčius, who had been an active writer in the 1930s, put out an underground newspaper in the Alytus region but died under torture after being captured, thus ending the newspaper.

Women also played an important role in Lithuania's underground press. Diana Glemžaitė, an artist and poet, wrote prolifically, and her poems appeared in many underground publications. She died when her bunker in the north of Lithuania was blown up by MGB agents in 1949. Some of the longest-lasting partisan publications were run or assisted by women, particularly when the armed struggle was starting to dwindle. Monika Alūzaitė started writing for underground publications as a student and was only twenty-one when she was captured in late 1952 after her attempt to kill herself failed.[7] She had published and edited eleven issues of the *Malda Girioje* ('Prayer in the Wood'), which averaged a circulation of 500 copies, and seven issues of *Kovojantis Lietuvis* ('Lithuanian Fighter') on rotary duplicators.[8] In January 1953, the editors of *Laisvės Varpas* ('Liberty Bell') and *Vyčių Keliu* ('On the Path of Knights'), including Elena Gendrolytė, a schoolteacher, committed suicide rather than face capture and torture. Irena Petkutė, a poet and literature teacher who edited *Laisvės Balsas* ('The Voice of Freedom'), killed herself when surrounded in August 1953.

After the guns fell silent

Underground publications long outlived the armed partisan movement, and the golden age of *samizdat* in the Baltic states was arguably well after the decline of armed resistance. The underground newspapers of the 1960s and 1970s were merely the next wave of resistance to Soviet occupation. Indeed, studies of underground publishing in the Soviet Union often focus more on that period than on the Forest Brotherhood era. More examples of primary sources survive in archives, and there are some very interesting archival collections of *samizdat* from the later post-partisan Soviet period. Readers interested in this period are directed toward the very significant *Chronicle of the Catholic Church in Lithuania*, which ran from 1972 to 1989. An online archive, in

English, is also available.[9] The underground resistance to Soviet occupation entered a new phase, but that is beyond the scope of this book.

11

CONTACTS WITH WESTERN
INTELLIGENCE SERVICES

The war waged by the Forest Brotherhood was seen by some as a small side act in the Cold War between East and West. As the Forest Brother groups somehow managed to continue their struggle, the existence of armed resistance behind the newly formed Iron Curtain became known to Western intelligence services. As well as the Baltic states, Poland, Ukraine, Romania, and Albania had armed anti-Communist resistance movements that were of interest to the West. Quite early on, intelligence agencies in Finland and Sweden wanted to know what was happening in their immediate neighbourhood, an interest that predates the war. As the brief amity between wartime allies wore off, US, UK, and French intelligence agencies began to take an interest in the Baltic region. Into this mix, we must add the presence of Baltic exiles in Sweden, Britain, the United States, and displaced persons camps in Germany. Various exile groups seeking a better fate for Estonia, Latvia, and Lithuania grew and began to agitate, both openly and clandestinely, for Western assistance to their cause.

The mere existence of any anti-Soviet resistance was potentially helpful to military and intelligence officials in the West. Partisan groups could be sources of intelligence, and their existence could serve to tie up Soviet military and security resources. A Soviet invasion of Western Europe would need a mobilisation effort and troop movements. Eyes and ears in Eastern Europe, including the Baltic states, could give the West enough warning to defend itself. In the event of a broader Third World War, these groups could cause havoc in the enemy rear areas or even foment a broader revolt. Further, a network in the Baltics could be used to infiltrate personnel deeper into—or move them out of—the Soviet Union. A few people in the West even thought that, eventually, the Iron Curtain could be rolled back in part by partisan uprisings.

This is a complex subject that remains shrouded in mystery. Some details are available in archival documents and books on Cold War espionage, but many other aspects of this period remain secret. A full accounting of Western efforts in the Baltics is still difficult to compile. While many CIA records are now declassified, we know as much of the MI6 operations through Soviet memoirs and defectors as we do through British primary source material. But as with many accounts of intelligence and paramilitary operations, this story is replete with interesting personalities.[1]

As I approach this part of the tale, I wish to issue three disclaimers. First, we should not view these events in isolation. In one sense, the tale of Western espionage interacting with Baltic partisans is a minor part of a big story. In the broader context of Western operations against Soviet Communism in the Cold War, these efforts did not amount to much. The major efforts of Western intelligence services were going into things like the Greek civil war, the Chinese civil war, and the Korean war, as well as dozens of lesser covert operations around the world. Even in European terms, the Baltic operations were small compared to efforts elsewhere. Second, as we will see, Western intelligence work in the Baltic states generally had little impact other than wasting a lot of time and money. Finally, my own research has churned up literally hundreds of archival documents that tell a lengthy tale of incompetence, bureaucratic wrangling, betrayal, false optimism, byzantine machinations, aggrieved exiles, and spies, that would take a whole other book to cover.

The nearest neighbours: Finland and Sweden

As a combatant in the war and constantly worried about Soviet invasion, Finland had a direct interest in what happened across the strait in Estonia. However, Finland's forced neutrality under strict Soviet conditions, which spawned the unique term 'Finlandisation', curtailed the ability of Finnish intelligence to operate in Estonia. However, a number of Estonians in the Haukka group had been infiltrated in by sea and parachute before the end of the war, and it is almost certain that some liaison and passing of intelligence continued by radio until the last members of the group were killed or captured, or gave up.

Ostensibly neutral Sweden had avoided entering the Second World War and maintained an often fraught neutrality. Sweden's intelligence services were no longer worried about Nazi Germany but were heavily concerned about the possibility of a new world war in Europe. Sweden's military intelligence service (Svenska Militär Tjanst) and civilian intelligence service (Allmän Säkerhetsenhet) took an active interest in the Baltic struggle for understandable reasons, as any Soviet threat to Sweden would likely involve or come through the occupied countries. Furthermore, along with West Germany, Sweden was a primary refuge for exiles fleeing the Baltic states, with over 30,000 Baltic refugees having taken refuge in Sweden. The Estonian government in exile operated in Sweden, as did diplomats still operating out of Latvian and Lithuanian diplomatic missions. Various exile groups set up shop in Sweden.

Sweden was a den of intrigue during the war. Various characters came on to the stage, and the Swedish intelligence services did liaise quite closely with British intelligence. This liaison effort continued after the war and expanded to include cooperation with the Americans. One character was an exiled Baltic German countess from Estonia, Margareta Stenbock, who fled her estate when the Soviets took over in 1940. She used Estonian sailors who had taken refuge in Sweden to form a courier network in small boats. She worked with both Swedish and British intelligence.[2]

The Swedish operation evolved largely as an intelligence collection and liaison operation, not a covert campaign to arm rebels. Swedish intelligence operated motorboats that could covertly cross the Baltic and drop off or pick up agents along the Latvian and Estonian coastlines. Lithuania's coastline was smaller, and fewer Lithuanians were available for recruitment in Sweden, so fewer missions involved Lithuania. Perhaps sixty missions took place to insert agents into the Baltic states. Gradually, this became a joint effort with the British and Americans.

However, Sweden was not uniformly pro-Baltic in all of its actions and had recognised the Soviet incorporation of the Baltic states into the Soviet Union. In early 1946, in a shameful act, the Swedish government deported 150 Latvian and Estonian former soldiers as well as nine Lithuanians to the Soviet Union, where they were mostly imprisoned in the Gulag.[3] The 1970 Swedish film *A Baltic Tragedy* covers this sad episode.

American and British intelligence—the background

The early roots of Western intelligence involvement in the Baltic partisan movement can be traced back to British intelligence. Although the United States had a few military attachés in the area, the Americans did not have a true foreign intelligence service before the war. The British, however, were active collectors of intelligence around the world.

During the Second World War, not much actually happened in terms of the Western allies and Baltic partisans. The UK's Special Operations Executive (SOE) and the US Office of Strategic Services (OSS) had conducted covert operations, cooperated with local agents, and aided resistance movements in many places in Europe during the war. But in order to avoid direct conflict with their Soviet wartime allies, these agencies did not generally operate in the Baltic states. I have only been able to identify one SOE mission in the Baltic states, in which a British RAF officer named Ronald Seth was parachuted into Estonia in October 1942. Given the eventual failure of this mission, it was aptly named Operation Blunderhead. His mission was to sabotage oil production from Estonian oil shale, but he was captured and turned into a German agent. His story is colourful and downright odd at times but outside the scope of this book as he had no contact with the Estonian resistance.[4]

Whereas wartime contacts allowed some significant liaison to be quickly re-established in places like Albania, efforts to reach out to Baltic partisans had to start from scratch. But Western intelligence agencies were behind in many ways. In the United States and the UK, the dismantling and dismemberment of the OSS and SOE was probably an expression of premature post-war optimism. Capability that would later have been useful in aiding Eastern European partisans was discarded, and it was often years before new capability was re-built. While the CIA was the eventual replacement for the OSS, it was only established two years after the OSS had been disbanded. There was no clear replacement for the SOE in the UK. The Cold War and the establishments and institutions used to fight it simply did not evolve quickly enough to be much use to Baltic patriots.

Much of the Western intelligence effort focused on liaison with exile groups, such as VLIK (the Supreme Council for the Liberation of Lithuania). Much of this was a colossal waste of time, as these groups turned out to have far fewer direct contacts than advertised with the resistance movements back in their home countries. Furthermore, many of them were divided by political dissension, and some of their members had troublesome wartime pasts, such as those who had collaborated with the Nazis. They also seem to have leaked like a sieve and were a security risk.

French intelligence appears to have played a small role in operations as well. The French intelligence services had to rebuild after the war as France re-established itself. France then had two governments, Vichy France in the southern unoccupied part of France and a government in exile, the Free French. This situation ended up producing rival intelligence agencies during the war. In the late 1940s, there was some attempt to develop Baltic contacts. However, it appears the French lacked the wherewithal to insert agents into the Baltic states. At least one agent, Lukša, was originally recruited and trained by the French but was ultimately handed over to the American CIA.

Britain, MI6, and Operation Jungle

Two MI6 officials, Harry Carr and Sandy McKibbin, stand out as the pioneers of Western intelligence involvement in the region. Carr was a native Russian speaker who was born in 1899 in Archangel, in the far north of tsarist Russia, where his father had been sent to manage a British-owned sawmill. A small but noted British expat community existed in tsarist-era Russia, and the Carr family had been in Russia for several generations. Carr was at boarding school in England when the First World War broke out. He was commissioned in the British Army just slightly too late to serve in the First World War. But the British, along with their allies, staged an ill-fated military intervention in the Russian far north during the Russian Civil War in 1918–19. Carr was assigned as an interpreter with British forces in Russia. However, the intervention failed for a variety of reasons. After leaving military service, he was quietly picked up by the intelligence services. By 1928, he was MI6's man in Helsinki, where he developed extensive contacts with Finnish intelligence.

During the war, Carr kept an eye on Baltic matters from Stockholm. Emigres were turning up in Sweden, coming to the attention of British intelligence there. During the war, the British did not operate directly in the Baltic states other than the ill-fated Blunderhead mission mentioned earlier. However, they had an awareness of the situation in the Baltic countries through open-source analysis. The UK's little-heralded Foreign Research and Press Service was the main source of information on the Baltic states.[5] By the time of the late 1940s partisan war, Carr was 'Controller, Northern Europe' for MI6.

McKibbin, Carr's assistant during the period of the work with Baltic partisans, was, in effect, a Baltic Scot. For centuries, some English and Scottish families had lived and worked in the Baltic states, often involved in activities like timber and grain trading during the tsarist era. Riga has an Anglican church and at one point had a British mayor, George Armitstead. McKibbin had been born in the Russian Empire and grew up, like Carr, in the timber business. In 1939, he had fled his Tallinn-based timber business and took refuge in Stockholm. Having been in contact informally in Tallinn with the small local MI6 station, he was easily enrolled formally into the service. His liaison efforts with Swedish intelligence resulted in close cooperation on Baltic partisan matters.

British liaison with Baltic groups eventually evolved into a full-blown intelligence operation called 'Operation Jungle'. Accessing the Baltic states was viewed as difficult, but Britain had long had experience with small boat operations, and the British operation became a largely nautical one. One of the earliest operations by the British took place in October 1945, when four Latvian partisans with radio sets were dispatched by speedboat from Sweden to the Latvian coast.[6] Given the context, this operation was likely in conjunction with Swedish intelligence. The four Latvians were captured by Soviet border guards almost immediately after landing, along with their radio sets and codebooks. By capturing the codebooks intact, messages that appeared to be authentic could be sent back to MI6. This established a pattern that was frequently repeated. Agents were recruited, trained, equipped, and inserted into the Baltic states only to fall into oblivion. Most agents, whether they were Swedish, British, or American, disappeared with little or no contact back to their handlers.

Operation Jungle seems to have been headquartered in London's St James neighbourhood at the old wartime 'Special Liaison Centre' at 14 Ryder Street, with rather a lot of back-office work and training being done in Chelsea, in a safehouse at 111 Old Church Street.[7] Another house in Holland Park in West London was also used for training. Many aspects of the British operation take on an air of thrift and economy. Part of the ethos behind using boats was due to this drive for economy, as it was vastly cheaper than trying to fly agents behind Soviet lines. The entire annual global budget for all British covert operations was only half a million pounds—perhaps 15 million pounds in today's money.[8]

Estonians, Latvians, and Lithuanians helped Carr and McKibbin run Operation Jungle. The Estonian section was headed by the Estonian officer Alfons Rebane, who remains one of the more intriguing characters in the tale of the Forest Brothers. His nickname, naturally, was 'the Fox'—Rebane means 'fox' in Estonian. Rebane had served with distinction as an Estonian Army officer before the war and had been thrown out of service after the 1940 Soviet occupation. He fomented resistance even before the 1941 German invasion, having fled to the forests to avoid deportation to Siberia.

After the German invasion, Rebane joined the Estonian Legion to fight the Russians. His war record was one of skill and bravery. Rebane resisted his unit's incorporation into the SS but was forced into it.[9] He was awarded numerous medals by the Germans, including the Knight's Cross of the Iron Cross, making him the most decorated Estonian in German service. What we do not know with any degree of clarity is anything about his possible war crimes or his own personal politics, beyond a general anti-Communist sentiment. Unlike many other Estonians fighting alongside the Germans, Rebane stayed with his unit and retreated from Estonia. He viewed guerrilla resistance as ultimately futile and felt that fighting the Soviets on the battlefield would be the best thing he could do for

Estonia. By the end of the war, his unit was in Czechoslovakia, where it was disbanded. Colonel Rebane eventually ended up in the British occupation zone, having fled possible repatriation to the Soviet Union and inevitable imprisonment thereafter. Carr and McKibbin spotted his usefulness, and by 1947 he was in Britain, working as an expert on Estonia for MI6. Rebane was selected for Operation Jungle and settled into work at the safe house on Old Church Street in Chelsea. Rebane headed the Estonian portion of Operation Jungle.

The Lithuanian section was headed by Stasys Žymantas. Dr Žymantas (born Žakevičius) had been a rapidly rising academic in the pre-war era and had offered rooms at Vilnius University for plotters of the 1941 uprising. He ended up as chair of the 'citizen's committee' in Vilnius during that ill-fated uprising. He appears to have played the Germans in that he assisted in the civic administration of Vilnius but was also active in the LLKS, which was anti-German. This group was involved in the production of an underground publication, *Laisvė Kovotojas* ('Freedom Fighter'), and helped resist Nazi development of a Lithuanian Waffen SS legion. He fled to the West when the Soviets reconquered Lithuania. Active in VLIK, the Lithuanian exile committee based in West Germany at the end of the war, Žymantas came to the attention of McKibbin. The Latvian section was headed by Rūdolfs Silarājs, who had been a pilot in the Latvian Air Force and had turned up in a refugee camp in Belgium at the end of the war. Silarājs has been portrayed in semi-fictional form in Latvian period dramas, somewhat muddling what we know about him.

Agents were recruited from practically every type of émigré. A large number of Baltic nationals were in displaced persons camps in the Allied occupation zones in West Germany. These people were largely former prisoners, former slave labourers, former soldiers in German-sponsored units, and refugees who had fled west ahead of the Soviet advance. There were the occasional former Nazi collaborators and deserter from the Soviet military laying low, pre-war émigrés, and Balts who had managed to fight for the Allies all knocking about in Europe. A number of exiles were in Sweden, in particular.

Agents were trained in Fort Monckton (an MI6 facility near Gosport), at the safe house, and likely at other locations. Some training is believed to have taken place in Scotland and Dartmoor. As the primary role of the inserted agents was meant to be liaison, much of the training was focused on communications techniques, such as morse code. Other forms of communication were used as well. Secret writing techniques were taught so that a seemingly innocuous postcard or letter to an address in the West could carry information. This was the backup to radio communication, but it was far less reliable.

A large part of the operational end of Operation Jungle was a small flotilla of motorboats operating out of German ports on the Baltic Sea in the British occupation zone. MI6 and the Royal Navy worked with a German naval officer named Hans Helmut Klose who had served in small patrol boats, the so-called 'E-boats', with some distinction during the war. After a brief spell as a POW, he was put to work in the German Minesweeping Administration, clearing wartime sea mines. It was in this role that he came to the attention of the British.

A new group called the 'British Baltic Fishery Protection Service' (BBFPS) was formed, but its nominal role in enforcing fishing rules was merely a cover for covert operations in the Baltic Sea. Klose worked with none other than the Royal Navy's Lt Commander John Harvey-Jones. After a distinguished wartime career at sea, Harvey-Jones had learned Russian and joined naval intelligence. (He later became chairman of Imperial Chemical Industries and a minor TV star in the early 1990s with *Troubleshooter*.) Several old German E-boats were modified and used by the BBPFS for Operation Jungle. If this plot sounds disturbingly familiar, it may be that you read it in fictionalised form in John le Carré's *The Secret Pilgrim* (1990).[10]

The way Operation Jungle worked in practice means that some level of cooperation with the Danish authorities is presumed to have taken place. The Danish island of Bornholm, to the east of the rest of Denmark, was the staging point for the BBFPS missions. Of course, it could have been a matter of the Danes being given the fisheries protection cover story and a wink and a nod. Or, the Danes being close Cold War allies, they may have actively assisted the missions.

Although the British and Swedes did not have as much activity with the Lithuanians, one of their missions involved a Lithuanian named Jonas Deksnys. Deksnys had been arrested by the Soviets in 1940 but was released during the 1941 uprising and was active in the Lithuanian Activists Front that was trying to establish a provisional government. He was active in anti-German underground work and published a newspaper. He was one of the founders of VLIK. The Germans arrested him and took him to Germany, where he was liberated at the end of the war. He went back to Lithuania in September 1945 and became active in the resistance. He was in contact with Markulis, whom readers will remember was a Soviet infiltrator. Several times, Deksnys went out of Lithuania and returned again, with Swedish assistance. In early 1949, the Swedes, with British assistance, infiltrated him and several others back in by speedboat. Suspiciously, he did not transmit a message back until November 1950. No useful intelligence came back from him, leaving people to wonder if he was accomplishing anything.

The CIA

The American CIA mounted similar operations in the Baltic states. There were numerous code names for CIA operations, including 'Aegean', 'Capstan', and 'Tilestone'.

In typical Washington fashion, the American government lurched from doing nothing and not having an intelligence service (the CIA only dates from 1947) to setting up a heavily resourced but ineffective beast. The United States had set up a whole bureau called, innocuously, the Office of Policy Coordination under Frank Wisner, a lawyer and wartime spy who had bravely headed up US intelligence operations in Romania.

The United States became involved in Baltic operations a bit later than the British and Swedes and became involved through their liaison with both countries. America did have a large number of Baltic people in various displaced persons camps or working on the American payroll in various military occupation roles in the American zone of occupation in West Germany, so it had a pool of potential recruits. CIA efforts in the field appeared to have concentrated more on Lithuania than on Latvia and Estonia. The Americans began a close relationship with VLIK—the principal Lithuanian exile group, which was operating in West Germany. General Plechavičius, the old general who had variously helped and not helped the Germans, liaised with the CIA and brought VLIK closer to the Americans than the British. It should also be noted that the CIA was involved in operations elsewhere, including Ukraine, alongside these efforts in the Baltic states.

The CIA operation was headed out of Germany, where it developed a large field station. George Belic was the CIA's man there. He was ethnically Russian and was born in Odessa in 1911. His father had fought and died in the White Army fighting against the Bolsheviks in the Russian Civil War. Young Belic fled to the United States in 1923 after the Bolshevik victory. He spoke fluent Russian. He had worked in US naval intelligence during the war and had been involved with Wisner in Romania. He was a skilled and effective covert operator. He had operational-level relations with McKibbin, of MI6, who looked down on his American colleagues as upstarts. The overall boss of CIA covert operations against the Soviets was Harry Rositzke, a former academic (a PhD from Harvard in German philology) and wartime American spy. Rositzke's relationship with his MI6 counterpart, Harry Carr, was not particularly cordial. At a major meeting in Washington in 1950, both sides accused the other of lying about operations.

At first, it seems that the CIA started piggybacking off Anglo-Swedish operations and inserted agents by sea. The CIA appears to have made a deal to financially underwrite the British speedboat effort in the Baltic Sea in return for intelligence information. Whether this was an effective return on investment seems unlikely. Some of the intelligence produced by the CIA operations was low-grade material. It was valid but mostly useless. A great example is a declassified Operation Tilestone report from November 1947 detailing documents smuggled out at great peril from Lithuania. These include such stunning revelations as a passport, a registration form for Communist Party membership, and the certificate accompanying a bravery medal.[11]

Eventually, the CIA Baltic operation turned to aerial operations, which did not need liaison with their British colleagues. Some of what we know about these operations comes from Rositzke's own memoir.[12] The CIA set up a covert air operation that used C-47 cargo aircraft and Czech pilots, veterans of the Battle of Britain, to covertly insert parachutists behind the Iron Curtain. The CIA appears to have successfully pulled off these dangerous parachute drops. America lost aircraft on other covert missions, but I have found no record of any aircraft being lost on Baltic operations. What Soviet air defence was doing is a mystery.

Operation Capstan

The apex of CIA operations in the Baltic states appears to have been Operation Capstan in 1950–1.[13] It also rates as, perhaps, a partial success, amid a general record of mediocrity and failure for missions to support the Forest Brothers, that successful liaison with the Forest Brotherhood was actually established for a period of time. Three Capstan airdrops were planned, and two of them occurred. The first involved the Lithuanian hero mentioned in previous chapters, Juozas Lukša, codenamed Daumantas in Lithuania but confusingly given the codename Skrajunas ('Flyer') by the CIA.

Lukša had escaped Lithuania and had been moving around Western Europe. He had many meetings with émigré groups. He wrote a memoir and got married. Originally, the Swedes had planned to reinsert him into the Baltic states, but he ended up not working for the Swedes. In Paris, Stasys Bačkis, the Lithuanian diplomat there, introduced Lukša to French intelligence. The French trained him in sabotage and parachute jumping, along with two other Lithuanians who had ended up in France, Jonas Kupstas and Jonas Kukauskas-Kukis. The French appear to have lacked the resources to infiltrate this team, and they were transferred to the CIA in Germany.

In Germany, Lukša was teamed up with two other Lithuanians to be sent back to Lithuania: Benediktas Trumpys ('Rytis'—Morning) and Klemensas Širvys ('Sakalas'—Falcon). Both had been taken to Germany as labourers and were liberated at the end of the war. They had both been working as general labourers for the Americans when they were recruited. On 4 October 1950, Lukša and the other two were parachuted into the Kaliningrad region, near to the Lithuanian border, with radio sets, German submachine guns, grenades, dollars, and roubles, as well as cyanide tablets for use in the event of capture.

Lukša established contact with his old comrades and resumed his old nickname Daumantas. His heroic return was lauded by the partisans as a sign that people in the West cared. He picked up where he left off and led partisan operations and sent information to the West. His last communication to the West was in early 1951, possibly due to radio problems. We now know that thousands of Soviet security forces were looking for him. As described in Chapter 10, he fell in the autumn of 1951. Trumpys and Širvys apparently fell out of contact with the CIA but are seen in a photo later in the month of October 1950. Trumpys died in action in May 1951, but this was not known to the CIA as this was after Lukša's last communications with US intelligence. Širvys stayed active until July 1952, when he was captured after being betrayed by a Soviet agent. He spent many years in the Gulag but lived to see Lithuanian independence, dying in 2003.

The second Capstan mission consisted of Julijonas Butenas (codename 'Steve', evidence that the CIA had had enough of poetic Lithuanian pseudonyms) and Jonas Kukauskas-Kukis, nicknamed 'Jack'. Butenas had been a journalist before the war, writing foreign policy columns for a daily newspaper in Kaunas. He fled the Soviets in 1940 and ended up in Berlin, as a minor figure associated with Škirpa and the LAF. After the German invasion, he worked on an underground resistance newspaper and was eventually arrested by the Germans and placed in a concentration camp. After the war, he got involved with VLIK and was recruited by the CIA. Butenas had flown on the first Capstan mission as jumpmaster for Lukša and the others.

Kukauskas-Kukis had been active in underground movements against both the first Soviet occupation and the Nazi occupation. In 1944, he made his way to Germany as a worker. The Abwehr had somehow latched on to him as a possible stay-behind partisan and trained him to be parachuted behind the lines, but his unit was never deployed. As a university student in Frankfurt in the late 1940s, he had been in contact with VLIK, who referred him on to the French, where he was trained alongside Lukša for a mission that never happened. Like Lukša, he was handed over to the CIA.

The second Capstan mission occurred on the night of 18 April 1951, and they were parachuted into an area south-west of Kaunas. The team made contact with partisans in early May. Kukauskas-Kukis communicated with the CIA on 15 June. The latter report indicated that the two had split up and that Butenas was dead but gave no further details. We now know that Butenas likely perished in May 1951. It appears that Kukauskas-Kukis was caught and turned by the Soviets. It is possible that he is the person who betrayed Lukša, and many Lithuanian sources make that claim. Kukauskas-Kukis continued to broadcast for some time, and there was considerable consternation at the CIA that he had gone over to the Soviets.

A third Capstan mission was planned but never executed. In 1951, the CIA recruited a Lithuanian refugee in Detroit, Michigan, named Česlovas Bankauskas. His partner was to be Balys Bedarfas, who had been recruited in Canada. The latter had been an associate of Kukauskas-Kukis for a period in Germany. The pair were trained, but this mission was never completed.

Treachery and perfidy

The problem for both the CIA and MI6 was that these brave and well-trained men often disappeared and were never heard from again. Some were arrested. Some were killed at the point of entry. Others simply disappeared into the mists of time. Some were turned under torture. A review of the whole operation after the fact shows that it was heavily betrayed and heavily infiltrated. Soviets could fight the secret war quite well, and in this affair they fought successfully.

Much of the effort to roll back the Iron Curtain was doomed to fail because of treachery. The Soviet intelligence services had infiltrated MI6, and it is here that a character named Kim Philby enters the tale. Readers have probably heard his name before. Philby was one of the 'Cambridge Five', a ring of spies recruited in the 1930s by the Soviet intelligence service that was active from the 1930s into the 1950s, having been recruited in Cambridge, England.[14] Philby had been working for the Soviets since 1934 and rose through the ranks of MI6.

In the immediate post-war era, while the various US and UK Baltic efforts were being developed and executed, Philby held roles in MI6 that placed him in positions to learn about the various efforts to 'roll back' the Iron Curtain. We now know some of the damage that Philby did in this regard based on Soviet-era sources. In his memoirs, Yuri Modin, who had been Philby's KGB controller, discusses Philby's access to the relevant secrets.[15] Oleg Gordievsky, who defected to the West, broadly confirms Modin's memoirs.[16]

In 1947, Philby was stationed in Istanbul and was involved in efforts to infiltrate agents into the Caucasus (Operation Climber) and Albania (Operation Valuable). Operation Climber was directly compromised by Philby, and he may also have sunk Operation Valuable. In 1949, at about the time when the CIA was starting its serious operations in the Baltic, Philby arrived in Washington to take up his post as, in effect, MI6's liaison officer with the US intelligence community.

In this role, Philby attended various Anglo-American coordination meetings. In particular, in February 1951 Philby attended a US–UK meeting on Baltic operations. Carr, the UK chief of Northern Europe operations, allegedly gave a detailed briefing of the Baltic operations. According to Modin, Philby sent this information straight to Moscow.[17] This was almost certainly not the only opportunity Philby had to compromise the Baltic operations. Modin goes into some detail about Philby compromising operations in Ukraine. It is questionable whether Philby deserves full credit for compromising all of the Baltic operations, as by the time he was in a position to do so, the Soviets were already alert to these attempts to insert agents. Perhaps Philby could give occasional details. Philby himself made a rare television appearance[18] on Soviet television in Latvia in which he claimed that he had little grasp of the finer operational details of the Baltic operations, which may not have been discussed at the higher-level meetings he attended. We do not know if he was being truthful or not.

Philby was by no means the only reason that Soviet intelligence succeeded against the Forest Brothers. Even before Philby, it seems that the Soviets knew about the general outlines of the US and UK operation. That early British mission in October 1945, which yielded radios and codebooks, was exploited in an interesting manner. The four Latvians went to their deaths without betraying anything.[19] But Soviet intelligence already had a useful prisoner in their hands named Augusts Bergmanis. He had served in the German Army's Latvian Legion as a radio operator but had secretly been using his equipment to communicate with Latvian exile organisations in Sweden. He had been captured at the end of the war. In exchange for better treatment, the Soviets induced Bergmanis to act as a double agent and assume the identity of one of the captured partisans.[20]

Using one of the captured radios and codebooks, Bergmanis started communicating with MI6. He was instrumental in the capture of several other teams of partisans. He gained the confidence of MI6 handlers. At one point, a team of Latvian Forest Brothers that was having technical problems with its radios was even sent to Bergmanis so that he could help them. Bergmanis' technical support consisted of arrest and torture.

Knowing the general outline of the UK operations, it was not difficult for the Soviet intelligence agencies to put likely candidates for US or UK recruitment into the right position to be noticed by the likes of Estonian intelligence officer Rebane and the others. One example of this is the case of Vidvuds Šveics.[21] He had been a student at Riga University before the war. He initially accepted the German occupation but become disillusioned with the Nazis and was recruited by the NKVD, who trained him as an agent. In October 1948, the Soviets arranged for him to 'escape' to Sweden, where he was recruited by MI6. He was trained as part of Operation Jungle and was chosen to lead an infiltration mission in the spring of 1949. After going ashore near Palanga, Lithuania, Sveics reported back to the NKVD, betrayed the other agents, but stayed in contact by radio with MI6, likely passing fake intelligence.

Deksnys, the agent who went ashore in January 1949, ended up switching sides and working for the Soviets somewhere along the way. Much US archival paperwork engages in handwringing about exactly where and when the betrayal happened, but Lukša, one of the few agents who survived for a long period and did not betray the Western intelligence agencies, radioed a brief message in morse code in November 1950: 'Deksnys in hands of MGB.'[22] Yet the British still communicated with Deksnys and sent an agent, codenamed 'Mike', to meet him in 1952. Mike eventually went off the air, betrayed by Deksnys. While it is possible that Deksnys might have been an infiltrator earlier on, it seems more likely that he cracked after being captured in January 1949. He died in 1982 in Vilnius, having spent the preceding period spying on Lithuanian intellectuals.[23]

The impact

From the viewpoint of actual support to the partisans, the Western efforts amounted to little. A minimal amount of material aid was received, with little beyond radio sets and personal firearms being received by the partisan units. The overall impression is that this was, in the end, a wrestling match between intelligence agencies. This tale of secret infiltration and betrayal wasted resources and had little effect on the actual resistance movements themselves. Indeed, by the time these operations had got into full swing, the number of Forest Brothers was very much on the decline.

We should keep a sense of proportion about the involvement of Western intelligence agencies in the Forest Brother movements. None of these movements were set up by foreign intelligence agencies. Much of the story is that of Western intelligence trying to establish contacts with groups that were already well down the path of partisan resistance or past their prime and on the way to oblivion.

The overall impact of the Western intelligence operations was mixed. It cost some lives, and for some of the people who survived, it ruined their lives. Some of the Western intelligence officers were emotionally broken by it. In practical terms, none of it helped the partisans very much, with the possible exception of Lukša, although he would have been better left alone to lead as he was likely betrayed by a fellow CIA-trained partisan. There was an awful lot of activity for very little gain, even if the whole affair did tie up a lot of Soviet counterintelligence and security assets. Perhaps some will see that as a small victory in a decades-long calculation of Cold War attrition. But by the same token, the effort tied up a lot of Western intelligence and covert operations resources too. It makes for an interesting story, but it was ultimately a waste of time and lives.

12

REVOLT IN THE GULAG

The peoples of the Baltic nations all ended up with significant portions of their population in the diaspora. The Baltic diaspora is mostly discussed in terms of exile and emigration to the West. Talk of Chicago as Lithuania's 'second city' or indeed as the largest one, was, in practical terms, no joke at one point. Exile and diaspora meant that places like Chicago or New York were a lifeboat for Baltic cultures during hard times.

But we have to understand that there was a different diaspora from 1940 onward, one that was within the Soviet Union. A large percentage of the Baltic population was imprisoned or taken into exile in places such as Siberia, Central Asia, and the Soviet Far East. Lithuanians, Latvians, and Estonians of every age, creed, gender, class, and occupation ended up in the Soviet penal system, either in camps behind barbed wire or in 'internal exile'.

Part of my own research for this book left me rather shaken one day in August of 2022. I found the online repository of records of Lithuanians deported, exiled, or imprisoned. I identified eighty-six people with my relatively rare and quite geographically specific Lithuanian surname (Kašėta). Many never came back. My own family members who had been sent off to exile or the Gulag were aged from one to seventy-three. My experience is not unique. Baltic families from Druskininkai to Narva will have similar experiences.

The Soviet removal of people from Baltic nations came in two punitive forms. The first was actual imprisonment in prisons and prison camps. The 'Gulag' is so named because of its acronym in Russian, meaning 'The Main Administration of Camps'. The Gulag was eloquently anatomised by Nobel Prize winner Aleksandr

Solzhenitsyn in *The Gulag Archipelago*. The Gulag consisted primarily of labour camps, although there were traditional prisons as well. The so-called 'Corrective Labour Camp' was the primary component of the Gulag.

People in the Gulag camps had been arrested and sentenced by the Soviet authorities. Many were convicted without trial. But even the trials that did happen did not follow any legal norm that would be recognised in a democratic country. Sentences of ten or twenty-five years were common. In practice, it took very little to be sentenced to the Gulag. Many offences were exceedingly minor or contrived. In many cases, torture and false confession condemned totally innocent people to harsh sentences of imprisonment. Even for actual offences, investigative standards were sloppy and the wrong persons arrested. Guilt by association was a common tactic as well. You did not need to be engaged in anti-Soviet activity to face arrest and forced labour. In practice, the Soviet security services could arrest anyone they wanted and ensure they were sent to a camp. Article 58 of the Soviet criminal code made almost anyone a criminal if the security services wanted to write the paperwork to justify their decision.

The other form of population removal was forced resettlement to distant areas of the Soviet Union. Many people refer to this forced resettlement as 'deportation' or 'internal exile'. Neither term is fully accurate. From the Baltic perspective, it was not 'internal' at all, as most exile destinations were literally thousands of miles beyond the border of their country. But if you were still in the Soviet Union, it was not really a deportation either. Internal exile was viewed as less of a punishment than imprisonment in the camps. It consisted of involuntary resettlement in other parts of the Soviet Union but under looser control than barbed wire and machine guns in towers. This could be in the form of an actual court sentence to a term of exile, or done 'by administrative means', a Soviet euphemism for extrajudicial processes that ranged from a lengthy file of paper to, literally, 'send that truck to Kazakhstan and dump them there'.

Forced resettlement was often more collective in nature than arrest and imprisonment. Whole families and farmsteads were corralled and deported. Walk through rural areas in the Baltic states and you come across old farmsteads that are now overgrown. Their occupants likely received such a fate. The 'internal exile' often amounted to weeks of transit under conditions that were often as harsh as those endured by the prisoners being taken to the camps. It involved either being sent to an existing settlement or being told to make a new one from scratch, often in extremely unforgiving environments. In some cases, this 'internal exile' was more lethal than being in a camp. There are many stories of freight rail cars of people dumped in the dead of winter in the middle of a forest and told to make a village. Families were often, but not always, kept together. (They were broken up in the Gulag camps.) Even new-born babies were deported. The oldest recorded deportees from Lithuania were born in the 1840s and thus in their late nineties when the deportations happened.

Exiles were generally under administrative controls but not under heavy guard. Escape was certainly possible, but there was usually nowhere to escape to, and without the right documents you could not move freely within the Soviet Union. Remote Siberia can be a prison without walls if it takes weeks to walk anywhere.

Statiev's book shows that between 1941 and 1952, 120,924 people were deported from Lithuania, most of whom were deported in 1948 and 1949. In 1948–9 alone, 20,702 were deported from Estonia and 42,133 from Latvia.[1] These figures refer solely to exiles, not people imprisoned in the penal system.

The severity of treatment varied greatly within both the imprisonment and resettlement schemes. Gulag veterans sometimes have arguments over which form of forced labour, which set of camps, or which period was worse. In practice, it was all bad, all the time, but the degree of 'bad' varied a lot, both subjectively and objectively. Conditions and misery, in fact, overlapped. Some forms of 'internal exile' would lead to more death, disability, and infirmity than some camps. There were camps with worse conditions than others, both deliberately and as happenstance of the work or the operating environment. Even within camps, some prisoners had better arrangements than others.

Both forms of population removal had multiple objectives. Some objectives were, obviously, punitive. The system was set up to punish real, perceived, or potential future opposition to the Soviet state. It was meant to physically remove obstacles to key Soviet policies, like collectivisation of agriculture, and physically incarcerate enemies of the Soviet state. It was meant for purposes of revenge, as Baltic peoples were viewed as having collaborated with the other side in the recent war, even if the Soviet Union had started out on the same side as the Nazis.

There were clear economic objectives to exile and imprisonment. The property of the deported people was seized, netting much valuable farmland and buildings. Forced labour, whether it was in terms of Gulag prisoners or relocated exiles, was used for thousands of different projects, including mining, construction, and lumber. The Gulag system and its auxiliary, the settlements of exiles, were an economy within the greater Soviet economy, working towards economic goals laid down by Moscow. New rail lines, dams, and entire sectors of natural resource extraction, such as nickel mining, relied heavily or even entirely on forced labour.

Finally, there were geopolitical objectives. Moving and dispersing entire ethnic groups broke up collectives of possible opposition. Moving people around could also be used to colonise parts of the Soviet Union that Moscow felt to be underpopulated or in need of development. It was cheaper and easier to populate areas of the Russian Far North, Far East, and Siberia by force than it would have been to induce people to move of their own accord. Religion could be suppressed by moving people to areas without places of worship or religious leaders. Ethnic identity could be suppressed by making sure that people were always in a minority and had to use Russian as their daily language to get by. Indigenous ethnic groups could be diluted by an influx of relocated persons from elsewhere in the Soviet Union.

Effect on the partisan movement

Imprisonment and forced relocation were some of the reasons that the Soviet Union gradually defeated the Forest Brothers. While some Forest Brothers died in battle, committed suicide before capture, died under torture, or were executed, many Forest Brothers and their supporters ended up sentenced to confinement. Besides these direct effects, Gulag imprisonment and forced relocation had many less direct effects on the Forest Brother movements. Farmers that supported them with food, shelter, and information were themselves imprisoned or deported. A farmer who has been sent to Magadan to work in a mine cannot leave a bucket of milk out for his cousin the partisan. In turn, other farmers learned from these examples and, over time, were less likely to support partisans for fear of imprisonment or exile. Within the Baltic states, forced relocation affected literally hundreds of thousands of people, draining entire areas of possible recruits as well as sympathisers and supporters.

The effect of the partisan movement on the Gulag

The Soviet authorities do not appear to have foreseen that imprisoning a lot of angry Baltic peoples would have an effect on the Gulag system as well as upon the Baltic countries. Yet taking a lot of Latvians, Estonians, and Lithuanians (as well as Poles and Ukrainians) with grievances, many of whom were veterans of armed struggle, and bottling them up in confinement and exile, clearly ran the risk of tensions spilling over. Before 1940, many, if not most, of the 'enemies of the state' locked up in the Gulag were normal people with that horrible label applied to them. But these partisans really were enemies of the state, and some of them were highly skilled fighters.

Labour camps and exile villages formed interesting ecosystems. Imprisoned freedom fighters encountered their compatriots imprisoned or exiled for manifold reasons or even none at all. Small microcosms of Lithuania, Latvia, and Estonia emerged in captivity as prisoners and exiles found people who could speak the same language. Baltic prisoners and exiles found themselves alongside others with powerful grievances against the regime. Many completely apolitical innocent people got swept up and deported or imprisoned for political crimes. But there really were people who were opposed to the regime, of every possible persuasion. Of particular interest to this narrative, there were also many Poles and Ukrainians, many of whom had been in resistance movements themselves. Chechens, Germans of many types including POWs, Kazakhs, Armenians, Crimean Tatars, members of every conceivable repressed religious sect, and others rounded out the mix in the Gulag.

Networks of like-minded people gradually formed within the camps, including Baltic networks.[2] Members of the more organised partisan groups might even try to maintain their affiliations while imprisoned. Baltic prisoners were active in making escape attempts in the late 1940s. Ukrainians and Poles also formed networks.

Cracks forming

In the years after the Second World War, at precisely the time when Baltic (and Polish and Ukrainian) partisans and patriots were being decanted into camps and exile, cracks started to appear in the Gulag system. An important aspect of the history of the Gulag was that the penal system also contained non-political prisoners. From 1945, a lengthy gang war between factions of traditional criminals, or non-political prisoners, broke out across the Gulag system. The authorities seemed unable to quash these so-called 'Bitch Wars' as different groups of conventional criminals, many of whom had been hardened by years of wartime military service, murdered each other in the camps. The overall climate of violence also made it possible for political prisoners to assassinate secret police informants with relative impunity, thus lessening the camp officers' awareness of what was going on.

In 1948, the Soviet Union set up a variety of 'special camps' that were strictly for political prisoners. By this point, there were many such prisoners in the Gulag system. However, this may have been a management error. There had long been a practice of using non-political prisoners, gangsters, and thieves, as well as networks of informants, to help maintain order in the camps. By setting up special camps, the ethnic networks became stronger. By 1953, Ukrainians, Poles, and Baltic nationals represented 40 per cent of the population in the 'special camps', and people from these ethnic backgrounds started to informally govern parts of the camps.[3]

The death of Stalin

Although the Gulag system is associated with Stalin, he did not create it, and it did not magically disappear when he died. But changes did start to happen after his death in March 1953. His henchman and chief oppressor, Lavrentiy Beria, was arrested and tried for treason and other offences. Beria's reputation as the head of the entire system of oppression meant that, for many people, he was the face of the worst excesses of Stalin's regime. At the end of 1953, Beria was executed. Many of Beria's underlings were purged.

Because of Beria's arrest and execution, people across the Soviet Union began to feel that the worst excesses of Stalinist oppression would be curbed. In East Germany, a workers' uprising was violently crushed in June 1953. Word of this uprising spread. There was some degree of optimism that things would get better. Rumours of amnesties abounded. An amnesty for non-political prisoners on short sentences caused envy among camp populations. There were also increasing amounts of self-doubt among the rank and file of the security services, including the guards and administrators. Former Gulag prisoner Alexander Solzhenitsyn put it aptly in *Gulag Archipelago*:

> They had no idea what was required of them and mistakes could be dangerous! If they showed excessive zeal and shot down a crowd they might end up as henchmen of Beria. But if they weren't zealous enough, and didn't energetically push the strikers out to work—exactly the same thing could happen.[4]

Whereas, in 1939, a camp guard who shot a prisoner for a minor offence might have even been given praise, by 1953 such a guard had to think if he was going to start a riot or get prosecuted for the exact same act.

Uprisings in the camps

Cracks started to appear even before Stalin's death. The Latvian scholar Leonards Latkovskis writes about minor uprisings in camps involving Ukrainian and Baltic prisoners in the Karaganda region, in Kazakhstan, in 1952 and early 1953. The camp authorities responded by sending the problem prisoners elsewhere. In 1952, 1,200 Baltic and Ukrainian prisoners were transferred to Norilsk and Vorkuta in the hope that this would break up their networks. It had the opposite effect. It caused word to spread that some form of uprising was possible while dispersing rebellious malcontents throughout the other parts of the Gulag system.[5] That the ringleaders were merely transferred and not executed gave a strong signal to some prisoners that agitation and organisation would only be lightly punished. After Stalin's death, it all started to boil over. At least three major Gulag uprisings with Baltic participants broke out.

Norilsk uprising

Norilag was a network of Gulag camps in the far north of the Krasnoyarsk region of Siberia. These camps were set up to support nickel mining operations, as the Norilsk area is one of the richest sources of nickel in the world. At one point or another during the history of the Gulag system, some 400,000 prisoners passed through the Norilsk camps. Many thousands died there. Eventually, camps sprang up that focused on things besides nickel mining, including copper mining, construction, railroad maintenance, and logging.

Soon after Stalin's death, a revolt kicked off in one of the Norilsk camps. Several prisoners had been shot by camp guards, inciting the inmates. Starting in late May 1953, over 16,000 prisoners went on strike. Committees were formed. Ukrainians appear to have been the ringleaders, but Estonians, Latvians, and Lithuanians played important roles in the strike committees. A commission from Moscow was sent to negotiate with the strikers but fled on the day that Beria was arrested. Prisoners were practising self-rule in the camp, and imprisoned priests were holding mass. A Lithuanian doctor, Juozas Kozlauskas, tended the sick and injured and confronted the camp authorities several times.[6]

Eventually, in August, the camp was surrounded by MVD internal troops. A crackdown occurred. Between seventy-eight and 100 prisoners were killed and 150 to 400 were wounded. Some of these figures come from a moving account of the revolt and crackdown in the memoirs of an American Jesuit priest, Father Walter Ciszek, who was imprisoned in the camp and participated in the strike.[7] As a Catholic priest, he ministered to many Lithuanians in the camps.

After the crackdown, conditions improved radically in the Norilag camps. Some of the strike committee's demands were actually implemented. Prisoner numbers were removed from prisoners' clothing. A modest wage was paid, and shops were set up so that some things could be bought with wages, like sugar, bread, and tobacco. Prisoners who met their work quotas could earn reductions in their sentences. Food rations improved, and prisoners were allowed to send one letter a month. The revolt had an effect.

Vorkuta uprising

The Vorkuta camps, the so-called Vorkutlag, were set up in 1932 in the Pechora River basin in the Komi region of North Russia. Coal mining was the principal activity, but many other types of forced labour also took place in a network of camps that grew to at least 130 camps.

Rumours of the East German uprising, word of Beria's arrest, and Baltic agitators from Karaganda arrived pretty much at the same time in Vorkuta. In July 1953, prisoners in one of the Vorkuta camps went on strike, demanding removal of bars from windows, the use of names instead of numbers, and the right to send letters. The rebellion quickly spread throughout the Vorkuta system. After some initial shootings to try to quell the riot, the prisoners threatened to blow up the coal mines if force was used. Eventually, other industrial activity, like brickyards, slowed down. Railroad workers, who were not prisoners, were starting to show sympathy for the prisoners. Over the course of a ten-day strike, hundreds of thousands of tons of coal production stopped. One witness of the Vorkuta uprising was an American prisoner, John Noble, who wrote about the ordeal after his release.[8] As with Norilsk, Baltic prisoners played a role in the uprising. The Lithuanians Vytautas Svilis, Eduardas Lugalys, Juozas Grušys, and Albinas Bliujis are specifically named as part of the strike committee.[9]

The negotiations were mostly a sham. On 31 July, the camp authorities started mass arrests, which were met with resistance and barricades. The next day, the unarmed prisoners stood firm and defiant. General Rudenko, who had been sent from Moscow to negotiate, ordered a massacre. Reports vary on the number of dead, but it seems that hundreds were killed and many hundreds more wounded. Latkovskis reports that the dead included two Latvians, ten Lithuanians, and four Estonians. One of the slain rebels was the Latvian Catholic priest Father Jānis Mendriks, from Latgale, who had been imprisoned for his ministry.

Despite the bloody crackdown, some changes occurred in the camps. More religion was tolerated in the Vorkuta camps, and the initial demands for the removal of bars from windows and removal of numbers from uniforms were met. Many agitators were sent to other bits of the Gulag system just to get them off the hands of the local Vorkuta administrators. This spread activists, many of them Baltic, and information around the wider Gulag system.

The Kengir uprising

The largest and best documented of all the Gulag uprisings occurred in a camp in Kengir, part of the Steplag complex in central Kazakhstan.[10]

For all the reasons explained above, tempers were already high in the Kengir camp. There were thousands of prisoners, in several different compounds, including a women's compound. However, the culture of casual lethal violence against the prisoners had not yet abated at Kengir. Tensions had risen after several prisoners were killed in early 1954, and some minor rumblings of resistance were stirring. Some work stoppages had clearly troubled the camp authorities. Because of their reluctance to use some of the more coercive techniques that had worked in previous years, the camp authorities decided to use an informal technique. They declared that the camp was no longer a 'special camp' and moved in hundreds of 'thieves'—hardened non-political prisoners. The authorities winked and nodded at the thieves and tacitly promised to overlook the rape of female prisoners.

History and experience would dictate that these non-political prisoners would revert to their predatory form and terrorise the political inmates. But that did not happen. Perhaps they realised they were seriously outnumbered. Perhaps the thieves had a newfound respect for political prisoners after hearing about rebellions elsewhere. The thieves saw that the former partisans carried knives, previously the sole domain of thieves. Or maybe upon being confronted with political prisoners who were actual enemies of the state and hard men themselves—Baltic Forest Brothers, Ukrainian partisans, and Polish Home Army members—the thieves realised they had no chance in a fight. So, they formed an alliance. If Solzhenitsyn is to be believed, the new arrivals refused to work and sun-bathed for weeks.

The new alliance plotted a rebellion. The prisoners revolted on 16 May 1954. They drove the warders out and built barricades.

Prisoners gradually took over and united the entire camp. They broke the barriers between the sub-camps, including the women's camp. Women got to see their husbands for the first time in ages. Imprisoned priests conducted masses and wedding ceremonies. Thanks to the Chekists, priests of every denomination were available in the camp. Despite what the authorities claimed would happen, no wave of rapes occurred. Indeed, the women prisoners enthusiastically joined the revolt. The guardhouse block was liberated, and prisoners toured the punishment blocks.

Most importantly, the 'service yard' was liberated. This had many types of technical workshops and months of stockpiled food. The prisoners elected a 'commission' to represent them and formed a self-government. Kites and balloons were used to send leaflets into the surrounding community. Imprisoned Chechens proved to be keen kite-fliers. Many engineers and technicians were among the prisoners. Machine shops turned out pikes and sabres. Although the guards had cut the power, generators were improvised. Radio broadcasts were made. A decision was made to stick strictly to the official food rations, but suddenly everyone got more food. This demonstrated that corruption had shorted the prisoners on food. They even spread rumours that the scientists and engineers were making secret weapons. 'Danger—Land Mines' signs were put up to scare the guards.

The elected leader was one Kapiton Kuznetsov, a former Red Army officer. He built a whole command structure, although the accounts make it clear that the Ukrainians had a parallel structure already in place that worked with Kuznetsov and his commission. Accounts specifically mention Lithuanians being part of the 'guard force' set up as part of the internal camp structure.

A group of negotiators was sent from Moscow. The prisoners' demands were relatively modest. They wanted bars to be removed, to be referred to by name instead of number, for certain camp guards to be investigated for murder, to be able to correspond with the outside world, and to have their cases reviewed. All of which was theoretically legally permissible within the Soviet constitution at the time. Indeed, Kuznetsov strongly held to the line that they were merely asking for their rights, not anything that could be considered 'anti-Soviet' behaviour.

Word was spreading, and the authorities were starting to panic. Would revolt spread to other camps? Into the civilian populace? Lots of deported people lived in the region. The situation gradually turned into a siege, with soldiers surrounding the camp. A democratic vote—ironically, the only democratic elections in 1954 in the Soviet Union were in Camp Number 4 in Kengir—to surrender or hold out was held, and the prisoners voted to hold out. The siege dragged on for forty days.

The inevitable crackdown started in the early hours of 26 June, heralded by illumination flares. Snipers took out the prisoners' sentries, many of whom were Lithuanian, who were then unable to spread the alarm. T-34 tanks, dogs, and around 1,700 soldiers entered the camp. Hundreds were killed; many hundreds more were wounded. The forty days of freedom were over. Some were tried and executed. Others were dispersed to other camps. But the winds of change were gradually felt across the Gulag system. And with the end of the Stalin era, the Gulag system shrank as it was reformed. Did Kengir play a role in that? It is difficult to say. But the authorities probably knew that they could not stand many more Kengirs. Steplag, in Kengir, was shut down in 1956.

The role of Baltic prisoners in the Kengir uprising, including incarcerated Forest Brothers, is now better documented than before. Because of the work of the Genocide and Resistance Centre in Vilnius, we know a lot about Lithuanian involvement in the uprising and the ensuing massacre. A total of 700 Lithuanians were at the camp, and research has been able to name many but not all of them. Thirty-five Lithuanians have been identified as part of the uprising's governing structures, and a further 224 are named as participating in the uprising. Many of them were women. At least six Lithuanians were killed in the massacre. A number of these Lithuanians were former Forest Brothers.

We know a bit about some of these Lithuanians. The Lithuanian lawyer Juozas Kondratas was a key part of the prisoners' governing structure. He was sentenced to an additional ten years for his role, which was investigating offences by the camp guards and bosses. Pranas Paulauskas wrote a newspaper called *Vytis* for Lithuanian prisoners. Vlada Milūtė suffered grievous injuries after being run over by a tank. Elena Grybinaitė is known as a chronicler of the uprising and lived until 2013. I found less about Latvians and Estonians in the Kengir uprising, but we know that they were there. Solzhenitsyn mentions a Latvian. Estonian records name several inmates in Kengir at that time. Deeper research would no doubt yield more names.

Actual enemies of the state

How does this fit into the overall story? These events show that the Forest Brotherhood managed to live on in the camps. Imprisonment moved the front of the war thousands of miles east. A quite different front in the war, perhaps, but still part of the same struggle against the same enemy. Of course, not all the Baltic participants in these uprisings—and the ones that likely happened but that we do not know about—were displaced Forest Brothers. But these rebellions brought new converts to the movement. New Forest Brothers (and Sisters) were made in the rebellions. Eventually, most of these people did indeed go home, with stories they could tell in hushed tones.

It is questionable whether these rebellions would have occurred without Baltic (and Polish and Ukrainian) prisoners. A vast hidebound system used to oppress normal people and call them 'enemies of the state' was not able to predict or quickly react to the trouble caused by actual enemies of the state. While their role was not the only role that was played in this drama, Baltic patriots played a key part in the unravelling of the Gulag.

PART 4

AFTER THE FOREST BROTHERHOOD

DEBATES, REVISIONISM, LEGACY

13

LAST OF THE BROTHERS

In some cases, it is possible to identify a specific event or point in time when a war ended. For Napoleon, it was Waterloo. The American Civil War ended at Appomattox Courthouse. The Second World War in the Pacific ended in a surrender ceremony on the USS *Missouri* in Tokyo Bay. It is altogether less obvious where and when the war of resistance in the Baltic states ended. The war did not even end with the failed Gulag uprisings, as armed conflict was still happening, albeit waning, while those revolts were taking place.

It could even be argued that the war lasted as long as the Soviet occupation, with the resistance merely shifting from armed resistance to various non-violent methods. The period from 1945 to 1955 was about guns and grenades and living in the woods. The period from 1955 onward was more about underground publications, passive resistance, and organising in ways that did not involve actual armed acts. While we could certainly term this as a 'struggle', it is hard to call it 'warfare'. There was never a point in time in the Soviet occupation of the Baltic states where there was not resistance of some form. But at some point, the struggle stopped being about living in the woods and having guns and more about fighting with words and ideas. The struggle that used words and ideas, from the 1960s into the 1980s, helped keep the idea of Baltic independence alive and gave a nucleus from which this entire region came back from a state of near death. But as this was a gradual shift in the centre of gravity, we cannot point to a specific place or time.

At some point, and it is hard to point to a time and a place, the Forest Brotherhood transitioned from armed resistance to small groups merely holding out and evading capture. As these small groups were gradually broken up, died, surrendered, fled, or otherwise declined in size and numbers, they were reduced to lone individuals eking out a spartan existence in the forests. Sovietisation and counterinsurgency tactics were, gradually and eventually, effective in choking the life out of the armed struggle. But how and when did the struggle end? There were likely Forest Brothers who died alone and unnoticed in the countryside. But there are also some answers to the question, as we have the advantage of records from the Soviet occupier to tell us about the last Forest Brothers in the three countries.

Estonia

The last battles fought by the Estonian Forest Brothers were some clashes involving three- or four-person cells in 1955 and 1956. General amnesties were declared in 1956 and 1957, and a number of partisans surrendered. By this point, the authorities knew that fake amnesties were counterproductive and that genuine amnesties resulted in people turning themselves in. Many were not even arrested, and many who did face arrest were released after questioning.

Estonian Forest Brothers managed to hold out alone or in pairs into the 1960s. In 1964, in the Jõgeva district, the brothers Aksel and Arnold Ojaste turned themselves in and were amnestied.[1] Arnold eventually led the Forest Brotherhood veterans' organisation well into the 2000s. One Jüri Keskküla was found in a hidden room on a farm on the island of Saaremaa in 1964, which had been his hideout since the German occupation. One of the last armed confrontations was in February 1965, when Raimond Mölder was tracked down by police. He wounded two police before he was captured.[2]

The last armed Forest Brothers to be captured were the Mõttus brothers, Hugo and Aksel. They had been hiding in a dugout near the Latvian border since the end of the Second World War. They were the last of their family and apparently kept sharp by reading books they stole from the local library. They had about 700 books stockpiled in barrels. In the summer of 1967, several police caught them in an ambush and seized their weapons. They were eventually sentenced to ten years' imprisonment.

A few holdouts managed to last until the 1970s. One man, Kalev Arro, passed himself off as a vagrant for decades. This was not easy, as vagrancy was illegal in the Soviet Union. He had been active with the Piho group of Forest Brothers. The rest of his group had been killed after a stand-off in 1949, but Arro had escaped. He lived in the woods for decades thereafter. In June 1974, two drunken tractor drivers confronted him, and Arro shot one of them dead. The other fled and summoned help. A manhunt ensued, and Arro was cornered. Armed with two Walther pistols and a knife, Arro was eventually felled in a shootout with the police.

The last known Forest Brother to be found in the wild was August Sabe (also spelled Sabbe in some accounts), son of a miller in the Pōlva district. After the Second World War, Soviet security agents tried to turn him into an informant. He gave no reports to the Chekists, and eventually they arrived at his family mill to deal with him. He fled, swimming up the millstream unseen.[3] Sabe joined the 'Orion' group of partisans in the area's forests. This group lasted until 1952, when Sabe was lucky enough to be left behind to look after the group's bunker and goods. The rest of the group was lured into a Soviet trap, but evidently nobody gave up Sabe's location.

Sabe had many friends in the area who could supply him with food. He was also a keen fisherman. Friends and relatives managed to circulate the rumour that he had died of tuberculosis. Eventually, though, villages were abandoned because of collectivisation. Old friends died, and he did not make new ones. Amazingly, Sabe survived until 1978. After reports of a mysterious armed man fishing in the local area, the local KGB chief mounted a plain-clothes operation. When confronted by the Chekists, Sabe fought with them and jumped into the Vōhandu River. He never came up for air, and his drowned body was eventually retrieved. Thus ended the partisan war in Estonia.

Latvia

In Latvia, deportations, collectivisation, amnesties, and counterinsurgency had ground the Forest Brothers into dust. However, there were small pockets of holdouts just as there were in Estonia and Lithuania. In 1953, the Soviets believed that fewer than 100 partisans were still active in Latvia. The last major group of Latvian Forest Brothers was in Vidzeme. The small group led by Stanislavs Zavadskis gave up in 1956 after a personal appeal from the chief of the Latvian SSR KGB. On New Year's Eve, 1959, one partisan named Arnolds Spārns was, possibly, the last armed Latvian Forest Brother to come out of the woods. He lived long enough to grant an oral interview that was recorded in 2011.

The endurance record for Forest Brothers is held by a Latvian. In 1995, after the last of the Soviet troops had finally left Latvia, a seventy-year-old man entered a rural police station in Pelēči parish and gave himself up, although there was now nothing that the police were going to arrest him for. His name was Jānis Pīnups, and he had a story to tell.

In August 1944, at the age of nineteen, Mr Pīnups had been forcibly conscripted into the Red Army. However, he was wounded in battle and left for dead. He woke up and took advantage of the situation to go home. Legally, he had been written off as dead, so he was not even considered a deserter that the authorities were looking for. A peaceful man, we cannot really consider him a guerrilla fighter. He did not take up arms. But he lived off the grid and below the Soviet radar for the entire length of the Soviet occupation of Latvia. For fifty years, his family kept him safe and fed. He even once got medical care from a Soviet clinic under an assumed name. He survived in a series of underground bunkers he had dug with help from his family. The Republic of Latvia restored his citizenship and awarded him a pension.[4]

Lithuania

Organised resistance lasted longer in Lithuania. Things finally seem to have fallen apart in 1953, when the MGB picked apart the remnants of the LLKS. In January, the last commander of the LLKS western region, Antanas Bakšys, was cornered and committed suicide. He had been deported to the Tula region in Russia but walked some 600 miles back to Lithuania to join the fight, a rare exception to the theory that population relocation suppressed partisan recruitment. In February 1953, Juozas Šibaila was betrayed by a captured partisan who gave up his location under torture. He and another partisan were killed. Sergijus Staniškis, the head of the eastern region, also fell in February. He had been a cavalryman in the Lithuanian Army and had fought hard as a partisan since 1945, rising through the ranks. An MGB manhunt found his bunker. Surrounded, he destroyed his documents and communications equipment and shot himself.

Another holdout was the leader of the movement, Juozas Žemaitis, who had been in hiding. Žemaitis had attempted to retire as chair of the LLKS after suffering a stroke in December 1951. But the organisation by was by then too fragmented to elect a replacement. In May 1953, his bunker location, near Jurbarkas, was betrayed. In an incident allegedly involving some sort of incapacitant chemical agent, Žemaitis was captured. After a show trial, Žemaitis was executed in Moscow at the infamous Butyrka prison. The LLKS was broken.

The only surviving LLKS leader was Vanagas—the American-born Ramanauskas, whose exploits have been detailed in Chapter 8. It is estimated that, in 1956, he was one of about forty-five partisans still in hiding. The Chekists had spent eleven years searching for this legendary figure. A senior security officer, Petras Raslanas, the perpetrator of the infamous Rainiai massacre, was put in charge of a squad to find Vanagas. Vanagas and his wife were laying low in an apartment in Kaunas, not in a bunker in the forest. One of Vanagas' old military school friends, Antanas Urbonas, had been secretly recruited as an informant. Ramanauskas and his wife were seized on 12 October 1956. He was tortured and eventually executed in late 1957. This is widely accepted as the end point of the armed resistance in Lithuania.

However, various partisan acts did continue for a time after Vanagas' death. Printed proclamations were posted anonymously, and there were a number of incidents of Lithuanian flags being raised. Pranas Končius ('Adomas'—Adam) had evaded capture when his group was surrounded in 1953 and continued to live in the woods for another twelve years. In July 1965, he died in a shootout with the KGB, although he may have killed himself to avoid capture. Kostas Lyuberskis ('Žvainys'—Firecracker), who had been a pilot for the small Lithuanian Air Force before the war, was caught and killed in October 1969.[5]

Finally, there was Stasys Guiga, codenamed 'Tarzanas', for which no translation is necessary. In his youth, he had been in the Riflemen's Union. He had spent the period from 1944 to 1952 fighting as a Forest Brother. He went to ground after his comrades were killed. He lived in hiding near the small village of Činčikos, north-east of Vilnius. A local woman, Onutė Činčikaitė, looked after him in exchange for clandestine help around the farm. He died of pneumonia in 1986. He was secretly buried and was only publicly acknowledged by local residents after independence.[6]

Transition to civil resistance

The Forest Brothers became ghosts. Signs of their activity faded away, replaced by rumours and hints of their presence. There were, certainly, men who were wanted by the authorities who could not be accounted for. Things went missing in rural areas. But the armed struggle faded from real life, if not from memory. To this day, the memory of partisan resistance remains part of popular culture. There are strong musical traditions in all three countries, and Forest brother folksongs have entered the canon of Baltic folk music. Names and symbols from the era percolate through to the present. It is not an accident that a drone donated in July 2022 by Lithuanians for the defence of Ukraine bears the name 'Vanagas'.

In all three countries, largely non-violent civil resistance movements slowly grew as the 1950s faded into the 1960s and 1970s. These dissident movements began to closely resemble those in other countries under Communist dictatorship in the Soviet Union and Eastern Europe. Some of the underground publications of the Forest Brothers reappeared in new form, produced by dissidents. In Lithuania and parts of Latvia, the Catholic Church continued to play a role in the resistance. The history of these movements and the later Soviet era is an interesting one, and part of the story of restoration of Baltic independence, which came to fruition in 1990 and 1991. However, it is a story for another book.

14

CRITICISMS OF THE FOREST BROTHERS

BANDITS? NAZIS? COLLABORATORS?

In February 2022, Putin's Russia invaded neighbouring Ukraine under the pretext that Ukraine was run by a 'Nazi regime'. Using the words 'Nazi' and 'fascist' in those parts of Central and Eastern Europe stirs the pot. The accusation of being a Nazi will sting. Yet we are dealing with a complex part of the world and a complicated period.

An entire swathe of Europe was caught between fascism and Communism. The far-right fascist movements of Europe, including the Nazis, claimed their enemies were Communists. Communists claimed their enemies were fascists and Nazis. Most people in Europe were not fascist, Nazi, or Communist. Much commentary is devoid of nuance or ambiguity. The events of this period cast shadows and leave ample scope for blind spots. A historian's duty is to get to the bottom of this and cast light into the shadows and peer into the blind spots. People who live in Britain or North America have the luxury of seeing the Second World War in Europe as a stark binary between good and bad. But if you were a Pole, a Ukrainian, a Finn, or a Lithuanian, for example, you had a variety of bad options, and often no good ones. Sometimes even making no decision at all was a bad choice too, because bad things happened to such people as well. The period from 1939 onward is a difficult one in this part of the world, and it is a grievous error to view it through the same prism that an American or British person would view it. People found themselves on different sides of the conflict without making any personal decision.

The events described in this book occurred in complicated times. In some interpretations of this period, the Forest Brothers are problematic. Some people have, historically, found it convenient to misrepresent them or even deny their existence. Looking at the commentary that has emerged since 1945, five critiques of the Forest Brothers emerge. I will take these critiques head-on.

The first is that the whole thing never happened. Many accounts of the history of this area that were written in the Soviet sphere of influence basically omit any reference to Baltic partisans. Large, detailed Soviet works on the history of the 'Great Patriotic War' say nothing on the subject. Some works that talk about partisans only talk about Moscow-sponsored irregulars and arrogate the term to apply only to such movements. This is not really a critique but a flat-out whitewash. Fortunately, such claims are now rare. This entire book is a rebuttal of this easily dismissed charge.

The second critique downplays the significance of the Forest Brotherhood movement in the broader context of the time. This is the implied critique in many works about the history of the region, even well-intended ones, that skip over or barely mention the topic. Perhaps it is too hard to address. For decades, there was little information that could be used by Western historians seeking to write a serious history on the subject. Someone writing about this in 1970 might have had little choice but to glaze over it. But we live in new times. There is information, and there is a lot of it if you try to look for it. There are two ways to address this critique. The first is that the Forest Brotherhood matters because it is part of the history of three small countries. It might not matter much to someone in New York or London, but that is not the definition of insignificant. The second response is that it matters very much, as I will argue in the conclusion of this book.

A third critique is that the Forest Brotherhood movements were only ever the pawn of Western intelligence agencies. A body of discourse that can best be described as conspiracist nonsense attempts to view much of the world's events since 1945 through the lens of American (and to a lesser extent, British) intelligence agencies. Such a view is inadvertently aided by intelligence and espionage books, many of which are actually very good and well resourced, that might give the reader a slanted perspective. If your only knowledge of Baltic partisans is a book, even a very good one, that mentions them in passing as part of a specialist tale of Cold War intelligence and espionage, you might pick up an odd idea or two along the way.

There were, indeed, contacts between Baltic resistance movements and Swedish, Finnish, German, British, French, and American intelligence agencies. This much is true. But to claim that the Forest Brotherhood was simply an arm of Western intelligence is ahistorical and deprives tens or hundreds of thousands of Baltic resistance fighters of their agency and legitimacy. Chapter 12 digs deep into this aspect of Baltic resistance. The timing was never right for the Forest Brothers to have been an arm of Western intelligence, as all of the major activity predates the Western intelligence officers even starting their work in this sphere. Furthermore, the West had other ideas. It largely wanted liaison and intelligence collection, not a partisan uprising. Finally, the West's intelligence efforts were riddled with informants and traitors. Attributing the whole thing to a Western plot inadvertently undermines the actual effectiveness of Soviet intelligence operations.

These three allegations are easily dismissed as facile. But the other two critiques deserve deeper examination and reflection, because they are at the heart of allegations, defamations, and libels used by enemies of the Baltic countries. But like many critiques and accusations, they have some grains of truth.

Bandits?

The most common trope in Soviet and then Russian sources has been to refer to the Forest Brothers as lawless criminals. They have been referred to as 'bandits' in numerous sources.[1] Other sources refer to them as criminals and antisocial elements.[2] Were they just bandits? The Forest Brothers were not bandits but were engaging in a political and military struggle. Words like 'bandit' and 'criminal' serve to remove politics and national identity from the debate. Admitting that someone is fighting a struggle for independence or even autonomy means admitting that people are fighting for ideas. The Soviets wanted to eradicate the very idea of Baltic nationhood. The Soviet brand of Marxism–Leninism attempted to declare a monopoly on truth and proposed a structure of society and flow of history. If you were on the wrong side of that structure and history, you were an enemy, and your ideas were wrong. It was much easier to brand the Forest Brotherhood bandits than combatants.

The Soviet usage of terms like 'bandit' and 'illegal' required a bit of circular logic. Forest Brothers are illegal because Soviet law says so. But rather a lot of people in the Baltic states never viewed Soviet laws and Soviet rule as legitimate. The Forest Brothers were illegal gangs of criminals in the eyes of a Soviet legal code that was not legal. The Soviet occupation of the Baltic states was always illegitimate. Therefore, the idea of what was or was not 'legal' is far from clear. The argument that they were all criminals because they were illegal groups is a pointless one that only works if you fully adopt a flawed set of premises.

The accusation can sting because bandits existed and actual banditry occurred. There really were bandits lurking about in the 1941 risings and early in the 1944–5 phase of the Forest Brotherhood struggle. Groups of opportunists fled to the forests along with patriots. Some degree of guilt by association is employed by those wanting to adopt the Soviet line. That partisan groups did at times steal in order to survive makes it slightly easier to paint them as simple thieves. Tales of Estonian train robberies make for good anecdotes, but they also inadvertently help the 'bandit' narrative. Of course, if the Soviets declared that absolutely everything was state property, and they did, then, by that definition, even picking a wild mushroom in the forest was theft in Soviet eyes. The banditry accusation only works if you deliberately distort the perspective.

However, the sheer difficulty of life in the wilderness tended to weed out criminals. As a practical matter, the opportunities for personal enrichment, theft, rape, and other forms of banditry were greater on the Soviet side. Looking through the events of the period, the true bandits were the rapacious Soviet Army units and the *istrebiteli* battalions that were actively engaged in banditry. The element of Baltic society that most closely resembles stereotypical bandits were the social elements heavily recruited into the Soviet occupation forces in 1944 and 1945, when acts of banditry were widely reported. More significantly, many rural residents and the Forest Brothers themselves viewed the partisan groups as a bulwark against banditry. The biggest bandits were the Soviets themselves, and the biggest act of banditry was stealing three entire countries.

The N word—'Nazi'

The most serious allegation is Nazism. This is a common trope. The Forest Brothers, and sometimes the entire nations of Lithuania, Latvia, and Estonia, are often described in Soviet or Russian nationalist discourse as Nazis or direct allies of the Nazis. It is the most searing of the accusations and the most hurtful. Part of this allegation involves a deliberate muddling of categories of people and loose logic. Some arguments proceed along a line of logic such as this: Some Lithuanians were, indeed, enablers of the Holocaust. The Lithuanian Forest Brothers were Lithuanians. Therefore, the Lithuanian Forest Brothers were Nazis. Almost nobody articulates the argument in such a direct manner, but that is the basic underlying logic.

The Nazi allegation comes in overlapping guises, and it is important to understand the anatomy of this body of criticism.

'They fought on the wrong side'

The simplest allegation is one that I hear from people in the West as well as the typical Soviet-era sources. Fundamentally, those making this claim argue that as the Soviets were against the Nazis in the war, anyone who fought against the Soviets must have been a Nazi. This strand of argument relies on the listener being ignorant. Western popular culture tends to downplay or ignore the fact that the USSR entered the war in Europe on the same side as Nazi Germany and was on that side of the war, actively supporting Germany, until June 1941. At the point at which the Baltic states fell under Soviet occupation in 1940, the Soviets were allied with Germany. The Balts were only ever allied with themselves. The big alliance around them shifted. They just wanted to be independent.

Those of us fortunate enough to have grown up in Western Europe or North America have a far more cut and dried view of the Second World War. There was the good side and there was the bad side. The problem for a lot of people in Finland and Eastern Europe was that, from their perspective, there was a bad side

(Nazis) and a different bad side (Soviets), and they were stuck in the middle. It seems unfair to project a false degree of moral clarity on to that situation. At the time the Forest Brotherhood started, the Nazis and Soviets were on the same side of the war. If you started out struggling against a Soviet Union allied with Nazi Germany, it's not your fault if Nazi Germany turned on the Soviets and kicked them out of the alliance, especially when the oppressor is still oppressing you.

'The Baltic states were fascist anyway'

Some Soviet-era commentary portrays the pre-war Baltic states as fascist dictatorships. This makes it easier to justify their 'liberation' and the repressive actions taken against them. As discussed earlier in the book, far-right politics and authoritarianism plagued all three countries in the 1920s and 1930s. But none of them descended into fascism, and they had few of the hallmarks of fascist regimes. Indeed, actual fascists were largely considered a menace to the right-wing governments of the time. It is a gross distortion to portray the three countries in the 1930s as 'fascist'. They were certainly authoritarian and less than democratic, but they were not fascist.

We should also not let legitimate critiques of pre-war regimes cloud the issue. It is possible to be in favour of Baltic statehood and independence without being a proponent of the pre-war dictatorship. By the time the partisan movements became a proper armed rural insurgency from 1945 onward, there were very few Forest Brothers aiming to restore the pre-war leadership. Estonians were fighting for the idea of Estonia; few were fighting to restore the Päts government. If a Lithuanian Forest Brother proposed a toast to Smetona, he might well have been laughed at. Even if the pre-war regimes really were fascist, that does not take away the legitimacy of the later independence movement. With regard to the Forest Brothers, this allegation is a red herring.

Furthermore, Nazi Germany had specific disputes and grievances with the interwar Baltic states. German–Lithuanian relations were antagonistic due to the Memel issue. Lithuania was the only country in Europe to jail Nazis in any quantity before the war. The treatment and fate of Baltic Germans was a lesser but not minor issue between Germany, Estonia, and Latvia during this period as well. There is no body of evidence to claim that, somehow, the three countries were pre-war allies of Nazi Germany.

Anatomising collaboration, cooperation, and coercion

The biggest allegation is also the most specific and the one with the most evidence behind it. People in all three countries fought on the side of the Germans. Other people helped the Germans in other ways. There is no doubt that some people in Estonia, Latvia, and Lithuania greeted the arriving Germans in 1941 as liberators. There is also no doubt that a lot of people in all three countries assisted the Germans in their execution of genocide. Some of the earlier hagiographic accounts of Forest Brothers downplay or ignore this period. But it is impossible to ignore the facts: to varying degrees, Baltic people aided the Germans, and they did so for a variety of voluntary and involuntary reasons.

Collaboration, in all its flavours, is a society-level issue in the Baltic states, and to apply it just to the Forest Brothers is simplistic. But if the Forest Brothers were a subset of society, so were collaborators of various types. Little good comes from trying to look away. Instead, it is useful to look into this.

For lack of a better term, there is a 'spectrum of collaboration' between Baltic peoples and the card-carrying Nazis and their apparatus. It is useful to dissect this beast of 'collaboration' and look at all its parts. This spectrum of collaboration ranges from actual Nazi party members and people who willingly did very bad things all the way to people who were conscripted or enslaved, often literally at gunpoint, and compelled to do things to help the Nazi regime. Everyone agrees that the former are collaborators. Reasonable people would consider the latter category as victims, not collaborators. In the Baltic states, there were more people in the latter category than in the former. But there are many shades of grey between these two extremes. So, let us look at the spectrum.

Actual Nazis

There's no getting around a basic fact that Baltic nationalism does not actually sit well with Germany's Nazi ideology of the era. Hitler's 'National Socialism' did not just have political beliefs. It had a worldview that was steeped in a particular ethnonationalist philosophy. The Nazi worldview had no place for Estonian, Latvia, or Lithuanian statehood. While Nazi racial theology did not place Balts on quite as low a rung in their artificial hierarchy as Slavs, there simply was not a place for Balts to have their own countries. The Nazi worldview saw the eventual settlement of those defined by their racial pseudoscience as ethnic 'Aryans' into the three Baltic states. There is no cause to think that such a plan would end well. The war ended before such plans could be put into full swing, as this hinged on conquering Russia and resettling Balts further east.

There were, nonetheless, certainly ethnic Germans in the three Baltic states who were Nazis. Rather a lot of Baltic Germans did not appreciate Nazi Germany's attitude toward them. Then there is the issue of the German state-sponsored repatriation of Baltic Germans in the late 1930s, another such campaign in the first period of Soviet occupation, and then the final German retreat from the Baltic states in 1944–5. These left very few Baltic Germans, of any political inclination, in the Baltic states. There were, both metaphorically and literally, boot prints on the bodies and quaysides as Baltic Germans, both Nazi and other, beat a hasty retreat out of the region in 1944. Very few Baltic Germans ended up in the partisan movements.

Even at the point where Nazi ideology came closest to accepting another ethnicity, in Estonia, the Estonians were not Nazis. The Holocaust scholar Anton Weiss-Wendt's probing analysis of the many Estonians who actively or passively cooperated with the Holocaust lays out a lot of acts of collaboration by Estonians. But even his analysis is clear: 'At no point in time, neither before nor during the war, did Estonians subscribe to Nazi ideology.'[3]

One salient point that can be examined is how the actual Nazi occupation treated Baltic resistance movements. The Nazi occupiers tolerated a narrow aspect of Baltic national identity, and only to the point that it helped them recruit collaborators to run the countries and exploit their resources, particularly labour.

Baltic fascists and anti-Semites of other stripes

Pre-war Estonia, Latvia, and Lithuania all had far-right movements and groups. As discussed earlier in the book, the pre-war authoritarian Baltic governments actually feared and suppressed movements further to the right. It is clear that the far-right groups that did exist provided recruitment fodder for the Nazi occupiers. The Pērkonkrusts movement in Latvia was the movement that most resembled Nazism. With a swastika (seemingly independently derived rather than copying the Nazis in Germany), odd salutes, grey uniforms, and black berets, they were essentially fascist in outlook and appearance. Gustavs Celmiņš, their leader, and many prominent members were active supporters of the Nazi occupation, although the German authorities proscribed the group. Some members aided the Holocaust. But the significant issue relevant to this book is that while some individual Pērkonkrusts members ended up in partisan units, they were not a major influence on the Latvian Forest Brothers. The Nazi occupiers did not trust these local far-right movements very much at all. In Lithuania, many of the Voldemaras movement were active in the 1941 anti-Soviet uprising. Nazi ideology did not allow much room for expression of nationalism or patriotism by rival parties, so even the Voldemaras movement was proscribed.

Anti-Semites of various other bents no doubt took advantage of the situation or, at a minimum, had their ideology exploited. Such examples, where we find them, must be called out for what they were. We can point to many examples of people in all three countries who helped the Nazis oppress their countrymen. More often than not, these people ended up leaving their country instead of fighting the Soviets. Some examples stand out. Jurgis Bobelis, the Lithuanian policeman who served as a commander in Kaunas under the Nazis, ended up in Germany in 1944 and never went back. An Estonian, Karl Linnas, helped run a concentration camp. He fled with the Germans, ended up in the United States, and was deported to the Soviet Union decades later by the Reagan administration. A number of Latvians cooperated in the Holocaust through an infamous unit called the Arajs Kommando, named after its leader, Viktors Arājs, a Latvian of mixed Latvian and Baltic German heritage. His band of men was responsible for about half of the Jews murdered in Latvia, under SS command. He did not stay to fight the Soviets. He ended up in Germany at the end of the war. He was eventually outed, and West Germany rightly tried and imprisoned him as a war criminal.

This is a tale that runs alongside the events of this book, but it is a different tale nonetheless.

There is much more of a grey area with some of the Forest Brothers who did serve in German-sponsored military or paramilitary units. When it comes to such units, it is not easy to make blanket statements about just how ethically and morally questionable any individual's service may have been. We can examine a particular individual's wartime service using two different gauges. First, what was the means by which they joined and their motivation? The second gauge is, did that unit engage in war crimes or crimes against humanity?

Many thousands of Baltic people fought in German military units, and some Estonians served in Finnish units. How do we reckon such people on a spectrum of collaboration? These people could be broadly divided into five categories. It is almost certain that there is a high degree of overlap between these categories. Any one individual may have had motivations or circumstances that put them in multiple categories. Each category is worth some further examination.

First, there were the willing recruits. The German invasion came on the back of a brutal occupation. Many people wanted revenge against their oppressors. Some were ideologically hell-bent against Communism. Some hated Russians, often for reasons that would be understandable given what they had just gone through. Others felt that it was pragmatic to be on the side of the winners in the war, and for the first year at least, the Germans looked like they were the winning side.

The second category was made up of people who joined voluntarily but were deceived into doing so by Nazi propaganda. It would be naïve to forget just how effective German propagandists were. Particularly in Latvia and Estonia, the Nazi regime had access to Baltic Germans who knew the local languages and culture well and could exploit existing fault lines. Germany's war with the Soviet Union was portrayed as a holy crusade against Communism, and the Communists had just spent a year oppressing everyone. Much Nazi propaganda went to great lengths to mine existing prejudices like historical anti-Semitism and worked hard to conflate Bolshevism with Jews.

The third category was made up of people who were needy. We should not forget that these were hard times. People joined up because of the opportunity to be fed, clothed, and paid. The living conditions in the German military and auxiliary units were not great, but they were better than nothing. Some people saw joining up as, if not a road out of privation, at least a better alternative.

The fourth category comprised conscripts and de facto conscripts. At some points during German manpower drives, many people were coerced into military service by being given a choice of military service or slave labour. In some cases, people were threatened with imprisonment or service. In other cases, people's families were threatened. Someone who 'voluntarily' joined a military unit as their only real option other than slave labour must be treated with some degree of leniency.

The fifth category were those who used the Germans for their own ends. Particularly in the latter period of the German occupation, many people could see which way the wind was blowing. The return of a harsh Soviet occupation was seen as a sad and frightening inevitability. The drafting of thousands of people into various 'self-defence' units as the Eastern Front approached the Baltic states meant that many people were actually looking ahead to partisan resistance. The German efforts in the latter part of the war were transparently desperate, and a number of people joined specifically to obtain weapons. There are even accounts of multiple enlistments by the same person to collect weapons. People joining German units to obtain resources for partisan resistance certainly cannot be judged harshly as Nazi collaborators.

Actual conduct

Any attempt to evaluate wartime service must also account for conduct. What actual deeds or misdeeds a particular individual did or did not do must be taken into account. There are a lot of grey areas, and it is, in fact, impossible to make blanket statements. The grey area is further muddied by desertion and infiltration. Baltic people deserted prolifically from military, paramilitary, and auxiliary units. In addition, some Balts actively infiltrated units, most commonly to gain information and equipment.

Let us look at some theoretically feasible 'grey area' cases as a thought exercise. Are the following people 'Nazi collaborators' and, if so, to what extent?

- A person participates in an uprising in 1941 and becomes part of an organised partisan unit that then becomes one of the auxiliary police battalions. The police battalion is posted to guard Jewish prisoners. The person doesn't like this and deserts.
- The same person, but their police assignment for the war is to guard the docks in Riga or serve in the fire brigade.
- An Estonian whose family members were sent to Siberia by the Soviets falls prey to German propaganda, is recruited into the Estonian Legion, and spends the rest of the war fighting in conventional actions on the Eastern Front.
- A Lithuanian gets dragged in off the streets and spends a year in Silesia in an armaments factory making ammunition.
- A Latvian who joins no group and does no military or paramilitary service but secretly informs both the NKVD and the Gestapo about people in his neighbourhood at various points during the 1940–5 period. Because the records are lost, nobody knows this ever happened.
- A Lithuanian who joins the Territorial Defence Forces, but who deserts to the forests after three weeks with a rifle, a warm coat, and a rucksack full of food and ammunition to await further developments.
- A former military officer signs up for a German unit but uses his personal influence to moderate the worst excesses of the occupation for his men and the area where he is assigned.

One can spend all day concocting such scenarios, and there will be, somewhere in history, examples of real people that match these notional examples. The Germans ruthlessly exploited locally recruited units, and a lot of people ended up being sent to do things that they had not expected to do.

Given these complexities, we should be careful to assess the full circumstances of a particular partisan who turns up in a Forest Brother unit after the German occupation. Many partisans had served, in one capacity or another, in German-run or German-sponsored military or paramilitary formations. This does not taint the movement itself.

Looking at the Forest Brotherhoods themselves

Broadly speaking, the political philosophies of Baltic partisan movements were pragmatic. These movements were wide tents. There were pockets of ideological motivation, but where they existed, they tended to be either religious (typically Roman Catholic, especially in Lithuania but also notably in one corner of Latvia) or adherents to pre-1940 political parties. However, we can specifically look at the handful of larger partisan organisations that did emerge and see what their beliefs were. We can look at documents like the Estonian RVL charter and the various declarations by Latvian and Lithuanian groups. We find a lot of patriotism and a desire to restore nationhood. What we do not find is much if any sympathy for the German occupier or sympathy for fascism in the creeds of these groups.

Work has also emerged, at least in Lithuania, examining the individual records of individual partisans. Some of the most recent scholarship digs into the actual statistics of the membership of Lithuanian partisan groups. The Lithuanian scholar Dainius Noreika has examined records thoroughly and assessed the composition of the Lithuanian partisan groups.[4]

Noreika analysed over 1,000 partisan biographies. Using this work, we can start to understand how many post-1944 Forest Brothers may have been involved with the German occupier, and in what role. Around 25 per cent of the partisans had been involved in the June 1941 uprising in some fashion: so, even if one were to disregard the entire June 1941 movement by association with the anti-Semitic pogroms that occurred on its margins, three-quarters of later Forest Brothers had not been involved in it.

Some 14.4 per cent of the partisans had served in armed units under the Nazis, but this includes 6.2 per cent who had served in 'self-defence battalions' and 4.3 per cent in the short-lived Lithuanian Territorial Defence Force. The self-defence battalions had quite varied service, and some were, indeed, used by the Nazi occupiers for war crimes and crimes against humanity, while others had less problematic service records. Many of those who joined the Territorial Defence Force, on the other hand, often did so in the very last phase of the German occupation in order to gain weapons and ammunition to fight the oncoming Soviets.

Noreika finds that only fifty-nine of the 1,000 partisans he studied were actively associated with aiding the Holocaust, mostly in arrest and transport roles. In particular, he calls out the record of Baltūsis (discussed in Chapter 11) as problematic. Does 5.9 per cent condemn the entire movement? This is a subjective judgement, and opinions will continue to vary. But for every Baltūsis, there seem to be many Lukšas.

It is a historian's duty to call out Nazi collaborators where we find them, and Noreika's work shows that Lithuanian scholars are serious about outing the abettors of genocide. But some degree of revisionism and possible falsification is also evident in accounts that make the 'Nazi' accusation. Noreika shows, for example, that the allegation that Žemaitis, Lukša, and Ramanauskas participated in the Holocaust is largely unsourced, often relying solely on a dodgy manuscript by a former NKVD official named Nachman Dushansky, who may have been trying to cover his own misdeeds. Interestingly, at the Soviet trials of Žemaitis and Ramanauskas, no claim was made that they were involved in Nazi atrocities.

Collaboration with the Soviet occupier

We should never let the Soviet Union claim a monopoly on the use of the word 'collaboration'. Those who claim that 'Balts were Nazis' tend to overlook those who collaborated or cooperated with the Soviet occupier. Some opportunists collaborated with both sides, as there is always a percentage of the population who watch which way the wind blows. As many, and possibly more, Baltic people actively fought on the side of the Soviets as were enrolled in German military formations.

A verdict?

Where does this leave us with the Forest Brothers? One of the great problems with the totalitarian ideologies of Naziism and

Soviet Communism is that they and their followers were practically everywhere in Europe in the 1930s and 1940s. No country was free of the scourge of far-right or far-left extremists. Historians should not single out the Baltic states for some sort of higher level of scrutiny than, say, Belgium, France, or Yugoslavia.

One useful concept for understanding the period comes from Holocaust studies. In his book *Versions of Survival: The Holocaust and the Human Spirit* (1982), Lawrence Langer gives us the concept of 'choiceless choice'.[5] This is the idea that people can be put in situations where all of the available options are bad. The broader geopolitics of the Baltic situation, which sandwiched the three countries between Naziism and Soviet Communism, and a myriad of specific situations and actions, put most people in the Baltic states in periods of hopelessness where all available decisions and outcomes were bad. In fact, the entire phenomenon of the Forest Brothers largely exists because, at various points, some people had an opportunity to escape the no-win choiceless choice situations, and the way out was armed partisan resistance.

So, were the Forest Brothers Nazis? No. Were there some bad people in the movement? Yes. Were there a lot? Probably not. Were there a lot of people with a questionable background? Certainly, but the whole mess of the times meant that a lot of people ended up with a questionable background by accident. Were the Forest Brotherhood movements fascist? No.

CONCLUSION

IMPACTS AND IMPLICATIONS

There is a swathe of Europe with a troubled twentieth-century history. From Finland down to Greece, a large slice of Europe was sandwiched between larger empires. Smaller nations and ethnic groups were stuck between larger ones that were often in conflict. The narrative played out differently in each of these places, and it had different impacts across the region. Indeed, as this book is being written, some of the tensions bottled up from the 1940s are still being litigated with bullets in a bitter war in Ukraine. Unweaving this carpet of history to look at the bits that represent Estonia, Latvia, and Lithuania is not easy.

I have found this period of history to be interesting, and if you have made it this far, I hope you have as well. But history is more than interesting stories. What can we learn from this period? How does the verdict of history read when we examine the spectrum of available information?

We know that Soviet-era accounts either ignore the Forest Brothers, treat them as bandits, or accuse the Baltic peoples of being Nazis, as discussed at some length in the previous chapter. The polar opposite of these Soviet accounts are patriotic and nationalist accounts published in the West during the Cold War, some of which verge on hagiography and martyrology. Given the oppression that Baltic peoples had suffered, there were and are legitimate grievances. These works, where they exist, tend to overlook the bad and accentuate the good. But these books have their place in the canon too. Estonians, Latvians, and Lithuanians, and those of an ethnic Baltic background, published books and articles discussing Soviet oppression in the Baltic states and made an effort to discuss the partisan resistance at a point when the subject had yet to receive much attention. The Lithuanian diaspora was larger in numbers, so the Lithuanian partisan resistance received somewhat more space in print than the Latvian and Estonian movements. In particular, the Lithuanian-American academic journal *Lituanus* was published in English. A number of academics of Baltic origins kept the subject alive in the West, and some of their scholarship has proved highly valuable in studying this period of history.

Some of the literature, particularly early in the Cold War, is unabashedly nationalist. Indeed, some statements in various books and articles make claims that have not been easy to substantiate. Emotions ran high, and it is my own belief that in a few places, there was a tendency towards polemic. The partisans were described as noble heroes fighting a glorious, if lost, cause. The occasional blind eye was turned on facts and situations that were inconvenient to the broader cause of Baltic independence. For example, some of the behaviour in the 1941 Lithuanian uprising was either downplayed or not mentioned at all in earlier accounts. One early work, Joseph Pajaujis-Javis' *Soviet Genocide in Lithuania* (1980),[1] totally denies German involvement in the 1941 uprising and pretty much ignores the German occupation. In later phases of resistance, numbers of partisans and numbers of Soviets killed were occasionally exaggerated, although this may have been out of lack of direct information.

The Baltic diaspora was a broad tent encompassing academics engaged in honest inquiry, the occasional scoundrel with personal deeds that they would want to hide or dilute, members of political parties from left to far right, and people with a particular axe to grind, but most often they were earnest people wanting the best for their country of origin. One can find examples of all of these in the émigré literature, including this author's own work from the late 1980s.

A third strain of historiography touches obliquely on the history of the Baltic states during this period. Holocaust studies have, at times, placed a fair bit of blame on Baltic collaborators for aiding and abetting the attempted extermination of the Jewish people. There are, to be certain, many people to blame and many fingers to point. As discussed in the previous chapter, there is a broad spectrum of activity and behaviour that could be construed as collaboration or cooperation with the enemy, and Holocaust scholarship has shed some light on this. Yet some discourse on the subject is reductionist, and reductionism is polemic. One can stake out a rigid position saying that everyone who carried a German rifle or wore a German uniform is as guilty as Himmler and Mengele. But surely this is reductionist. The man frog-marched into the Waffen SS by a conscription effort disguised as 'recruitment' is, at base level, a victim. If he went on to do bad things, then indeed he did bad things. But the enslavement of someone, and there was a lot of enslaving going on, should not lead to victim-blaming.

Holocaust studies point to some truly foul examples of human conduct worthy of condemnation. But one occasionally comes across oversimplification and controversy. Despite the numerous Baltic names among the Righteous at Yad Vashem who risked everything to save Jews, and, indeed, the well over 100,000 Balts who served in Soviet uniform fighting against Nazis, some of the Holocaust literature on the Lithuanians, Latvians, and Estonians comes close to bigotry and racism. I have been on the receiving end of abuse for my Lithuanian roots, even though part of my own family tree were likely Lithuanian Jews from Jurbarkas. If this book serves any purpose at all, it should help to elucidate the many shades of grey during the period. Nobody's cause, let alone Holocaust remembrance, is served by oversimplification.

Efforts to commemorate characters like Adolfas Ramanauskas and Alfons Rebane after the restoration of independence prompted criticism from some groups and individuals. Ramanauskas was criticised because he had fought in the 1941 Lithuanian uprising. Rebane was criticised because he fought for the Germans. But actual evidence of misconduct or war crimes by these two men is not to be found, even under great scrutiny. So does this amount to guilt by association? Or are there enough scoundrels to be found without tarring others?

The fourth wave of historical interpretation is better sourced, better conceived, and ultimately more useful. In more recent decades, the re-emergence of Estonia, Latvia, and Lithuania as independent states has led to a cultural renaissance that has extended into the study of recent history. This was coupled with extensive access to archival materials from the Soviet regime, many of which were seized at independence. Further archival materials were made available in the 1990s when Russia was less authoritarian than it is at present. Many thousands of documents and photographs consequently became available to scholars for the first time. Just as importantly, the retreat of the old occupiers meant that people were free to tell their stories. After all, this is not scholarship about the French Revolution but a period of history within living memory.

It is no exaggeration to say that the amount of material available to scholars, albeit mostly in languages other than English, has increased a hundred-fold in the space of a few years. It has taken decades for archivists and scholars to go through the trove of old papers, and discoveries will continue to be made years into the future as old files are finally read. It is also now true that much of this material is available electronically and rather generously made available for all of us. There is a significant language barrier, but even this is being overcome by relatively accurate online translation software. A hardcopy document in Lithuanian that you had to travel to Vilnius to read would have been largely inaccessible to most scholars. But now more of this material is available for a few minutes of online effort. What do these archival materials and fresh accounts from survivors and witnesses tell us?

The post-independence scholarship fills in many cracks and gaps. Thousands of documents add names, dates, and places and have brought to light many of the atrocities committed by the Soviet occupiers. From a broader Baltic perspective, an area of scholarship that had been heavily centred on Lithuanian partisans broadened, and we all learned more about Estonian and Latvian resistance movements. We also got to see many photographs and underground publications, which had been carefully filed away as evidence by the secret police.

The nature of totalitarian states is, fundamentally, bureaucratic. The Soviet state took a tsarist-era bureaucratic infrastructure of oppression and made it broader and more powerful. The state security organs of the USSR kept excellent records, many of which survive intact. This vast body of records confirms several key points. The Soviet occupations were truly awful: torture, murder, deportation of innocent civilians, expropriation of property, and myriad other crimes are documented in forensic detail. The old KGB files are truly damning. An émigré article in the 1960s might have said '3,000 people were deported from X district' and someone else might claim that the figure was an exaggeration—of course a nationalist account would say that. But if you are confronted with an official KGB file with 2,898 names of real people on it and actual dates of arrest, then the criticisms fade away. The archival material put meat on the bones of previous accusations. The state records and, especially, the attempts to document human memories from survivors and witnesses also yield up many hitherto unknown accounts of individual heroism by brave partisans.

The Soviet archival records have shown that the 'official' Soviet narratives of the era were replete with fiction. The portrayal of the resistance movement as apolitical bandits or Nazis is dishonest given that the Soviet archives were full of copies of resistance newspapers explaining their political beliefs. Nor were the movements small. As noted in earlier chapters, Soviet documentation clearly shows the extent of the movement, and it was not small. Partisans themselves and their sympathetic friends and relatives in the West claimed that the Baltic states were being butchered. In the end, the state archives provided the receipts to prove it.

It is also clear from the archives that 'collaboration' was not just a word to be used in the Second World War about cooperation and complicity with the Germans. Estonians, Latvians, and Lithuanians collaborated with the Soviet occupiers. While everyone knew this was happening, the archives provided information on who the collaborators were. The Soviet state sought to permeate society with informants. The records have gradually yielded names and reports. Some families were embarrassed to find that a relative had been an informer. As with other places under Soviet rule, it is important to remember that many people were given little choice but to cooperate with the authorities. Many of these informant reports are full of time-wasting nonsense. Spending hours wasting the time of secret policemen chasing ghosts and red herrings is, in fact, a valid tactic of resistance to totalitarianism. Thus some of these 'informants' were heroes in their own way.

Since 1990, scholarship has also sought to grapple with some of the nuances and grey areas, including the legacy of the Holocaust, collaboration with the Nazis, and collaboration with the Soviets.

Serious scholars saw the limitations of the earlier outlook and have not been afraid to confront hard questions. Professor Saulius Sužiedėlis, whose lengthy career put him in both the old emigration and post-1990 spheres of scholarship, aptly writes that '[t]he emphasis on martyrology and victimhood has, over the years, helped construct a rigid pattern of collective memories impervious to any revision based on new research'.[2] Episodes with ample grey areas, like the 1941 Lithuanian uprising, were opened to new scrutiny, much of which has been discussed earlier in the book.

Impacts: how it mattered

A final argument I occasionally receive, even within the year I've spent writing this book, was that the whole thing simply didn't matter. Those making this argument usually claim that as the defeat of the Forest Brothers was inevitable, there is little point studying the movement. An early version of this argument was originally couched in determinist terms by Marxist–Leninists, who, as a matter of doctrine, argued that history followed scientific laws and that Soviet Communism was on the right side of history as a scientific fact, as if it were a physical law of the universe. History has, ironically, proven that view to be bankrupt. But from a vantage point less prone to Marxist–Leninist obscurantism or Soviet revisionism, do these critics have a point? Were the Forest Brothers doomed? They probably were. But being 'doomed' does not mean that there was no point to their struggle or that it was not important. Just because someone is defeated does not mean that the effort had no impact.

Whether or not 'something mattered' is actually a difficult question to answer. When we are talking about the things that thousands of people in the Forest Brotherhood did, the answer to that question is that it mattered to them. People sacrificed their lives and lived in harsh conditions, sometimes for years. Human psychology is such that people do not do that sort of thing voluntarily unless it matters to them. Fighting for freedom, or even just staying alive or finding ways to protect one's family or friends, is an important motivation. Of course it 'mattered'. The more interesting question is why did it matter? What impacts did the movement have?

CONCLUSION

Protecting people and mitigating human suffering

The Forest Brothers often did what they could to protect the rural population from some of the worst excesses of the Soviet regime. There are numerous incidents of theft and looting being prevented as well as examples of Forest Brothers taking part in reprisals against Soviet officials and their collaborators. In some places for some periods, it is feasible that fear of partisan reprisal inhibited some of the crimes against the population in the immediate post-war era. It is easy to point to instances when some Forest Brother activity did protect people and reduce human suffering. Particularly in Latvia and Estonia, some partisan activity allowed people to flee the Soviet Union to Sweden or Finland. There are people who avoided deportation because of partisan activity. Certainly, deportations in some rural districts were slowed down. There are almost certainly people who avoided death, detention, or rape because a particularly vicious Soviet soldier or official was killed.

There is a natural counterargument to this claim, as some partisan activity elicited draconian responses. Did various Forest Brother deeds provoke a harsher response than what may otherwise have happened? The nature of the partisan struggle is such that it is improbable that any historian can quantify these effects and work out how it all balances out. My response to the counterargument is that some planned repressions and reprisals against the population were likely pushed back until after Stalin's death, at which point the Soviet state had a reduced arsenal of atrocity and perfidy. Regardless, the ultimate calculation on this will have to be left for the future.

Reducing the legitimacy of the occupation and keeping national identity alive

The Soviet Union was not merely occupying Estonia, Latvia, and Lithuania; it was trying to eradicate their national identities. The existence of armed partisans actively contesting foreign occupation and, importantly, using the language and symbols of the pre-war republic were direct challenges to this policy. Resistance to occupation reduced the perceived legitimacy of the occupation. The existence of movements that openly proclaimed Estonian, Latvian, and Lithuanian identity in a non-Soviet, non-Communist context helped to keep the idea of national identity alive. The memory of a brave if ultimately futile partisan resistance has formed part of the national identity of each of the three countries. The resistance kept the idea of independence alive long after the last partisans died or were captured. Never underestimate the value of a 'well, at least we went down fighting' narrative in national folklore.

The decades since the restoration of the Baltic states' independence have seen the dedication of a multitude of monuments to figures from the Forest Brotherhood era. Surviving Forest Brothers were granted recognition and pensions. The names of institutions and streets have been changed to commemorate figures from the era. That these names are even known at all is evidence, to some degree, that memories persisted.

Information warfare

The prolific production of underground publications served to provide information to the population. It could be argued that partisan efforts to keep the population informed through leaflets and periodicals kept Baltic populations better informed on the actual situation and world news than, say, Russians in the heartland of the Soviet Union. Providing people with an alternative to the Soviet view, which attempted to monopolise news and interpretation of events, was a worthy achievement. It is clearly significant that some alternative voices were still in print five or even seven years after the Soviets reoccupied the Baltic states.

Delaying collectivisation and demographic change

One hypothesis is that partisan resistance delayed Sovietisation and Russification of the three Baltic states by slowing the collectivisation of agriculture. Numerous scholars have made this assertion over the years. Partisan resistance certainly did not stop collectivisation efforts, but it slowed them down considerably. It is possible that partisan resistance had enough of a delaying effect on the Soviet transformation of Baltic society and economy for it to have had some lasting effects in the following decades. By forcing the Soviet authorities to take longer and devote more security forces to dispossessing farmers, the Forest Brothers postponed the inevitable. But even this postponement meant that fewer non-native people were brought in from other parts of the Soviet empire.

This raises an important question. Did Baltic resistance affect the demographics of the Baltic states? There was, in the post-partisan era, a concerted Soviet effort to resettle non-Baltic peoples, especially Russians but also other nationalities, into the Baltic republics of the USSR. Balts widely believe that part of the rationale for this was to dilute nationalism and national identity in the region. Did the partisan movement reduce or delay the Russification of the Baltic states? Even just delaying things by a few years until Stalin's death, which led to a slight reduction in coercion and repression, may have made a difference.

Certainly, it is easier to point at the case of Lithuania. Lithuania was less industrialised than Estonia or Latvia, both at the beginning of the Soviet occupation and at the end. There was less scope for mass importation of factory labourers and their families. It was more agrarian. It had a larger partisan movement, by any of the relevant measures, and the partisan movement directly opposed collectivisation of agriculture. For several years, the Lithuanian Forest Brothers deliberately targeted rural non-Lithuanian colonists arriving from the Soviet Union. Did such tactics work? Did they delay demographic change just enough so that, by the 1980s, there was still a degree of homogeneity and national identity in the three 'Baltic republics' of the USSR? I believe that this is a defendable hypothesis in the case of Lithuania.

Eroding the Gulag?

It is also possible to hypothesise that there was an impact from the imprisoned Baltic partisans through their role in the various Gulag uprisings in the mid-1950s, described in Chapter 13. This is a much harder impact to evaluate. We know that Baltic partisans were active participants in Kengir and other uprisings. However, it is hard to prove or disprove this hypothesis. Others were involved as well, especially Poles and Ukrainians. Might these uprisings have happened without Baltic participants? Were these Balts essential to the uprisings? Did Baltic participation make any difference to what happened? Furthermore, what actual effect did the uprisings have on the broader course of history? Again, these issues are debatable, but we can indeed document Baltic involvement in this part of history. The gradual reduction in the Gulag system's cruelty because of the uprisings is likely to have meant that more Estonians, Lithuanians, and Latvians survived captivity and then eventually returned to their homelands. This is an interesting idea but one that is difficult to quantify.

Buying time

In the end, many of these possible impacts and implications have an underlying component. The Forest Brothers bought time and delayed things. In the end, brave men and women sacrificed themselves to buy days, weeks, months, or years for their countrymen. Buying a few days' time could mean the ability to send a family member into the forest to avoid arrest or even send them on a boat to Sweden. Buying weeks could allow people to hide their valuables from looters. Buying months could mean getting in a harvest and laying in enough food to last a winter. Buying a year or two might drag things out long enough for something to happen, like Stalin dying and the regime suddenly becoming less repressive. Delaying the collectivisation of farms and hindering the settlement of others helped keep three nations alive as entities with a shared identity, culture, and language in their own homeland. In the Soviet Union, this was not a given. In the end, the greatest impact of the Forest Brothers was measured in terms of bought time, which had impacts in many different ways.

Implications for the present

What can the Forest Brotherhood teach us that is relevant in the present day? As this book is being written, a violent conflict rages not far from the Baltic states, between Russia and Ukraine. It is a war over two competing visions for the region. Is this a region only to be dictated to by the larger countries around it? Putin would have us think so. However, this is a region where a lot of different groups of people have equally valid claims to nationhood and statehood, and the broader trajectory of history in the twenty-first century is that we have ways to accommodate the statehood of small and medium-sized countries, even if they are surrounded by larger ones.

The Forest Brothers' struggle teaches several military lessons. While we know these lessons from both earlier and later conflicts, the Forest Brothers serve as confirmation of much received wisdom about insurgencies. First, an insurgent movement, even one operating at a low operational tempo, can only last so long without new recruits and a source of subsistence. Dead, wounded, and captured partisans must be replaced for a movement to endure. Partisans have to eat. Controlling the rural population ended the insurgency.

Second, a partisan movement in a small country will only get so far without some form of external support. External support could, in part, make up for lack of domestic recruitment and subsistence and provide essentials like training, arms, and even new recruits from elsewhere, such as émigrés from exile. The Forest Brothers did not receive such support. The efforts to reach out to the Forest Brothers from the West were too late and too little to make any difference. They were, largely, focused on liaison, communications, and intelligence collection, not on promoting an effective insurrection.

The third lesson is that counterinsurgency is costly. The Soviet military and security services expended a lot of effort to grind down the Baltic partisans. It took seven or eight years. It took, at times, an estimated thirty security forces personnel for each partisan to wear down the insurgency while maintaining Soviet rule. There were several operations where literally thousands of troops were involved in manhunts for a dozen or fewer insurgents. The Soviet authorities had the resources to achieve this. Rarely was such a magnitude of effort available or sustainable in conflicts like the Algerian struggle against the French, or the various insurgencies in South East Asia or Latin America, or, indeed, the Soviet adventure in Afghanistan.

Could these military lessons apply in, say, Ukraine? Certainly. The Ukrainians' will to fight has been demonstrated repeatedly. A population could support it. Ukraine has external borders that front upon NATO countries. External support to a Ukrainian partisan resistance would certainly be feasible. A Ukrainian diaspora, which now numbers in the millions, could infiltrate thousands of partisans into occupied areas. Could a single Ukrainian partisan tie down thirty Russian soldiers? It was possible in 1946, and there is little reason to suspect it would not be possible today. Would garrisoning the whole of Ukraine to such an extent be feasible for the Russian state for a period of years? Almost certainly not. At the time that I started writing this book, I feared that Ukrainians would have to resort to a partisan resistance. By the time I write this conclusion, Ukraine has done quite well in conventional fighting. But the lesson still stands—how could Russia conceivably garrison a country that large?

There are also lessons that are broader than the strictly military ones. From a broader perspective, fighting for a difficult or even 'lost' cause against insurmountable odds still has some impact if you end up delaying bad things from happening. The Forest Brotherhood bought time and dragged events out until after Stalin's death. Perhaps it might not have mattered if Stalin had lived a few years longer. But perhaps it mattered just enough to stretch out the process of Sovietisation and demographic change.

The other and possibly biggest lesson that the Forest Brotherhood movement shows us is that ideas matter. The countries of Estonia, Latvia, and Lithuania exist on a map and in daily life because enough people believe in the idea of their country and identify with it. For long periods, it was impossible for anyone to say 'Here I am in Estonia, as an Estonian, speaking Estonian, with an Estonian passport' because there was no independent Estonia. Today, a Circassian or a Crimean Tatar does not have this possibility. Countries, states, and nations—which are overlapping but not identical things—exist because of ideas about identity. One of the greatest crimes of the Russian Empire and the Soviet Union was the attempted and nearly successful robbery of Baltic identity.

But the attempted robbery of the idea of Baltic identity was ultimately unsuccessful. The ideas survived. The Forest Brothers were an expression of these powerful ideas. The Forest Brotherhood movement was an important part of these countries' survival. By expressing these ideas, dynamically, for a period of years, the Forest Brothers were a living embodiment of a different idea from the ruling Soviet one. As long as the Forest Brothers were still alive, even only in memory, the idea of independent Estonia, Latvia, and Lithuania remained alive too.

CONCLUSION

After the guns fell silent, the hidden bunkers were discovered, and all but a few hardened holdouts were killed or captured, people remembered the Forest Brothers even if they were not allowed to talk about them. The memory of the Forest Brothers served to keep the ideas alive long enough to be realised once again. This story mattered. And it still does.

NOTES

INTRODUCTION

1. Readers interested in this period are directed to the excellent book *The Baltic States in Peace and War, 1917–1945*, University Park, PA: Pennsylvania State University Press, 1978, edited by the Lithuanian-American scholars V. Stanley Vardys and Romuald Misiunas.
2. Jaan Tōnisson's death at the hands of Stalin's secret police is presumed, but the exact date is unknown.
3. The full name was Eesti Vabadussõjalaste Liit, roughly 'Union of the Participants of the War of Independence', known colloquially as the Vaps movement because the term for a single member was *vaps*.
4. Mara Kalnins, *Latvia: A Short History*, London: C. Hurst and Co., 2015, p. 123.

1. NIGHTFALL

1. The non-fiction works of Patrick Leigh Fermor and the fictional writing of Stefan Zweig and Eric Ambler capture the spirit of the age.
2. For an excellent account of Nazi–Soviet cooperation, see: Roger Moorhouse, *The Devils' Alliance: Hitler's Pact with Stalin, 1939–1941*, London: Hachette, 2014.
3. Ibid., pp. 20–2.
4. Ibid., p. 35.
5. Alexander Statiev, *The Soviet Counterinsurgency in the Western Borderlands*, Cambridge: Cambridge University Press, 2013, pp. 167–8.
6. See: 'Lietuvos gyventojų tremtys ir kalinimas Sovietų Sąjungoje', https://www.lietuviaisibire.lt

2. 1940 AND 1941

1. Laur Viirand, 'Staabi- ja sidepataljon käis külas Raua tänava lahingus osalenud veteranil', *Eesti Rahvusringhääling*, 25 November 2016, https://www.err.ee/578023/staabi-ja-sidepataljon-kais-kulas-raua-tanava-lahingus-osalenud-veteranil

2. Ilza Arklinka, 'Artistic Controversy Erupts around President's Memory', *Baltic Times*, Riga, Latvia, 1 November 2001, https://www.baltictimes.com/news/articles/5663/

3. Romuald Misiunas and Rein Taagepera, *The Baltic States: Years of Dependence, 1940–1990*, Berkeley: University of California Press, 1993, p. 19.

4. Ibid.

5. Tiit Noormets, 'The Summer War: The 1941 Armed Resistance in Estonia', in *The Anti-Soviet Resistance in the Baltic States*, ed. Arvydas Anušauskas, Vilnius: Genocide and Resistance Research Centre of Lithuania, 2006, pp. 186–208.

6. 'Metsavennad pidasid maailma ajaloos ainulaadset Suvesõda', *Postimees*, Tallinn, Estonia, 27 March 2004.

7. Riho Rõngelep and Michael Hesselholt Clemmesen, 'Tartu in the 1941 Summer War', *Baltic Defense Review* 1, no. 9 (2003): 165–82, here p. 170.

8. Noormets, 'Summer War', p. 189.

9. Ilze Pētersone, 'Klusie varoņi, kas viņi bija: lielākā pretpadomju pagrīdes organizācija "Tēvijas sargi"', *Latvijas Avīze*, 26 May 2018.

10. Juris Ciganovs, 'The Resistance Movement against the Soviet Regime in Latvia between 1940 and 1941', in Anušauskas, *Anti-Soviet Resistance in the Baltic States*, pp. 122–30.

11. Valentinas Brandišauskas, 'Anti-Soviet Resistance in 1940 and 1941 and the Revolt of June 1941', in Anušauskas, *Anti-Soviet Resistance in the Baltic States*, pp. 12–15.

12. Parliament of Lithuania, 'Kazys Škirpa', 22 February 2006, https://www3.lrs.lt/pls/inter/w5_show?p_r=4160&p_d=2792&p_k=1

13. Paddy Ashdown, *Nein! Standing up to Hitler 1935–1944*, New York: HarperCollins, 2018.

14. 'The Einsatzgruppen: Report by Einsatzgruppe A in the Baltic Countries, October 15, 1941', accessed online in translation at https://www.jewishvirtuallibrary.org/report-by-einsatzgruppe-a-in-the-baltic-countries-october-1941

15. Ciganovs, 'Resistance Movement against the Soviet Regime', p. 129.

16. Valdis O. Lumans, *Latvia in World War II*, vol. 11, New York: Fordham University Press, 2006, p. 266.

17. Rõngelep and Clemmesen, 'Tartu in the 1941 Summer War'.

18. Mart Laar, *War in the Woods*, Washington, DC: Compass Press, 1992, p. 16.

3.	THE SECOND WORLD WAR

1.	Geraldien von Frijtag Drabbe Künzel, '"Germanje": Dutch Empire-Building in Nazi-Occupied Europe', *Journal of Genocide Research* 19, no. 2 (2017): 240–57.

2.	Readers wishing for a deeper dive into Nazi slave labour are encouraged to read Ulrich Herbert, *Hitler's Foreign Workers: Enforced Foreign Labour in Germany under the Third Reich*, Cambridge: Cambridge University Press, 1997.

3.	John H. E. Fried, 'The Exploitation of Foreign Labour by Germany', Montreal: International Labor Office, 1945, pp. 264–5.

4.	Yitzhak Arad, *The Holocaust in the Soviet Union*, Lincoln, NE: University of Nebraska Press, 2020, p. 109.

5.	In none of the three countries should one necessarily take the number of battalions as a face-value figure. Some battalions were short-lived, and some people were transferred from battalion to battalion.

6.	E. Brūvelis et al., eds, *Latviešu Legionāri/Latvian Legionnaires*, Riga: Daugavas Vanagi, 2005, pp. 16–17.

7.	Perhaps a future book can explore this in a more detailed manner. The Finnish journalist Jukka Rislakki discusses the situation of Latvia in *The Case for Latvia: Disinformation Campaigns against a Small Nation*, Amsterdam: Rodopi, 2008.

8.	Alexander Statiev, *The Soviet Counterinsurgency in the Western Borderlands*, Cambridge: Cambridge University Press, 2010, p. 77.

9.	Estonian International Commission for Investigation of Crimes Against Humanity, 'Phase II: The German Occupation of Estonia 1941–1944', Tallinn, 1998.

10.	Arūnas Bubnys, 'The Holocaust in Lithuania: An Outline of the Major Stages and Their Results', in *The Vanished World of Lithuanian Jews*, ed. Alvydas Nikžentaitis, Stefan Schreiner, and Darius Staliūnas, Amsterdam: Rodopi, Brill, 2004.

11.	Romu Platforma, 'Roma Genocide', http://www.romuplatforma.lt/en/holocaust

12.	A deeper exploration of Estonia and memory of the Holocaust can be found in Anton Weiss-Wendt, *Murder without Hatred: Estonians and the Holocaust*, Syracuse: Syracuse University Press, 2009.

13.	Ibid., p. 767.

14.	Mečislovas Mackevičius, 'Lithuanian Resistance to German Mobilization Attempts 1941–1944', *Lituanus* 32, no. 4 (1986): 1–7.

15.	Yad Vashem: The World Holocaust Remembrance Center, 'In Cellars, Pits and Attics: Robert and Johanna Seduls', https://www.yadvashem.org/yv/en/exhibitions/righteous/seduls.asp

16. Žanis Lipkes Memorial, https://lipke.lv/en
17. The Righteous among the Nations Database: Kutorgienė Elena (Buivydaitė), https://righteous.yadvashem.org/?searchType=righteous_only&language=en&itemId=4043723&ind=0
18. Lithuanian Catholic Academy of Science, Clergy Database, https://www.lkma.lt/lddb/israsas.php?id=1878
19. Yad Vashem: The World Holocaust Remembrance Center, 'Anna Borkowska', https://www.yadvashem.org/righteous/stories/borkowska.html
20. Readers interested in a deeper dive into this subject are directed to this excellent book: Lester Eckman and Chaim Lazar, *The Jewish Resistance: The History of the Jewish Partisans in Lithuania and White Russia during the Nazi Occupation 1940–1945*, New York: Shengold Publishers, 1977.
21. Statiev, *Soviet Counterinsurgency in the Western Borderlands*, pp. 75–7.
22. Genocide and Resistance Center of Lithuania, 'Pirčiupiai Žudynes', http://genocid.lt/centras/lt/2631/a

4.   THE END OF THE SECOND WORLD WAR. OR NOT?

1. Kaarel Piirimäe, 'From an "Army of Historians" to an "Army of Professionals": History and the Strategic Culture in Estonia', *Scandinavian Journal of Military Studies* 3, no. 1 (2020): 100–13.
2. Laar, *War in the Woods*.
3. Evid Uustalu, *For Freedom Only: The Story of Estonian Volunteers in the Finnish Wars of 1940–1944*, Don Mills, Ontario: Northern Publications, 1977, p. 5.
4. Vincent Hunt, *Blood in the Forest: The End of the Second World War in the Courland Pocket*, Solihull: Helion and Company, 2017, pp. 116–30.

5.   PROFILE OF A PARTISAN

1. It takes a bit of effort to be equitable in writing an account such as this. When I first started researching the subject of Baltic partisans in my youth, there were many accounts of Lithuanian partisans available in English, largely through the efforts of the sizeable Lithuanian diaspora in the United States who wrote both serious works and martyrology accounts. I could find relatively little, even at the Library of Congress, about Latvian and Estonian partisans, other than brief mentions of the 'there were also Forest Brothers up there too' sort. It should be noted that the Forest Brotherhood movement was, by all available information (including from Soviet sources), larger in Lithuania than in Estonia or Latvia. Furthermore, the Latvian and Estonian diasporas in the English-

speaking West were much smaller, so there were fewer articles, stories, and publications in circulation.

As a Lithuanian American, I've spent thirty years collecting books and scraps of paper on the Lithuanian partisans. This situation left me with a surplus of material on the Lithuanian resistance and a deficit on the others. The research efforts for this book sought to remediate this deficit. I should also note that while I can read Russian and can, with difficulty, work my way through written Lithuanian, I have had to rely on electronic translation methods for some Estonian and Latvian language sources.

2. Juozas Lukša, *Forest Brothers: The Account of an Anti-Soviet Lithuanian Freedom Fighter*, Budapest: Central European University Press, 2009, p. 100.

3. Statiev, *Soviet Counterinsurgency in the Western Borderlands*, 99–102.

4. Domantė Platūkytė, 'Women Partisans among Lithuania's Forest Brothers: From Lovers to Fighters', LRT, 12 September 2020, https://www.lrt.lt/en/news-in-english/19/1227079/women-partisans-among-lithuania-s-forest-brothers-from-lovers-to-fighters

5. For a deeper exploration of women in the Baltic partisan movements, see: Sanita Reinsone, 'Forbidden and Sublime Forest Landscapes: Narrated Experiences of Latvian National Partisan women after World War II', *Cold War History* 16, no. 4 (2016): 395–416.

6. Baltic News Network, 'WWI Hand Grenade Found in a Chimney of a House in Riga', 16 January 2013.

7. Alfonsas Eidintas et al., *The History of Lithuania*, Vilnius: Eugrimas Pub. House, 2016, p. 256.

8. Lionginas Baliukevičius, *The Diary of a Partisan*, Vilnius: Genocide and Resistance Centre of Lithuania, 2008, p. 129.

9. Nijolė Gaškaitė, *Lietuvos partizanai: 1944–1953*, Vilnius: Union of Lithuanian Political Prisoners and Exiles, History Section, 1996, p. 344.

10. In the seminal (alas, Lithuanian language only) work on the history of the Lithuanian partisan movement, Marijona Žiliūtė of the Jurbarkas region is singled out for her heroism and skill as a field nurse. Ibid., p. 96.

11. Laar, *War in the Woods*, pp. 132–5.

12. Ibid., pp. 231–8.

13. Ibid., p. 142.

14. Arvydas Anušauskas, 'A Comparison of the Armed Struggles for Independence in the Baltic States and Western Ukraine', in Anušauskas, *Anti-Soviet Resistance in the Baltic States*, p. 65.

15. Ibid., pp. 67–8.

16. Laar, *War in the Woods*, pp. 78–9.

17. Lukša, *Forest Brothers*, pp. 186–94.
18. Laar, *War in the Woods*, p. 150.

6.   ESTONIA

  1. Ibid., pp. 69–70.
  2. Estonian Ministry of Defence, 'Minister of Defence Luik Remembered Courageous Resistance Fighters', 22 September 2020, https:// kaitseministeerium.ee/en/news/minister-defence-luik-remembered-courageous-resistance-fighters
  3. Enno Tammer, 'Õhkijamemm: Kaua me seda pronkssõdurit kardame!', *Postimees*, Tallinn, Estonia, 27 May 2006.
  4. Some accounts, including Mart Laar, spell his surname as Orav.
  5. Laar, *War in the Woods*, pp. 116–19.
  6. Ibid., p. 118.
  7. Ibid., p. 115.
  8. Laar, *War in the Woods*, pp. 172–3.
  9. Ott Tammik, 'Six Forest Brothers Laid to Rest', Estonian Public Broadcasting, 21 August 2012, https://news.err.ee/110471/six-forest-brothers-to-be-laid-to-rest
 10. Laar, *War in the Woods*, pp. 84–5.
 11. Pekkit Erelt, 'Raha või elu!', *Eesti Ekspress*, Tallinn, 8 October 2009, https://ekspress.delfi.ee/artikkel/69244765/raha-voi-elu
 12. Laar, *War in the Woods*, p. 126.
 13. Statiev, *Soviet Counterinsurgency in the Western Borderlands*, p. 136.

7.   LATVIA

  1. Although sources on the Latvian Forest Brothers in English are more widely available than in the past, I had a narrower body of literature and documents to draw from in the preparation of this book. A biography of a Latvian soldier who became a partisan, Roberts Dāvīds Timermanis, provides a useful amount of information on the early years of the partisan movement. See: Ēriks Jēkabsons and Reinis Ratnieks, *Latvian Soldier's Story: Roberts Dāvīds Timermanis (1909–1945)*, Riga: University of Latvia Press, 2020.
  2. Perhaps the best source in English that attempts to summarise the Latvian resistance movement is Aleksandrs Kiršteins, ed., *The Unknown War: The Latvian National Partisan's Fight against the Soviet Occupiers 1944–1956; The Battle and Memorial Sites of the National Partisans*, Riga: Latvian National Partisan Association, 2011.
  3. Ilze Pētersone, 'Netaisnība, kas jālabo', *Latvijas Avīze*, 18 May 2019.

4. Gaidis Landratovs, 'Resistance-Related Mission Essential Tasks Implementation in Latvia Armed Forces Soldiers Training', PhD diss., US Army Command and General Staff College, Fort Leavenworth, Kansas, 2020.

5. Kiršteins, *Unknown War*, p. 41.

6. Landratovs, 'Resistance-Related Mission Essential Tasks Implementation', p. 133.

7. Jēkabsons and Ratnieks, *Latvian Soldier's Story*, p. 139.

8. Tālrīts Krastiņs, 'The Bear Hunter', 2003. Interview. Transcript online at http://lpra.vip.lv/lachu_medn.htm

9. Peter Grimm and Eckart Reichl (dirs), *Forest Brothers: The Partisans of the Īle bunke*, 2014. See: https://www.forestbrothersmovie.com/home.html

10. Reinsone, 'Forbidden and Sublime Forest Landscapes', p. 398.

8.   LITHUANIA

1. Nijolė Gaškaitė-Žemaitienė, 'The Partisan War in Lithuania from 1944 to 1953', in Anušauskas, *Anti-Soviet Resistance in the Baltic States*, p. 35.

2. Dainius Noreika, 'Who Were the Lithuanian Partisans?', in *The Unknown War: Anti-Soviet Armed Resistance in Lithuania and Its Legacies*, ed. Arūnas Streikus, London: Routledge, 2022, pp. 48–72.

3. Nijolė Gaškaitė-Žemaitienė, 'The Partisan War in Lithuania from 1944 to 1953', in Anušauskas, *Anti-Soviet Resistance in the Baltic States*, p. 30.

4. Nijole Gaskaite et al., *Lietuvos Partizanai 1944–1953*, Kaunas: Laisves kovu archyvo priedas, 1996, p. 55.

5. Genocide and Resistance Centre of Lithuania, 'Virtuku Kautynes', 19 July 2005, http://genocid.lt/datos/virtuku.htm

6. Because of various anti-Semitic acts at the edges of the 1941 uprising, this leads to a controversy as to whether Ramanauskas engaged in any atrocities against Jewish people. On the one hand, hagiographic accounts make Ramanauskas a national hero. On the other hand, some people have sought to brand everyone who had anything to do with the 1941 uprising a genocidal accomplice of the Nazis. Once one digs into this controversy, it is clear that even the assiduous archivists who have gone a long way to name the Nazi collaborators have not been able to link Ramanauskas to any tragedies in Druskininkai in 1941. The only reference to Ramanauskas being part of the anti-Semitic acts in Druskininkai is a single unsourced work by an NKVD officer well after the fact. For a discussion, see: 'A Response to E. Zurof regarding A. Ramanauskas-Vanagas', Lithuania Tribune, 13 May 2019, https://lithuaniatribune.com/a-response-to-e-zurof-regarding-a-ramanauskas-vanagas

7. Auksutė Ramanauskaitė-Skokauskienė, *Adolfas Ramanauskas: Partisan Commander General*, Kaunas: Naujasis Lankas, 2007.
8. Adolfas Ramanauskas, *Daugel Kritu Sunu*, self-published, 16 February 1952. Reprinted by Genocide and Resistance Centre of Lithuania. Available online at http://www.partizanai.org/failai/html/daugel_krito.htm.
9. Ibid., pp. 392–3.
10. Later scholarship has confirmed his narrative, and a more modern edition has extensive cross-references and footnotes to place his work in the historiography of the movement.
11. Stephen Dorril, *MI6: Fifty Years of Special Operations*, London: Fourth Estate, 2000.
12. Dainius Noreika, 'Kalniškės mūšis: Laisvės kovų paveikslo detalė', *Genocidas ir rezistencija* 31, no. 1 (2012): 86–111.
13. Istorija.lt, 'The Second Sovietisation of Lithuania', https://istorijai.lt/antroji-lietuvos-sovietizacija/
14. Lukša, *Forest Brothers*, pp. 196–7.
15. Vilutienė, Aldona, 'Anelė Julija Senkutė', in *Visuotine Lietuviu Enciklopedija*, https://www.vle.lt/straipsnis/anele-julija-senkute
16. Lukša, *Forest Brothers*, p. 331.
17. Eidintas et al., *History of Lithuania*, p. 256.
18. Anušauskas, 'Comparison of the Armed Struggles for Independence', pp. 65–7.

9. THE SOVIET SIDE OF THE EQUATION

1. Pavel Sudoplatov et al., *Special Tasks: The Memoirs of an Unwanted Witness; A Soviet Spymaster*, London: Warner, 1995.
2. Lukša, *Forest Brothers*, pp. 98–9
3. Statiev, *Soviet Counterinsurgency in the Western Borderlands*, pp. 220–1.
4. Jeffrey Burds, *Советская агентура: Очерки истории СССР в послевоенные годы (1944–1948)*, Moscow: Sovremennaia Istoriia, 2006, pp. 209–17.
5. Statiev, *Soviet Counterinsurgency in the Western Borderlands*, p. 235.
6. Ibid., pp. 233–5.
7. For those deeply interested, Alexander Solzhenitsyn's *Gulag Archipelago* contains an elaborate catalogue of coercive techniques employed by the Soviet authorities.
8. Matthew Rendle, 'Mercy amid Terror? The Role of Amnesties during Russia's Civil War', *Slavonic & East European Review* 92, no. 3 (2014): 449–78.
9. Statiev, *Soviet Counterinsurgency in the Western Borderlands*, pp. 202–3.

10. Henrichs Strods, 'The USSR MGB's Top Secret Operation "Priboi" ("Surf") for the Deportation of Population from the Baltic Countries', Occupation Museum of Latvia, http://lpra.vip.lv/priboi.htm

11. Statiev, *Soviet Counterinsurgency in the Western Borderland*, p. 258.

12. Genocide and Resistance Centre of Lithuania, 'Justinas Lelešius', 2012, http://genocid.lt/UserFiles/File/Atmintinos_datos/2012/2012_lelesius_biogr.pdf

10. UNDERGROUND PRESS

1. Genocide and Resistance Centre of Lithuania, 'LLKS Declaration', http://www.genocid.lt/centras/lt/1166/a/

2. A copy of this document is available at: https//epartizanai.archyvai.lt/dokumentai/3/doc6983

3. Gaskaite et al., *Lietuvos Partizanai 1944–1953*, p. 55.

4. Laar, *War in the Woods*, pp. 147–55.

5. Vineta Rolmane, 'The Resistance in Latvia during the Nazi Occupation (July 1941–May 1945)', in Anušauskas, *Anti-Soviet Resistance in the Baltic States*, pp. 143–4.

6. Gaskaite et al., *Lietuvos Partizanai 1944–1953*, pp. 63–90.

7. Nijole Gaskaite, 'The Partisan War in Lithuania', in Anušauskas, *Anti-Soviet Resistance in the Baltic States*, p. 35.

8. Gaskaite et al., *Lietuvos Partizanai 1944–1953*, pp. 67–8.

9. *Chronicle of the Roman Catholic Church in Lithuania*. Online archive at https://lkbkronika.lt/en

11. CONTACTS WITH WESTERN INTELLIGENCE SERVICES

1. For deeper discussions of this period, see: Stephen Dorrill, *MI6: Fifty Years of Special Operations*, London: Fourth Estate, 2000, and Peter Grose, *Operation Rollback: America's Secret War behind the Iron Curtain*, Boston: Houghton Mifflin, 2000.

2. For a deep treatment of Sweden's history in this era, see: Lars Stöcker, *Bridging the Baltic Sea: Networks of Resistance and Opposition during the Cold War Era*, Lanham, MD: Lexington Books, 2018, p. 57.

3. The 1970 Swedish film *A Baltic Tragedy* covers this sad episode.

4. David Gordon Kirby, *Operation Blunderhead: The Incredible Adventures of a Double Agent in Nazi-Occupied Europe*, Brimscombe Port, Stroud: The History Press, 2015.

5. Ben Wheatley, 'The Foreign Research and Press Service: Britain's Primary Source of Intelligence from the German-Occupied Baltic

states during the Second World War', *Intelligence and National Security* 28, no. 5 (2013): 655–77.

6. Grose, *Operation Rollback*, p. 35.
7. Laas Lievat, 'Vignettes from the Soviet Past: On Assignment from MI6', *Eesti Elu*, 28 November 2014, https://eestielu.com/vignettes-from-the-soviet-past-on-assignment-from-mi6/
8. John Prados, *Safe for Democracy: The Secret Wars of the CIA*, Lanham, MD: Rowman and Littlefield, 2006, p. 53.
9. Toivo Miljan, *Historical Dictionary of Estonia*, 2nd edn, Lanham, MD: Rowman & Littlefield, 2015, pp. 382–3.
10. John Le Carré, *The Secret Pilgrim*, London: Penguin, 2011.
11. Central Intelligence Agency, 'Dispatch WSSA-158-Tilestone 0024', 25 November 1947, declassified in 2007, https://www.cia.gov/readingroom/document/5197c264993294098d50e022
12. Harry Rositzke, *The CIA's Secret Operations: Espionage, Counterespionage, and Covert Action*, London: Routledge, 2019.
13. Central Intelligence Agency, 'Study, Review, Analysis of All CAPSTAN Agents' Personal Histories, Contacts, and Associates', 23 March 1953, declassified 2007, https://www.cia.gov/readingroom/document/5197c263993294098d50df07
14. The other members were Donald Maclean, Guy Burgess, Anthony Blunt, and John Cairncross.
15. Yuri Modin with Jean-Charles Deniau, and Aguieszka Ziarek, *My Five Cambridge Friends*, London: Headline, 1994, pp. 186–90.
16. Andrew Christopher and Oleg Gordievsky, *KGB: The Inside Story of Its Foreign Operations from Lenin to Gorbachev*, New York: HarperCollins, 1990, pp. 316–22
17. Modin, *My Five Cambridge Friends*, p. 188.
18. Grose, *Operation Rollback*, p. 163.
19. Laar, *War in the Woods*, p. 208.
20. Grose, *Operation Rollback*, pp. 35–6.
21. Ibid., p. 36.
22. Central Intelligence Agency, 'Joint CIA/SIS Inquiry into Security of Existing Operations in Lithuania', 25 June 1953, declassified 2007, https://www.cia.gov/readingroom/docs/AECHAMP%20%20%20VOL.%201_0020.pdf
23. 'Jonas Deksnys', https://www.vle.lt/straipsnis/jonas-deksnys

12. REVOLT IN THE GULAG

1. Statiev, *Soviet Counterinsurgency in the Western Borderland*, pp. 176–7. It should be noted that the Lithuanian figure does not include 1940 and

1953. The 'Lithuania Siberia' archive (http://www.lietuviaisibire.lt/) shows 114 forced relocations in 1940 and 56 in 1953.

2. Leonard Latkovskis, 'Baltic Prisoners in the Gulag Revolts of 1953', *Lituanus* 51, no. 3 (2005): 5–39.

3. Ibid.

4. Aleksandr I. Solzhenitsyn, *The Gulag Archipelago, Volume Three*, New York: Harper & Row, 1976, p. 289

5. Latkovskis, 'Baltic Prisoners in the Gulag Revolts'.

6. Ihor Siundiukov, 'A Spirit that Breaks Shackles', *Dien* (Kyiv), 6 October 2009, https://day.kyiv.ua/en/article/ukraina-incognita/spirit-breaks-shackles

7. Walter Ciszek, *With God in Russia*, New York: McGraw-Hill, 1964.

8. John Noble, *I Was a Slave in Russia*, Broadview, IL: Cicero Bible Press, 1961.

9. Latkvoskis, 'Baltic Prisoners in the Gulag Revolts'.

10. Several excellent resources exist on the Kengir uprising. Solzhenitsyn devotes an entire chapter in vol. 3 of *The Gulag Archipelago* to describing the uprising. More recently, the Lithuanian Genocide and Resistance Museum in Vilnius held an exhibition on Lithuanians in the Kengir uprising. The book that accompanied the exhibition is a gold mine of information specifically describing the involvement of Lithuanians in this siege: A. Vyšniūnas, R. Driaučiūnaitė, and A. Tarabildienė, *Lietuviai Kengyro sukilime: 1954 m. gegužės 16—birželio 26 d*, Vilnius: Lietuvos gyventojų genocido ir rezistencijos tyrimo centras, 2019. There is also a website explaining the Lithuanian role in Kengir: https://urm.lt/default/en/how-the-gulag-broke-down-kengir-uprising-of-1954 Further mention of the revolts is in Anne Applebaum, *Gulag: A History*, New York: Doubleday Books, 2003. A Russian account is also interesting: 'Chronicle of the Uprising in Steplag', https://polit.ru/article/2004/05/18/steplag

13. LAST OF THE BROTHERS

1. Valdo Pand, 'Valdo Pand and Forest Brothers', Estonian State Radio, 21 January 2016, https://vikerraadio.err.ee/800354/reporteritund-pealkirjata-saade-valdo-pant-ja-metsavennad

2. Estonian War Museum, 'Estonian War Museum: Metsvennad', https://estmark.org/poliitika/eesti-sojamuuseum-metsavennad

3. Laar, *War in the Woods*, pp. 203–6.

4. 'A Film Will Be Made about a Latvian Who Hid in the Forest for 50 Years', *Jauns* (Riga), 20 July 2010, https://jauns.lv/raksts/zinas/212250-taps-filma-par-latvieti-kurs-50-gadus-slepas-meza

5. Genocide and Resistance Centre of Lithuania, 'Kostas (Konstantinas) Liuberskis', October 2014, http://genocid.lt/UserFiles/File/Atmintinos_datos/2014/10/201410_liuberskis_biog.pdf

6. Genocide and Resistance Centre of Lithuania, 'He Died 25 Years Ago', n.d., http://genocid.lt/centras/lt/1294/a/

14. CRITICISMS OF THE FOREST BROTHERS

1. Neil Taylor, 'A History of the Baltic Region, 1860–1991', in *Understanding the Baltic States: Estonia, Latvia, and Lithuania since 1991*, ed. Charles Clarke, London: C. Hurst and Co., 2023, p. 29.

2. Inga Zakšauskienė, 'Historical Propaganda in Pro-Kremlin Media: The Case of the Collapse of the Soviet Union', in Clarke, *Understanding the Baltic States*, pp. 232–3.

3. Weiss-Wendt, *Murder without Hatred*, p. 341.

4. Noreika, 'Who Were the Lithuanian Partisans?', pp. 48–72.

5. Lawrence Langer, *Versions of Survival: The Holocaust and the Human Spirit*, New York: State University of New York Press, 1982.

CONCLUSION

1. Joseph Pajaujis-Javis, *Soviet Genocide in Lithuania*, New York: Manyland Books, 1980.

2. Saulius Sužiedėlis, 'The Burden of 1941', *Lituanus* 47, no. 4 (2001): 47–60.

SELECTED BIBLIOGRAPHY

Andrew, Christopher and Oleg Gordievsky. *KGB: The Inside Story of Its Foreign Operations from Lenin to Gorbachev.* New York: HarperCollins, 1992.

Anušauskas, Arvydas. 'A Comparison of the Armed Struggles for Independence in the Baltic States and Western Ukraine'. In *Anti-Soviet Resistance in the Baltic States*, edited by Arvydas Anušauskas. Vilnius: Genocide and Resistance Research Centre of Lithuania, 2006.

Applebaum, Anne. *Gulag: A History.* New York: Doubleday Books, 2003.

Arad, Yitzhak. *The Holocaust in the Soviet Union.* Lincoln, NE: University of Nebraska Press, 2020.

Baliukevičius, Lionginas. *The Diary of a Partisan.* Vilnius: Genocide and Resistance Centre of Lithuania, 2008.

Baltic News Network. 'WWI Hand Grenade Found in a Chimney of a House in Riga'. 16 January 2013.

Brandišauskas, Valentinas. 'Anti-Soviet Resistance in 1940 and 1941 and the Revolt of June 1941'. In *The Anti-Soviet Resistance in the Baltic States*, edited by Arvydas Anušauskas. Vilnius: Genocide and Resistance Research Centre of Lithuania, 2006.

Brūvelis, E. et al., eds *Latviešu Legionāri / Latvian Legionnaires.* Riga: Daugavas Vanagi, 2005.

Bubnys, Arūnas. 'The Holocaust in Lithuania: An Outline of the Major Stages and Their Results'. In *The Vanished World of Lithuanian Jews*, edited by Alvydas Nikžentaitis, Stefan Schreiner, and Darius Staliūnas. Amsterdam: Rodopi, 2004.

Burds, Jeffrey. *Советская агентура: Очерки истории СССР в послевоенные годы (1944–1948).* Moscow: Sovremennaia Istoriia, 2006.

Central Intelligence Agency. 'Dispatch WSSA-158—Tilestone 0024'. 25 November 1947. Declassified in 2007. https://www.cia.gov/readingroom/document/5197c264993294098d50e022

SELECTED BIBLIOGRAPHY

————— 'Joint CIA/SIS Inquiry into Security of Existing Operations in Lithuania'. 25 June 1953. Declassified 2007. https://www.cia.gov/readingroom/docs/AECHAMP%20%20%20VOL.%201_0020.pdf

————— 'Study, Review, Analysis of all CAPSTAN Agents' Personal Histories, Contacts, and Associates'. 23 March 1953. Declassified 2007. https://www.cia.gov/readingroom/document/5197c263993294098d50df07

Ciganovs, Juris. 'The Resistance Movement against the Soviet Regime in Latvia between 1940 and 1941'. In *The Anti-Soviet Resistance in the Baltic States*, edited by Arvydas Anušauskas. Vilnius: Genocide and Resistance Research Centre of Lithuania, 2006.

Ciszek, Walter. *With God in Russia*. New York: McGraw-Hill, 1964.

Dorril, Stephen. *MI6: Fifty Years of Special Operations*. London: Fourth Estate, 2000.

Eckman, Lester and Chaim Lazar. *The Jewish Resistance: The History of the Jewish Partisans in Lithuania and White Russia during the Nazi Occupation 1940–1945*. New York: Shengold Publishers, 1977.

Eidintas, Alfonsas, Alfredas Bumblauskas, Antanas Kulakauskas, and Mindaugas Tamošaitis. *The History of Lithuania*. Vilnius: Eugrimas Pub. House, 2016.

Erelt, Pekkit. 'Raha või elu!' *Eesti Ekspress*, Tallinn. 8 October 2009. https://ekspress.delfi.ee/artikkel/69244765/raha-voi-elu

Estonian International Commission for Investigation of Crimes Against Humanity. 'Phase II: The German Occupation of Estonia 1941–1944'. Tallinn, 1998.

Estonian Ministry of Defence. 'Minister of Defence Luik Remembered Courageous Resistance Fighters'. 22 September 2020. https://kaitseministeerium.ee/en/news/minister-defence-luik-remembered-courageous-resistance-fighters

Fried, John H. E. *The Exploitation of Foreign Labour by Germany*. Montreal: International Labor Office, 1945.

Frijtag Drabbe Künzel, Geraldien von. '"Germanje": Dutch Empire-Building in Nazi-Occupied Europe'. *Journal of Genocide Research* 19, no. 2 (2017): 240–57.

Gaškaitė, Nijolė. *Lietuvos partizanai: 1944–1953*. Vilnius: Union of Lithuanian Political Prisoners and Exiles, History Section, 1996.

Gaškaitė-Žemaitienė, Nijolė. 'The Partisan War in Lithuania from 1944 to 1953'. In *The Anti-Soviet Resistance in the Baltic States*, edited by

Arvydas Anušauskas. Vilnius: Genocide and Resistance Centre of Lithuania, 2006.

Grose, Peter. *Operation Rollback: America's Secret War behind the Iron Curtain*. Boston: Houghton Mifflin, 2000.

Herbert, Ulrich. *Hitler's Foreign Workers: Enforced Foreign Labour in Germany under the Third Reich*. Cambridge: Cambridge University Press, 1997.

Hunt, Vincent. *Blood in the Forest: The End of the Second World War in the Courland Pocket*. Solihull: Helion and Company, 2017.

Jēkabsons, Ēriks and Reinis Ratnieks. *Latvian Soldier's Story: Roberts Dāvīds Timermanis (1909–1945)*. Riga: University of Latvia Press, 2020.

Kalnins, Mara. *Latvia: A Short History*. London: C. Hurst and Co., 2015.

Kirby, David Gordon. *Operation Blunderhead: The Incredible Adventures of a Double Agent in Nazi-Occupied Europe*. Brimscombe Port, Stroud: The History Press, 2015.

Kiršteins, Aleksandrs, ed. *The Unknown War: The Latvian National Partisans' Fight against the Soviet Occupiers 1944–1956; The Battle and Memorial Sites of the National Partisans*. Riga: Latvian National Partisan Association, 2011.

Laar, Mart. *War in the Woods*. Washington, DC: Compass Press, 1992.

Landratovs, Gaidis. 'Resistance-Related Mission Essential Tasks Implementation in Latvia Armed Forces Soldiers Training'. PhD diss., US Army Command and General Staff College, Fort Leavenworth, Kansas, 2020.

Langer, Lawrence. *Versions of Survival: The Holocaust and the Human Spirit*. New York: State University of New York Press, 1982.

Latkovskis, Leonard. 'Baltic Prisoners in the Gulag Revolts of 1953'. *Lituanus* 51, no. 3 (2005): 5–39.

Le Carré, John. *The Secret Pilgrim*. London: Penguin, 2011.

Lievat, Laas. 'Vignettes from the Soviet Past: On Assignment from MI6'. *Eesti Elu*, 28 November 2014. https://eestielu.com/vignettes-from-the-soviet-past-on-assignment-from-mi6/

Lucas, Edward. *Deception: Spies, Lies and How Russia Dupes the West*. London: Bloomsbury, 2012.

Lukša, Juozas. *Forest Brothers: The Account of an Anti-Soviet Lithuanian Freedom Fighter*. Budapest: Central European University Press, 2009.

Lumans, Valdis O. *Latvia in World War II*. Vol. 11. New York: Fordham University Press, 2006.

Mackevičius, Mečislovas. 'Lithuanian Resistance to German Mobilization Attempts 1941–1944'. *Lituanus* 32, no. 4 (1986): 1–7.

Miljan, Toivo. *Historical Dictionary of Estonia*. 2nd edn. Lanham, MD: Rowman & Littlefield, 2015

Misiunas, Romuald and Rein Taagepera. *The Baltic States: Years of Dependence, 1940–1990*. Berkeley: University of California Press, 1993.

Modin, Yuri, Jean-Charles Deniau and Aguieszka Ziarek. *My Five Cambridge Friends*. London: Headline, 1994.

Moorhouse, Roger. *The Devils' Alliance: Hitler's Pact with Stalin, 1939–1941*. London: Hachette, 2014.

Noble, John. *I Was a Slave in Russia*. Broadview, IL: Cicero Bible Press, 1961.

Noormets, Tiit. 'The Summer War: The 1941 Armed Resistance in Estonia'. In *The Anti-Soviet Resistance in the Baltic States*, edited by Arvydas Anušauskas. Vilnius: Genocide and Resistance Research Centre of Lithuania, 2006.

Noreika, Dainius. 'Kalniškės mūšis: Laisvės kovų paveikslo detalė'. *Genocidas ir rezistencija* 31, no. 1 (2012): 86–111.

———— 'Who Were the Lithuanian Partisans?' In *The Unknown War: Anti-Soviet Armed Resistance in Lithuania and Its Legacies*, edited by Arūnas Streikus. London: Routledge, 2022.

Pajaujis-Javis, Joseph. *Soviet Genocide in Lithuania*. New York: Manyland Books, 1980.

Pētersone, Ilze. 'Klusie varoņi, kas viņi bija: Lielākā pretpadomju pagrīdes organizācija "Tēvijas sargi"'. *Latvijas Avīze*, 26 May 2018.

———— 'Netaisnība, kas jālabo'. *Latvijas Avīze*, 18 May 2019.

Piirimäe, Kaarel. 'From an "Army of Historians" to an "Army of Professionals": History and the Strategic Culture in Estonia'. *Scandinavian Journal of Military Studies* 3, no. 1 (2020): 100–13.

Platūkytė, Domantė. 'Women Partisans among Lithuania's Forest Brothers: From Lovers to Fighters'. LRT, 12 September 2020. https://www.lrt.lt/en/news-in-english/19/1227079/women-partisans-among-lithuania-s-forest-brothers-from-lovers-to-fighters

Prados, John. *Safe for Democracy: The Secret Wars of the CIA*. Lanham, MD: Rowman and Littlefield, 2006.

Ramanauskaitė-Skokauskienė, Auksutė. *Adolfas Ramanauskas: Partisan Commander General*. Kaunas: Naujasis Lankas, 2007.

Ramanauskas, Adolfas. *Daugel Kritu Sunu*. Self published, 16 February 1952. Reprinted by Genocide and Resistance Centre of Lithuania. http://www.partizanai.org/failai/html/daugel_krito.htm

Reinsone, Sanita. 'Forbidden and Sublime Forest Landscapes: Narrated Experiences of Latvian National Partisan Women after World War II'. *Cold War History* 16, no. 4 (2016): 395–416.

Rendle, Matthew. 'Mercy amid Terror? The Role of Amnesties during Russia's Civil War'. *Slavonic & East European Review* 92, no. 3 (2014): 449–78.

Rislakki, Jukka. *The Case for Latvia: Disinformation Campaigns against a Small Nation*. Amsterdam: Rodopi, 2008.

Rolmane, Vineta. 'The Resistance in Latvia during the Nazi Occupation (July 1941–May 1945)'. In *The Anti-Soviet Resistance in the Baltic States*, edited by Arvydas Anušauskas. Vilnius: Genocide and Resistance Research Centre of Lithuania, 2006

Rõngelep, Riho and Michael Hesselholt Clemmesen. 'Tartu in the 1941 Summer War'. *Baltic Defense Review* 1, no. 9 (2003): 165–82.

Rositzke, Harry. *The CIA's Secret Operations: Espionage, Counterespionage, and Covert Action*. London: Routledge, 2019.

Solzhenitsyn, Aleksandr. *The Gulag Archipelago, Volume Three*. New York: Harper & Row, 1976.

Statiev, Alexander. *The Soviet Counterinsurgency in the Western Borderlands*. Cambridge: Cambridge University Press, 2013.

Stöcker, Lars. *Bridging the Baltic Sea: Networks of Resistance and Opposition during the Cold War Era*. Lanham, MD: Lexington Books, 2018.

Strods, Henrichs. 'The USSR MGB's Top Secret Operation "Priboi" ("Surf") for the Deportation of Population from the Baltic Countries'. Occupation Museum of Latvia. http://lpra.vip.lv/priboi.htm

Sudoplatov, Pavel et al. *Special Tasks: The Memoirs of an Unwanted Witness; A Soviet Spymaster*. London: Warner, 1995.

Sužiedėlis, Saulius. 'The Burden of 1941'. *Lituanus* 47, no. 4 (2001): 47–60.

Tammer, Enno. 'Õhkijamemm: Kaua me seda pronkssõdurit kardame!' *Postimees*, Tallinn, Estonia, 27 May 2006.

Tammik, Ott. 'Six Forest Brothers Laid to Rest'. Estonian Public Broadcasting, 21 August 2012. https://news.err.ee/110471/six-forest-brothers-to-be-laid-to-rest

Taylor, Neil. *Estonia: A Modern History*. London: C. Hurst and Co., 2020.

———— 'A History of the Baltic Region, 1860–1991'. In *Understanding the Baltic States: Estonia, Latvia, and Lithuania since 1991*, edited by Charles Clarke. London: C. Hurst and Co., 2023.

SELECTED BIBLIOGRAPHY

Uustalu, Evid. *For Freedom Only: The Story of Estonian Volunteers in the Finnish Wars of 1940–1944*. Don Mills, Ontario: Northern Publications, 1977.

Vyšniūnas, A., R. Driaučiūnaitė, and A. Tarabildienė, *Lietuviai Kengyro sukilime: 1954 m. gegužės 16–birželio 26 d.* Vilnius: Lietuvos gyventojų genocido ir rezistencijos tyrimo centras, 2019.

Weiss-Wendt, Anton. *Murder without Hatred: Estonians and the Holocaust*. Syracuse: Syracuse University Press, 2009.

Wheatley, Ben. 'The Foreign Research and Press Service: Britain's Primary Source of Intelligence from the German-Occupied Baltic States during the Second World War'. *Intelligence and National Security* 28, no. 5 (2013): 655–77.

Zakšauskienė, Inga. 'Historical Propaganda in Pro-Kremlin Media: The Case of the Collapse of the Soviet Union'. In *Understanding the Baltic States: Estonia, Latvia, and Lithuania since 1991*, edited by Charles Clarke. London: C. Hurst and Co., 2023.

INDEX

INDEX

INDEX

INDEX

National Committee of the
Republic of Estonia, 62
national identities, 2–3, 4, 6–7,
15, 204, 225, 230, 245–6, 250
National Renaissance Front
(Romania), 20
Nazi Germany (1933–45), xvii–
xviii, 9, 14, 20–21, 51–71,
73–82, 109–10, 227–37
Abwehr, 39, 40, 41, 74, 110
Austria annexation (1938), 20,
22
Baltic Germans, repatriation of
(1939–40), 30–31
Baltic States, occupation of,
see Reichskommissariat
Ostland
collaboration with, xviii, 20,
44, 45, 46, 49, 53, 59–61,
76, 85, 121, 138, 204
Czechoslovakia annexation
(1938–9), 20, 22
deserters, 77–8, 86, 88, 100,
136
ethno-nationalism, 230
France, invasion of (1940), 25,
26
Holocaust (1941–5), *see*
Holocaust
information, control of, 174
Memel crisis (1939), 14, 22–3,
228
Molotov–Ribbentrop Pact (1939),
23–4, 37, 204, 227
Poland, invasion of (1939), 24
police state, 65
propaganda, 65
racial pseudoscience, 52, 62,
230

recruitment/conscription,
55–9, 61, 63–5, 75–6, 79,
80, 86, 241
retreat (1944–5), 73, 109–10,
123–4
Rhineland remilitarisation
(1936), 22
Schutzmannschaften, 56
slave labour, use of, 54, 58,
233
Soviet Union, invasion of
(1941), 32, 42–50
weapons from, 91
Neifalta, Jonas, 145–6
Neifaltienė, Albina, 145
Netherlands, 52, 67–8
Nevsky, Alexander, 173
New Britain, Connecticut, 141
New Latvians, 39
New York, United States, 36, 201
nickel mining, 204
NKGB, 154
NKVD, xx, xxiii, xxiv, 154,
160–62, 234
Ants the Terrible and, 117
Baltic occupation, first (1940–
41), 30, 31–2, 35, 38, 40,
54
Baltic occupation, second
(1944), 82
Battle of Île (1949), 129
Battle of Kalniškės (1945),
145–6
Battle of Määritsa Farm
(1946), 119
Battle of Stompak Marsh
(1945), 126–7
counterintelligence, 198–9
covert operations, 162–3

285

food, surveillance of, 162
Forest Brothers' targeting of,
    96, 112
German invasion (1941),
    42–3, 44
German retreat (1944), 110,
    112
human intelligence, 160–62
infiltration operations, *see*
    infiltration operations
informers, 30, 69, 145,
    160–62, 167, 243
interrogation and torture, 162
Latvian Self Defence, conflict
    with, 125–6
Lukša arrest (1941), 143
omnipresence, 159
Pargas and, 119
Veverskis execution (1945), 136
Noble, John, 209
Noreika, Dainius, 131, 235, 236
Norilag, Siberia, 208–9
Norilsk, Russia, 129, 207, 208
Northern Ireland, 149
Norway, 36
Novosibirsk, Russia, 155

Office of Policy Coordination
    (US) 192
Office of Strategic Services (OSS),
    186–7
oil industry, 186
Ojaste, Aksel and Arnold, 218
Old Believers, 5
Omakaitse, 57, 112, 118
omnipresence, 159
On the Path of Knights, 181
Operation Bagration (1944), 73,
    109–10

Operation Barbarossa (1941–5),
    32, 42–50, 65
Operation Blunderhead (1942),
    186, 188
Operation Capstan (1950–51),
    194–6
Operation Climber (c. 1947), 197
Operation Jungle (1949–55),
    188–92
Operation Priboi (1949), 168
Operation Tilestone (1946–8), 193
Operation Valuable (1949), 197
Operation Vesna (1948), 168
operations (Forest Brothers),
    96–107
    assassinations, 99, 103, 113,
        118, 127–9
    collaborators, retaliation
        against, 103
    conscription resistance, 102–3
    electoral interference, 103–4,
        113
    information operations, 105
    liaison and communication,
        105–6, 135
    prisoner liberation, 102, 117
    repression, protection from,
        101
    Sovietisation, delay of, 101–2
    supply gathering, 99
    symbolic acts, 104–5, 113
    tactics, 99, 133–4
    targets of, 97–9, 112, 133–4
Oras, Vambola, 116
Order of the Red Banner, 59
Organisation of Latvian National
    Partisans, 125
Organisation of Ukrainian
    Nationalists (OUN), xvi